"The lives and experiences of sisters from all over the world are a rich treasure trove of wisdom to nurture and inspire the reader. For far too long the voices of Catholic sisters have gone unheard. Now sisters appreciate that it takes both humility and courage to share reflections on what they have heard, seen, touched, tasted, and smelled. When shared, these transformational experiences and personal insights witness to faith, hope, and love in a complex and fractured world. *Wisdom from the Global Sisterhood* offers material for a synodal type reflection at personal/group levels. The texts which have emerged from the lives and reflections of sisters can be dialogical partners as we seek to find resonances within and identify God's grace-filled presence in our own lives."

— Patricia Murray, IBVM, executive secretary, International Union of Superiors General (UISG)

"*Wisdom from the Global Sisterhood* is a rich array of essays organized in ten themes capturing the insight, experience, and voice of sisters across the globe. It is a moving testimony (and reminder) of how sisters are creating and sustaining the Church in both great cities and hidden villages in a multitude of languages and cultures."

— Tom Gaunt, SJ, executive director, Center for Applied Research in the Apostolate (CARA)

"*Wisdom from the Global Sisterhood* provides powerful and inspiring evidence that religious life is alive and well in the twenty-first century. The authors' voices—from around the world and from a spectrum of communities—reveal the remarkable scope of women's spiritual and ministerial gifts to the church and to the world. The reflection questions that accompany each piece are additional testimony to the writers' generosity. Here's to many more decades of Global Sisters Report!"

— Margaret Susan Thompson, Syracuse University

"A splendid collection of personal stories infused with spiritual experience, human trials, and pastoral sensitivity. These heartfelt chapters come from and project a global vision and feminine embrace that women religious bring to the joys, hopes, and pain of humanity. It is a book that speaks truth to the power of love for God and neighbor and gently guides us to continue our journey together in faith, hope, and courage. What a gift. I couldn't put it down."

— Rose Pacatte, FSP, director, Pauline Center for Media Studies, Rome Office

"*Wisdom from the Global Sisterhood* celebrates ten years of documenting the spirituality and justice work of Catholic women religious worldwide. Stories from seasoned sisters like Mary John Mananzan, Nancy Sylvester, Margaret Gonsalves, and next-generation leaders like Corbin Hannah and Tracey Horan convey the rich contributions of nuns. Questions and photos with each essay invite more personal and communal reflection. Congratulations to Global Sisters Report and *ad multos annos*."

— Diann L. Neu, cofounder and codirector of WATER, Women's Alliance for Theology, Ethics, and Ritual, and author of *Stirring WATERS: Feminist Liturgies for Justice*

"The integrity and reputation of the Global Sisters Report is a key incentive to read this book in its entirety. Gathering the vivid insights and global experiences of Catholic Sisters from varying charisms quickly invites the reader to want to learn more about vocations to religious life. This book is ideal for those discerning a vocation, especially the meaningful reflection questions after each article. It is also a timeless treasure for everyone who is seeking to understand the significance of answering God's endless call to become a sister."

— Deborah Borneman, SSCM, National Religious Vocation Conference Director of Mission Integration

Wisdom from the Global Sisterhood

Contemporary Reflections by Catholic Sisters

A selection of columns from

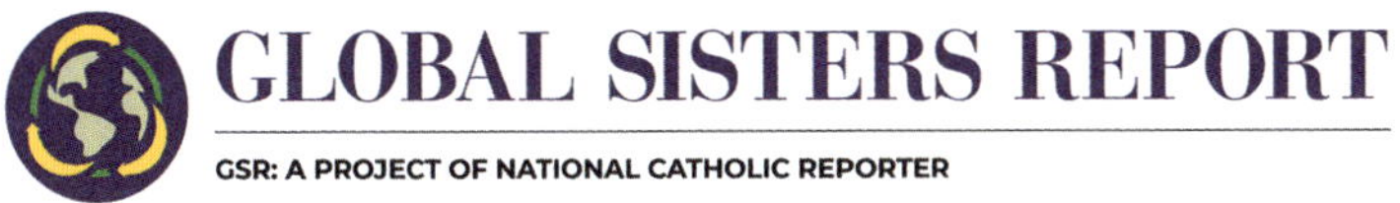

Edited by

Srs. Joyce Meyer, Michele Morek, Helga Leija, and Jan Cebula

Introduced by

Sr. Joyce Meyer, Sr. Jane Wakahiu, and Gail DeGeorge

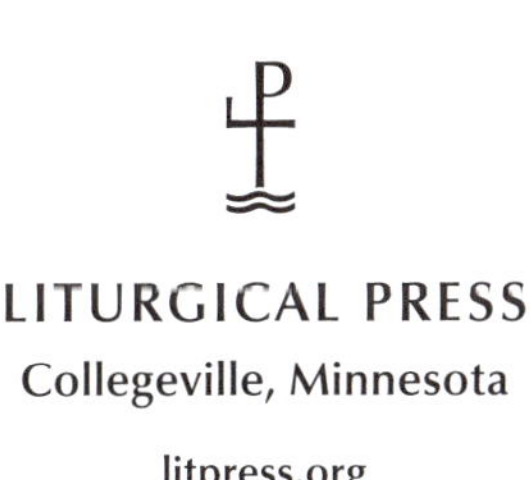

Collegeville, Minnesota

litpress.org

Illustrations on pages 1, 29, 67, 95, 127, 153, 179, 211, 237, and 267 used courtesy of Getty Images.

1 2 3 4 5 6 7 8 9

Library of Congress Cataloging-in-Publication Data

Names: Meyer, Joyce, 1943– editor.
Title: Wisdom from the global sisterhood : contemporary reflections by Catholic sisters / edited by Srs. Joyce Meyer [and three others] ; introduced by Sr. Joyce Meyer, Sr. Jane Wakahiu, and Gail DeGeorge.
Description: Collegeville, Minnesota : Liturgical Press, [2024] | Summary: "In Wisdom from the Global Sisterhood, Catholic sisters from across the world share their insights about prayer, grace, grief and healing, ministries, and a variety of topics. From the thousands of columns published since it began in April 2014, Global Sisters Report's editors share some of the publication's columns to celebrate the enduring life and ministry of these women of faith"—Provided by publisher.
Identifiers: LCCN 2024002174 (print) | LCCN 2024002175 (ebook) | ISBN 9798400801334 (trade paperback) | ISBN 9798400801341 (epub) | ISBN 9780814688915 (pdf)
Subjects: LCSH: Nuns. | Catholic Church. | Monasticism and religious orders for women. | BISAC: RELIGION / Christian Living / Calling & Vocation | RELIGION / Christianity / Catholic
Classification: LCC BX4200 .W48 2024 (print) | LCC BX4200 (ebook) | DDC 271/.9—dc23/eng/20240429
LC record available at https://lccn.loc.gov/2024002174
LC ebook record available at https://lccn.loc.gov/2024002175

Contents

Introduction

This book with Liturgical Press is a high point in the 10-year history of Global Sisters Report. It includes some of the thousands of published columns by Catholic sisters around the world, many of whose voices would not be heard nor insights shared were it not for Global Sisters Report. The commitment of the National Catholic Reporter, as Global Sisters Report's parent company, has been a tremendous support to this effort.

I can only thank God and the creativity of our journalists, lay women and men and sisters from around the world who have brought to life the often hidden and unrecognized lives of Catholic sisters. These women are dedicated not only to faith development but to every aspect of human development, and not only to Catholic communities but to any faith or non-faith community they are called to serve.

The story of Global Sisters Report's beginnings is important to review. The seeds for the website were planted with a small attempt by the Conrad N. Hilton Fund for Sisters to highlight significant projects of sisters worldwide in a 2009 book called "Seeds of Hope: Sisters in Action Around the World." The purpose was to bring attention to best practices of development but also to raise up the creativity and ingenuity needed for this work.

The idea was picked up by Thomas C. Fox, then-publisher of the National Catholic Reporter, who came to me as the then-executive director of the Conrad N. Hilton Fund for Sisters, to seek a grant to publish such stories in the National Catholic Reporter. After receiving positive affirmation for this effort, Tom came again seeking a much larger grant that would include reporting and publishing stories online, an amount beyond my budget. I referred him to the Conrad N Hilton Foundation, which asked for a feasibility study. Tom took this on and invited me to partner with him in gathering sisters from around the U.S. who agreed that having global visibility would be very positive for women's religious life. At that time, I was doing some work in Africa, so I invited Tom to accompany me to Kenya and Uganda to experience the vibrancy of women's religious life on that continent. On our way home, we stopped in Rome to visit Vatican dicasteries to let them know of our plans.

In April 2014, within months of receiving the grant from the Hilton Foundation, Global Sisters Report began. These past 10 years have been a marvelous adventure of seeking out the sisters' stories of their lives and ministries in far distant parts of the world. We have read their stories—written in their own voices and by journalists—and those stories continue to inspire and encourage others.

The future looks bright as more and more sisters are contributing to Global Sisters Report and we are able to reach into new and often unheard-of parts of the world where the presence of sisters brings hope and joy. Thanks to the Hilton Foundation and other generous donors. We continue to need your financial and moral support.

Sr. Joyce Meyer, Presentation of the Blessed Virgin Mary,
International Liaison to Sisters, Global Sisters Report

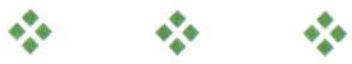

We are thrilled to applaud Global Sisters Report (GSR) as you mark the 10th anniversary with a book that pays tribute to the incredible work of Catholic women religious. The Conrad N. Hilton Foundation's Catholic Sisters Initiative is honored to support GSR's impactful journalism, which shares inspiring and untold stories of Catholic women religious worldwide. Over the past decade, GSR has expanded its coverage and global reach, documenting the rich tapestry of religious life, faith, hope, diversity, and culture and introducing new features, including *Community News* and *GSR in the Classroom*, a project that showcases the mission and ministry of women religious around the world for middle school and high school students.

In addition, Global Sisters Report provides an important platform for sisters to share about spirituality, mission, ministry, religious life, and other topics. The sisters' columns add a unique dimension to Global Sisters Report, and it is laudable that this anniversary book draws upon examples of those columns.

We are proud to continue our partnership, promoting ethical journalism as GSR continues to amplify the voices of these remarkable women. GSR's stories provide a unique and invaluable insight into the compassionate and transformative work of sisters in creating networks of collaboration that address societal issues. We invite readers to discover the profound impact of sisters as they bring hope, compassion, and service to communities – and walk the synodality path supporting the most vulnerable. Our gratitude to GSR for embodying a mission of solidarity to shine a light on the prophetic witness, tenderness, and humanitarian efforts of women religious globally, particularly in their support for migrants, refugees, trafficking survivors, healing the sick, teaching, and climate-related issues.

Sr. Jane Wakahiu, LSOSF, PhD
Associate VP of Operations & Head, Catholic Sisters Initiative,
Conrad N. Hilton Foundation

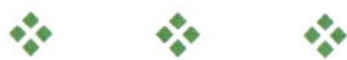

We are honored to bring this book to fruition with the help of Liturgical Press for the 10th anniversary of Global Sisters Report, a website publication of National Catholic Reporter. Since April 2014, Global Sisters Report has been reflecting the lives, missions, ministries and spirituality of Catholic women religious around the world. Through the stories journalists write and the columns sisters contribute, Global Sisters Report is a mosaic of the richness of religious life. The wisdom of the sisters is a gift we can all learn from—hence, this book.

In selecting the columns to be included, it quickly became apparent that it would be impossible to convey the wide variety of topics the sisters have written about. We reviewed thousands of columns to choose the ones in this book, grouping them into sections we thought would have wide appeal. For ministries, for example, the sisters do so many – but since so many congregations are involved in anti-human trafficking, we included some columns about that ministry in particular. We also included some columns from our most recent and ambitious series, "Hope Amid Turmoil: Sisters in Conflict Areas." This book is intended to give readers a sampling of the variety of sisters' ministries, with lessons and messages that can be carried with you. We invite you to become regular readers of Global Sisters Report at GlobalSistersReport.org to continue to learn from the sisters.

This book includes reflection questions with each of the columns. They can be used for your own contemplation or in small group settings.

We would like to thank all the sisters who write for Global Sisters Report, particularly those who agreed to have their columns included in this book. We are appreciative of sisters around the world who carry out the Gospel message in so many ways and varied ministries.

Thank you also to all those at Liturgical Press who helped with this project. Our appreciation also to Denise Simeone, former editor of *Celebration*, and an experienced retreat facilitator, for her work on the reflection questions, and to Brittany Wilmes, for her role as Global Sisters Report's production editor for this project. Our thanks also to Srs. Jan Cebula, Michele Morek, Helga Leija and of course, Joyce Meyer, for their efforts to nurture our sister writer-columnists. We also thank Sr. Jane Wakahiu of the Conrad N. Hilton Foundation and the Foundation itself, the Thomas and Dorothy Leavey Foundation, and our donors for their support of Global Sisters Report. Finally, we are grateful to Julia Ladner, whose generosity was instrumental in making this book possible. We are honored to be part of her legacy of goodness and generosity.

Gail DeGeorge
Editor, Global Sisters Report

Scan to learn more about Global Sisters Report. 

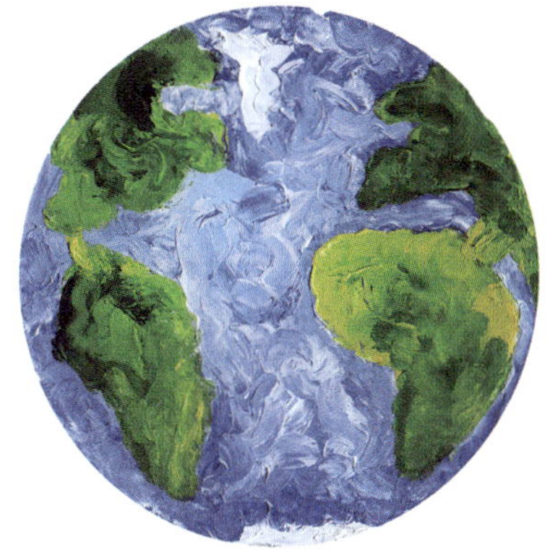

Prayer and Presence

Being consciously in God's presence is not only possible when I sit in prayer, but also when I practice seeing the goodness of God in everything around me—whether I'm walking, working or sitting.

Teresa Anyabuike

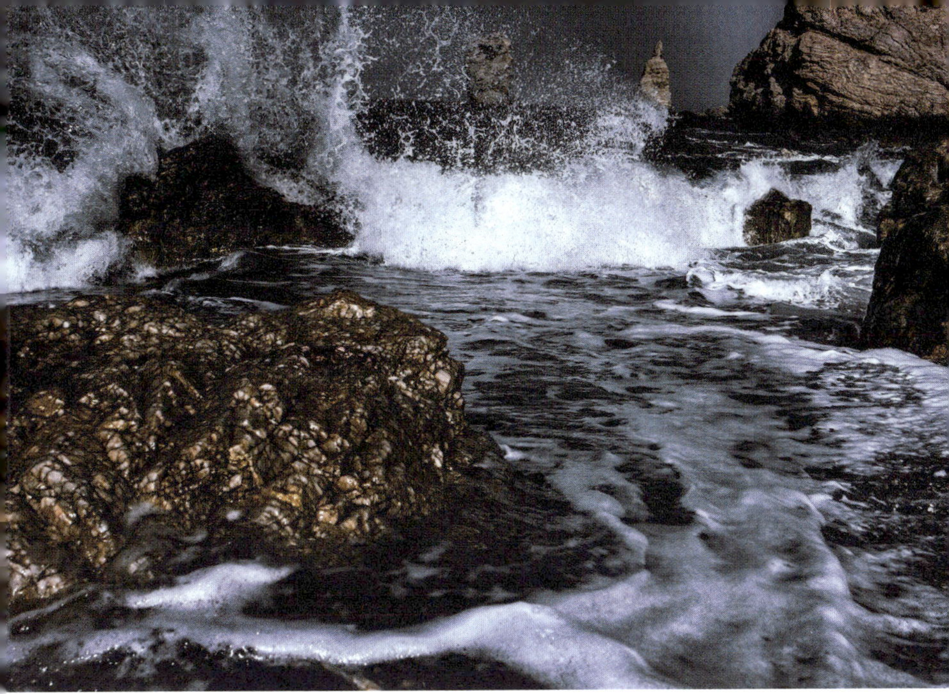

(Pixabay/Antonios Ntoumas)

Four effective habits for calming the tempests in your spirit

By Kathryn James Hermes

A friend told me recently that many of her colleagues were feeling depressed. The 24/7 access to news on their phones and through social media was somehow robbing them of energy and life.

I look around, and it is true. Many people exhibit signs of exhaustion, discouragement and confusion. They are suffering from all kinds of storms that rage through their minds and hearts. I walk with these people who are inundated with words—words piled upon words—as a #MediaNun, mostly *without* a lot of words.

Healing, I believe, takes place when our senses are directed inward *without* a lot of words. When we do not run from the raging fury of the inner storms of anger or fear but instead stand in their midst with silent courage and serenity, refusing to be propelled into action by what we feel, healing takes place.

Below are four habits you can develop to restore calm if there is a "tempest in your spirit."

1 - Develop the habit of waiting. Ultimately, we are happy when we are connected to our deepest inner source. Through our senses, we either empty ourselves *or* we enrich ourselves with the beauty of an inner life. One person can read a story on the internet and dash off a passion-filled comment that is embarrassingly lacking facts and reflection. Another can read the same story and be drawn to prayer, compassion, and to that deeper space within where God wordlessly has made a home. This person's comments and commentary contribute clarity to the conversation.

One important way to develop an inner life is to wait before speaking (or responding to that email or dashing off a comment). Wait, even if you do not feel anything or hear anything. Often, our inner life is like a shy child. It needs to be sure that you will respect it and honor it before it has the courage to make itself visible.

Waiting makes space for something deeper, something beautiful, something that is beyond our reactions.

2 - Develop the habit of awareness. As we wait, we discover that the tempests we thought were only *outside* ourselves are also *inside* ourselves.

Events we encounter trigger responses that are "charged" or "springing from the passions" within our own hearts. We often think and talk about these world or family situations in a cynical, angry, or discouraging way. Even though talking this way may make us feel important, informed, or helpful, the more we repeat these types of conversations, the more we strengthen the underlying passions. In effect, these "charged" thoughts appeal to the unpurified desires of our hearts. We are in danger of little by little becoming ourselves what we ridicule with our words.

By practicing awareness, we realize that we are subject to all manner of delusions, anxieties, and passions.

3 - Develop the habit of serenity. Serenity is the ability to disengage from the power of the tempest without acting on its suggestions.

Let's say you are thinking that a particular event or situation shouldn't be happening. When you think this thought, notice what you are feeling. What are the sensations, emotions, thoughts? Write them down. How are you affected by this thought that the event should not be occurring? What is the cost of having this thought? Could the opposite of this thought also actually be true? And finally, do you *really* know that this shouldn't be happening now?

When we disengage from the tempest within, we become free. Often without realizing it, we have become identified with a thought or feeling that isn't completely true or freeing. Through the serenity we gain by pondering the questions above, we become liberated from their power and can choose a wiser and more serene response to the situation at hand.

4 - Develop the habit of seeing with the eyes of God. We sell ourselves short when we look at people and situations only through the eye of our own storms. Here's a simple process for taking the poison out of the passion-charged thoughts and desires that create the drama of the overwhelming tempests:

As you become aware of your anger, sadness, frustration, or cynicism, you might have the grace to sense that there is also a deeper "I" within you.

Seek to be present to this "I" who is also experiencing the event or situation. This "I" is deeply present to the reality, but it has no thought or judgment in its regard. This "I" feels called to accept what *is* happening to us within that greater plan of God's design that is mysteriously beyond what we can grasp. Doing this does not mean that you condone or resign yourself to a situation; rather it is to open you up to what is also real—to the perspective of God. When we have stepped outside of the boundaries of the storm and stand within the heart of God, we look at the person involved and say, "You are precious to me." Observe what unfolds within you as the person who was the "problem" becomes "precious to you."

Looking at the world from within the mind and heart of God and at the people who take part in the drama of our tempests as precious and held in life by God's breath profoundly shifts our inner space. It sometimes can even "pull the plug" on the storm entirely, and all that is left is love.

Any number of issues in our country and our world trigger reactions within our minds and hearts. We can join the cacophony of voices speaking out of fear, anger, and cynicism making them stronger, or we can step aside and speak wisely, powerfully, and prophetically with the heart of God, with words our world needs to hear.

These four habits will strengthen you and gradually transform you into both mystic and prophet. When people decide they want to come out of the fury of the storm, you will find them coming to you. They will choose to come to you for warmth, support, and strength because you are no longer part of the tempest everyone is in, but a person of wisdom and peace.

October 10, 2016

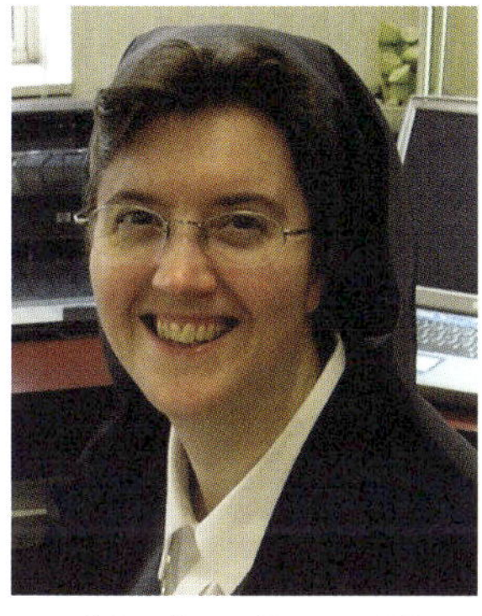

Sr. Kathryn James Hermes is a Daughter of St. Paul, an author, and is blessed to be able to spend all her life living Jesus and giving him to the world. Two of her titles, *Surviving Depression: A Catholic Approach* and *Reclaim Regret: How God Heals Life's Disappointments*, spring from her own experience of healing and love for spirituality. You can find her at touchingthesunrise.com.

Reflection

Contemplate your own inner storms/tempests, such as times of exhaustion, discouragement and confusion. How have you found healing and calm in the midst of those times? Who has been a person of strength and wisdom for you when you needed it?

Consider the four habits the author suggests. Perhaps journal with each one or find a personal way to explore the possible purpose or outcome for each habit. Which would be the easiest for you? The hardest? Where would you like to start?

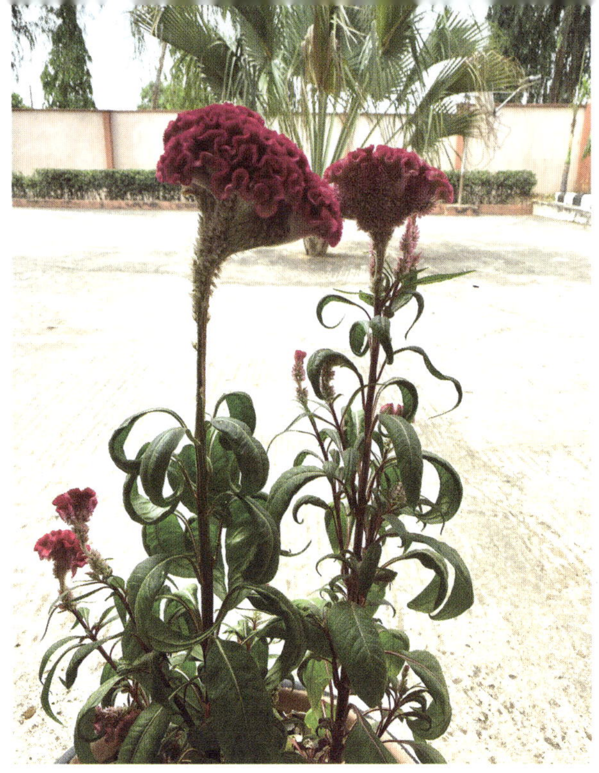

"Being consciously in God's presence is not only possible when I sit in prayer, but also when I practice seeing the goodness of God in everything around me," Teresa Anyabuike writes.

(Courtesy of Teresa Anyabuike)

Learning to be in God's presence always

By Teresa Anyabuike

Being in God's presence moment by moment is the most fulfilling experience I've ever had. It is hard to describe or express. One can be calm and at peace even in the midst of disturbing moments—not that you don't feel unease about it, but you just won't allow your feelings to take over.

I believe it's all God's grace in action when I permit God to take charge of the situation. Being consciously in God's presence is not only possible when I sit in prayer but also when I practice seeing the goodness of God in everything around me—whether I'm walking, working or sitting. This might sound difficult, but it is possible.

In everything I do, if mercy, love and compassion are missing, then I am not dwelling in God's presence nor being aware of God's abiding presence in my life and the lives of others. I must exhibit mercy in dealing with my sisters and brothers. That is one of the ways to see God in them.

In everything I do, wherever I find myself, I can create a peaceful atmosphere. The energy I use to practice this attitude of godliness is insignificant compared with the muscles or energy I use in showcasing negative attitudes within and around me. *How good it is for sisters and brothers to dwell together as one* (Psalm 133:1).

I try to be consciously aware of and dwell in God's presence in my daily encounters with myself, my sisters and brothers, and with all of creation. When I meet someone, I pray silently in my heart, asking God to help me see the beauty of God's presence in the person. So, relating with that individual will be awesome and wonderful.

We can actually grow in being in the presence of God, and being consciously aware that God is dwelling in us. We can be in touch with our feelings and open up space in us for God to fill. Once I realize that God dwells in me and I'm constantly in God's presence, my attitude towards my sisters and brothers will be that of love, joy, compassion and patience.

Recently, a security guard was sharing with me about the working conditions in his workplace. I sympathized with him because there was no compassion in the conditions he described to me: His work does not have a human face. I wished his company had compassionate conditions for their workers; it would have gone a long way toward putting a smile on the face of the security guard.

Sometimes the working conditions in our own establishments lack a human face, and it may be difficult for our workers to experience God's presence working with us. These conditions need to be reviewed: If our staff is not happy working with us, but have to work because jobs are not easy to come by, we must be concerned. We must exercise charity and learn why they are not happy working. Our workers ought to find God through their work for us, and the working conditions we provide for them ought to reflect God.

I feel concerned about the expressions on the faces of my sisters in the community and those with whom I work. When I notice that their facial expressions have changed from what I knew previously, I try to find out why. I believe we are all companions on a journey and need to look out for one another, even though sometimes it might be seen as not minding one's own business. No matter how it is interpreted, we are our sisters' and brothers' keepers. Just find a gentle way to care for one another.

Once when I was returning from a journey, I saw a little Muslim girl trying to cross the road. I could see how hard it was for her because of the moving vehicles. I simply asked her if she needed help and she nodded her head. I held her hand and helped her cross the road. You could see the smile on her face. I was happy I helped her because I saw God in her.

There's no limit to the kindness we should show to one another. It is a daily struggle for me, especially when I am hurt when I try to show love and compassion. But I fall on my knees in

God's presence to help me do good at all times, as St. Julie Billiart* found the goodness of God in all events of her life.

July 13, 2023

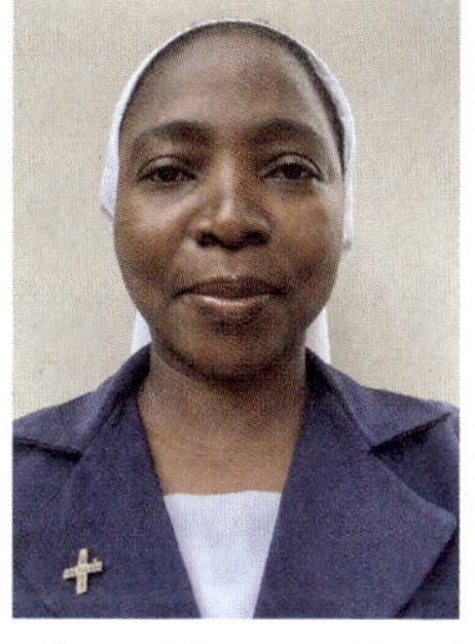

Teresa Anyabuike is a Sister of Notre Dame de Namur living in Abuja, Nigeria. For a time, she was the coordinator of a Catholic community self-help association, a department of the Justice, Development and Peace Mission in the Ilorin Diocese. She also served as a website manager for her Congregation. Currently, she is working as a social worker in advocacy against social injustice.

Reflection

Think of an experience in which you felt God's presence. How can you carry that presence with you into other aspects of your daily life?

How can you be attentive to those around you and thus become an instrument of sharing God's presence with another?

* *Sisters of Notre Dame de Namur consider St. Julie Billiart their foundress. Julie Billiart (12 July 1751 – 8 April 1816) was a French nun, saint, and educator. She was born in Cuvilly, a village in Picardy, in northern France.*

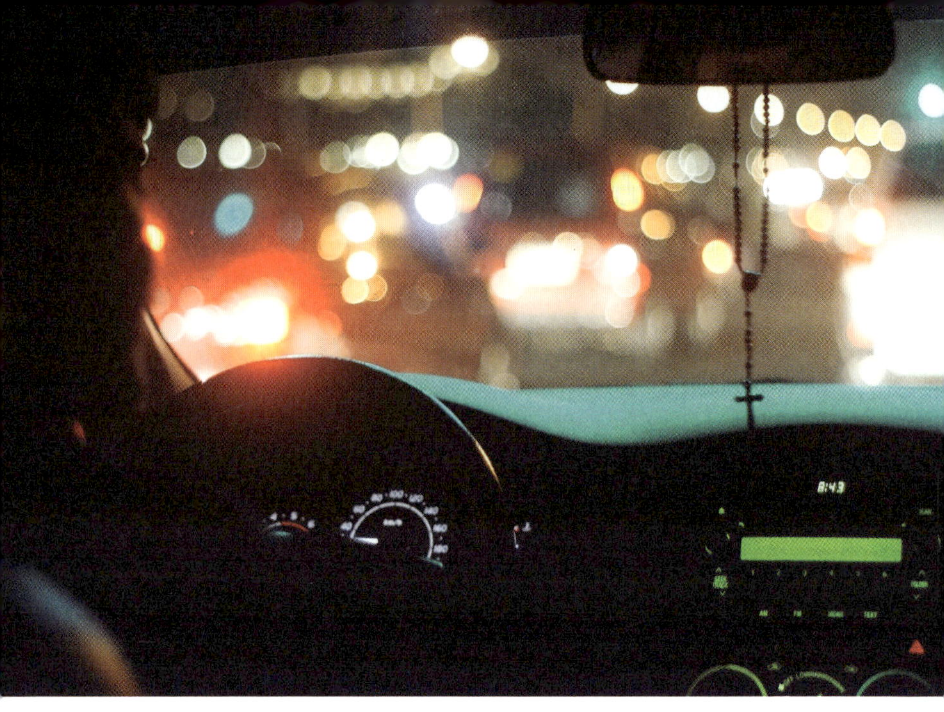

(Pixabay/Victrixia Montes)

Living on a prayer: A nun's guide to self-help

By Quincy Howard

I recently read that more Americans pray in their car than in a place of worship. My initial reaction was, "that tracks." Then it got me thinking about my own prayer journey . . . and yes, much of it was by car.

When I began discerning with the Dominican Order, I did not know how to pray at all. I had been a non-practicing Catholic for more than 25 years and was largely unaware of my spirituality. Thank God, I was still able to hear the call—and to respond—despite myself.

My subsequent experience with the sisters has been one of rapid growth and deep probing. With the guidance and support of wise companions, I've explored the divine presence in this world, witnessed it at work through my sisters and the church, and searched for it within myself.

The breadth and depth of approaches to prayer that the Catholic tradition offers is something I relish. Perhaps most familiar are the devotionals committed to memory and shared by Catholics across the globe. But there is a stunning range of ways to worship, to center, to engage with the sacraments, to sing praise, to lament and to seek intercession.

As my prayer life has deepened over the years, I've stumbled upon a prayer formula that has become one of my central tools of resilience and accountability. Sharing it feels vulnerable—like opening my inner room to the public—but gifts are meant to be shared, and it's been a gift for me. It is a tried-and-true personal prayer about God's call for me and how I respond. And, yes, I often pray it in the car!

The Personal Prayer

> I forgive, revoke, release and repent of all the contracts and agreements, the vows and promises, any programs, prisons, permissions and strongholds that distort my Divine Image in this world, distract me from my true path, diminish my connection with the Spirit, or dull my imagination or inhibit my gifts from being fully brought to bear in this world.
>
> Whether I've made them collectively or individually, allowed them to take hold willingly or unwillingly, or cling to them consciously or unconsciously,
>
> I forgive them now and send them back to where they came from.
>
> So shall this be thought, having been said, make it so.

This first part is about "clearing the deck" so that I'm praying from a true and attentive place—it breaks through the noise and sets an intention to ditch my baggage. Usually, my prayers alone are silent and only spoken out loud when I'm reading or reciting in a communal setting. Speaking this particular prayer out loud, by myself, keeps me focused and present in a way that feels like a first baby step toward manifesting it.

The second part, below, is an invocation for help attracting what I need and being my truest self in challenging times when truth can feel hard to discern. In my Trinitarian view, God provides circumstances and encounters to respond to; Jesus helps me contend with my brokenness and human failings (hence his is the longest!); and the Spirit inspires and guides me.

God

Gracious God, bring me insights, graces and protections.

Bring information to guide my thoughts, my words, my attention, my choices and my next right steps on my true path.

Bring filters of protection to shield me from information that doesn't serve me and from distractions that would lead me astray from God's call for me.

Thank you, God, for what I don't know: for mystery, for possibility and for the movement of the Holy Spirit in this world.

Help me to always be humble: mindful of how much I don't know and aware of how little I control.

Help me to always be hopeful: trusting that the Divine Advocate is always at work on our behalf, sustaining that faith in others, and emboldened by the power of my imagination and my gifts when I fully bring them to bear.

Jesus Christ

Sweet Jesus, bring me healing, freedom and wholeness.

Bring healing from the wounds and the hurts, healing from my brokenness, healing from the blindness that prevents me from seeing more clearly, healing for my strained and broken relationships.

Thank you, Jesus, for your model of healing, of reconciliation, of mercy, forgiveness and non-violence.

Bring freedom from any worldviews, systems, dogmas or narratives that limit my Divine Image from shining forth. Liberate me from any self-made prisons and self-imposed smallness. Free me from the fears and anxieties that plague me and from the judgments that are put upon me, those that I put upon others and those that I put upon myself.

Thank you, Jesus, for your model of courageous freedom to recognize, speak and live in truth.

Help me to become whole: to reclaim those aspects of myself that I have distorted, hidden, rejected or lost. To reclaim and integrate them as the blessings originally bestowed on me. Align how I act and speak with how I want to be. Help me to live with integrity, in right relationship with God, with others and with Creation.

Thank you, Jesus, for your model of unity and wholeness.

And thank you, Jesus, for your freedom to sacrifice, thus revealing the Paschal Mystery always at work in the world to make things whole.

Help me to be a friend to that Mystery: to accept, cherish, honor and salvage all that is falling away and the deaths to come. Help me to recognize, to nourish, to share and to manifest the life that is seeking to be born in its place.

Sweet Jesus, help me to walk your way with integrity and grace and to be your disciple at work in this world.

Holy Spirit

Divine Advocate, bring me a new and discerning heart.

Bring wisdom and courage so that I can know and do God's will for me.

Thank you for your presence in my life, for your invitations, for your inspiration, for your guidance and for your steadfast companionship.

Help me to be a wise discerner—always looking to you for my next right step.

Help me to be patient—waiting for your guidance and holding my ego at bay from prematurely driving forward.

Help me to be bold and creative—fully bringing to bear my imagination and my gifts to follow your guidance.

Help me to be a steadfast companion to you—always open to your guidance, attentive to your stirrings, ready for surprises, and responsive to your call.

I developed this prayer over the past decade; it grew in iterations from prayers that spoke to me. It takes about 20 minutes to recite thoughtfully. Since it reflects my theology, such as it is in 2023, I hope it will continue to develop and deepen over the decades to come. It's written on my heart and I offer it up here. Take what you like, leave the rest, and feel free to fine tune it for your own image(s) of God.

June 23, 2023

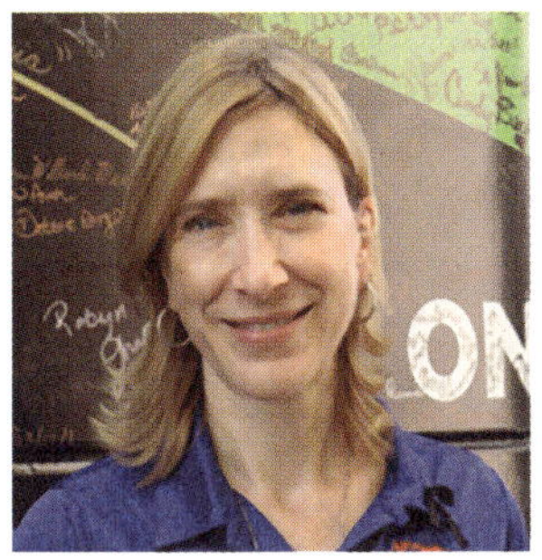

Quincy Howard is a Dominican Sister of Sinsinawa. She lives in Wisconsin, doing planning work on behalf of her congregation. She recently ended a ministry on Capitol Hill as a federal policy advocate for social justice.

Reflection

What means of prayer have been a part of your experience either from your own or other faith traditions or from the memory of childhood prayer and mystery? How has it changed over your life?

With trust, the author shares a personal prayer she has used for her own personal spiritual journey. If you are willing, try using the prayer that Sr. Quincy has offered by spending 20 minutes each day for a week to pray it thoughtfully. What surfaced in you during the week? Would you make changes to fine tune it for yourself or perhaps write your own from your heart?

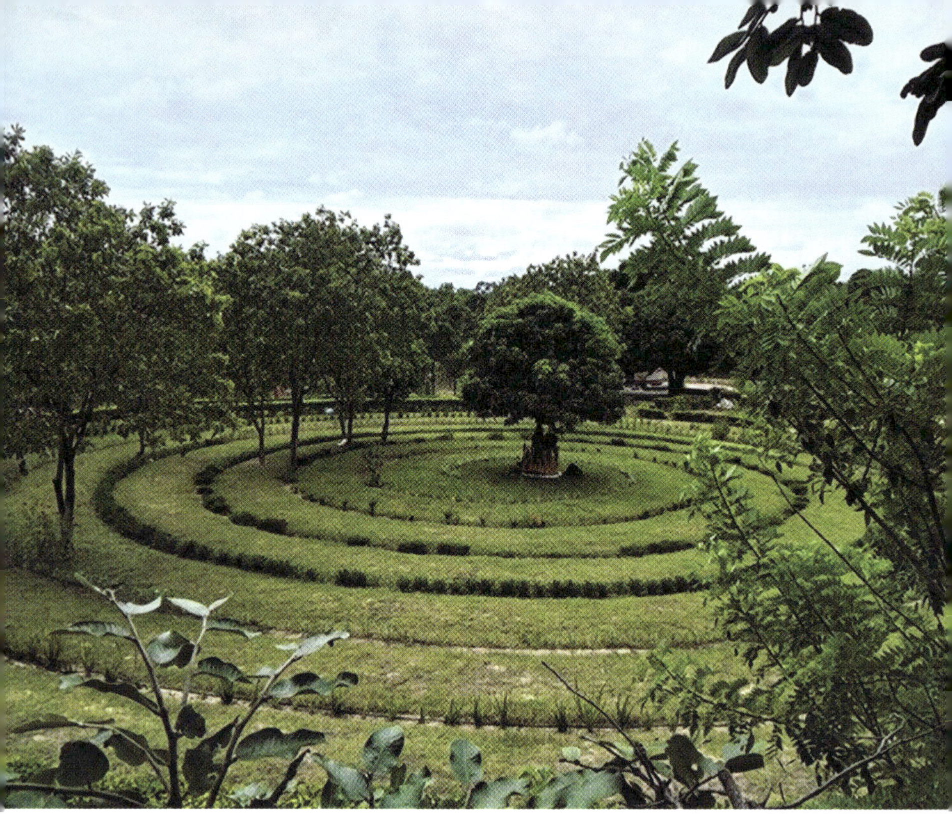

The heart of the Garden of Oneness, a natural sanctuary built by the Presentation Sisters and the local community in Zambia.

(Courtesy of Andrew Chunga)

Listening to the heartbeat: God's, ours and the world's

By Teresita Abraham

Often in the Garden of Oneness here in rural Zambia, we take moments of silence to honor the core of our being by placing our hand on our heart to feel our heartbeat and to be aware that the Heart of God is beating inside us. It is the same heart that beats in all creation: beings of land, sea and sky.

How often have I seen a twinkle in the eyes of people when we share that we are made of God, to know we are Holy Ground and are beloved of God! On one occasion, when we were practicing stillness together, a woman reflected, "How come we often use too many words when we pray, and how lovely it is to be in stillness together."

Stillness helps us to be in tune with the sound of the Spirit at the core of life itself, giving meaning and purpose to life. Spirituality is that which resonates with the sound of the Presence within us, helping us to breathe with the Great Spirit who is breathing within us all the time and within all things. The Spirit herself will pray in us, with sighs too deep for words.

Spirituality is about leaning on the breath of God in the realities of our lives. One of my own sisters in the Presentation family, Raphael Consedine, sums it up: "leaning heart to heart on the One who pulses life in the lowliest and least of all that lives." This leaning is spirituality.

How do we experience this everyday God? In everyday life? How can we listen to the heartbeat of God in the ordinary events of our day?

Each time we walk the Sacred Web in the garden, we take moments to breathe together to appreciate the gift of breath, which we so often take for granted. We remember with gratitude the tiny bacteria that created a revolution in our Earth story and changed the poisonous oxygen into that which is life-giving. The ability to breathe is one of the miracles of life and one of the greatest expressions of love. Love of God breathed us into being in the home of our parents, in the heart of Mother Earth.

Praying is breathing together, breathing with the Spirit. The image of Pierre Teilhard de Chardin, "breathing together of all things," invites us to listen to the heartbeat of God in all creation.

We are connected to all of life through breath, and "God is the breath of all breath" (Kabir).

Spirituality is listening to our own heartbeat because what happens deep in our hearts affects us and affects everything else. Spirituality is also listening to the heartbeat of the world—its joys and hopes, griefs and anxieties, especially of those who are made poor and suffering. Listening gives us the courage to see, feel and act with and on behalf of the poorest, lowliest and the most lost of all that lives, including peoples, nations, species and Mother Earth.

Spirituality also includes how we respond to the hard things of life—our own and others'—and our world, both locally and globally. When we listen to the aches and pains of our own hearts, our own lives, and are faced with the struggles of life, spirituality helps us to be more compassionate and attentive to the pains of our brothers and sisters in our neighborhood and in our world.

Last year, when some of the local people were here in the garden helping to clear the grounds, I noticed a little girl with a child on her back. When I asked what grade in school she was in, I was told she was not yet in school. She is 10 years of age. My heart ached for her. Since then, I have found two more girl children who are not in school. One is 12 years of age. I think it is a sad state of affairs that at this time and age, we can allow this to happen; that our children, our future generation is not able to see the doorstep of a school because of poverty. Since then, we have had these three children back in school thanks to the help of a kind friend and sharing from our own personal allowance. Last Sunday, during the church service, one of these little ones sat beside me and whispered in my ear with eyes beaming with joy, "I got a book.' "

Listening to the realities of life around us and responding to them is spirituality in action. Taking one small step to change one small situation in the life of a child demands listening to the heartbeat of God in another. The other is an extension of our own self.

Listening to the heartbeat takes practice. I consider it a spiritual practice. Practice, we know, becomes a pattern of life, of behavior. A number of years ago, I was at an Earth Wisdom Gathering with some 400 people of all faiths and walks of life. During a tea break, I was asked by one of my companions, "What is your spiritual practice?" I was taken aback! Gosh. What is my spiritual practice, I asked myself. Did I have one? It was a wake-up call to me to be attentive to my spiritual practice.

Spiritual practices are not just for monks or for monasteries or hermitages. They are meant for each of us to stay connected to the Ground of Our Being, to nourish us. Our spirituality does not grow if we do not nourish it. We each need to develop our own practices, whether meditation, yoga, centering prayer, attentiveness to breathing, mindful walking, or watching the sunrise/sunset.

Every part of creation is beating with the heart of God and is also practicing by its very being, fulfilling its place in the community of life. When we practice, the whole of creation practices with us. When we sit to meditate, the whole of creation sits with us in some mysterious way.

Pilgrim, listen . . . the Heart of God is beating all around you.

December 12, 2016

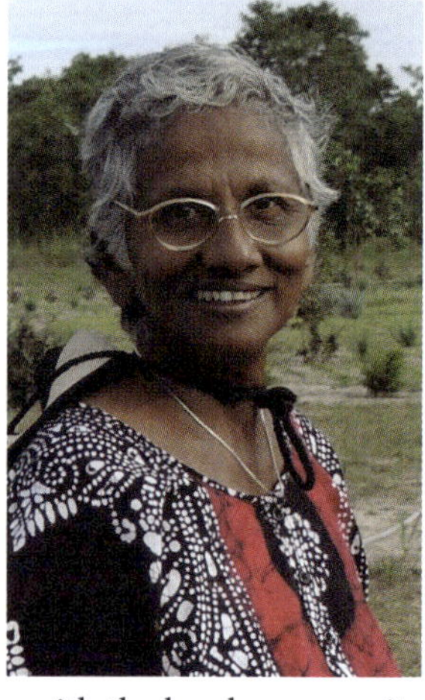

Teresita Abraham is a Presentation Sister from India living in rural Zambia. She is passionate about the new creation story and the spirituality of being in communion that seeks God in the inter-connectedness of all life. The Presentation sisters together with the local community worked with the natural surroundings to create the Garden of Oneness, a sanctuary of peace and harmony, where she lives and works.

Reflection

Feeling the Heart of God beating within us, being in tune with the sound of the Spirit, leaning on the breath of God, listening to the heartbeat of God in all creation—all of these rich images invite us to a deeper reflection of God's presence in our very being. What do these images offer you as a way to imagine or even deepen your spirituality?

Do you need a wake-up call that invites or challenges you to be attentive to your being, your source of life, and your spiritual practice? If it needs a jump start, what could help?

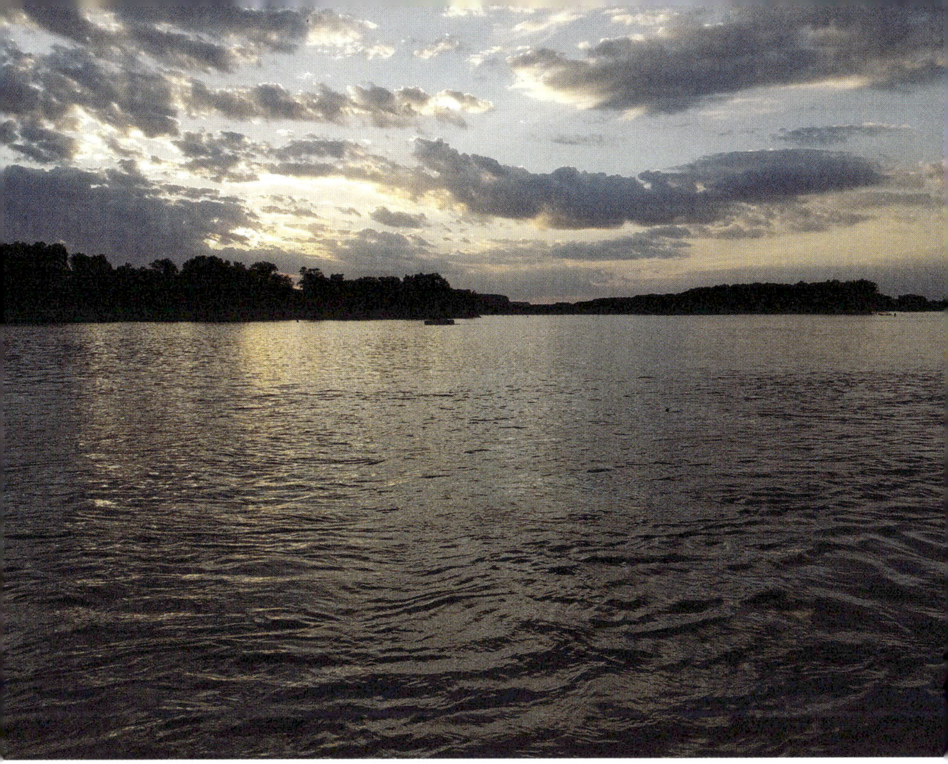

The Mississippi River near sunset. (Courtesy of Julia Walsh)

Praying with the power of paradox

By Julia Walsh

I am on the shore of the Mississippi River. I can't see into the water in this light. I can't see the bottom of the river, or much more than the movement of the surface and the reflection of sky bright upon the ripples and waves.

I know something of this body of water, its power for life and destruction, its broadness and strength—but I've never before encountered these particular droplets joining together into the one mass that flows in front of me. It is at once so familiar and completely new.

I've never traveled to the source of this mighty stream nor to its end. I only know a slice of this water. I've crossed this river hundreds of times, but only a section, really—the bridges between the Twin Cities and Dubuque. This region—often called the Upper Mississippi Valley—feels most like home to me compared to any other place I have been.

The presence of this stream during different eras of my life has convinced me I know this river well, has put me into relationship with it, has established an affection for it within me. Only reluctantly, awkwardly, can I admit that I can only know part of this great river: much of its vastness and force will forever remain a mystery to me.

Sometimes I think I know God. I can easily make big proclamations about who and what God is and isn't. I arrogantly inflate my knowledge and often try to define or explain God to others—in the same way I falsely think I know the Mississippi River.

But I haven't actually experienced the whole of the Mississippi River and likely never will. And I will never know all of God. The vastness of God shrinks me.

Sometimes I think I know people. I can easily judge and decide what type of person somebody is by their dress or mannerisms, occupation or preferences. If they don't vote or think or pray like I do, then they must not be good friend material. If they ever hurt or disappoint me—I shrink the potential or possibility for a future bond between us.

Only reluctantly, awkwardly, can I admit that I can only ever experience a part of a person—and much of them will forever remain a mystery to me.

At this juncture in history, when the tendency of the human mind is to sort and categorize, to label and judge, the Spirit prompts us to abandon our definitions. It's a good time to strip away the trappings of difference, to drop the masks and costumes that cover our chances for communion. With all our coverings on the cutting room floor, we can then be free of anything that causes us to make others into enemies instead of friends.

Weeks ago, during Mass on Pentecost Sunday, I heard the Gospel proclaimed. The good news was that the risen Jesus joined the disciples who were behind a locked door and told them twice, "Peace be upon you."

As I listened, my imagination put me in that room right with all the other disciples. I interrupted Jesus, my critical mind thinking overtime. "What do you mean by peace, Jesus?" I wanted analysis, explanations. I wanted clear definitions.

Jesus gently put his hand on my shoulder. He calmed me and spoke a thousand words through one simple gesture of love. The answer to every question I'm trying to ask is being powerfully present.

I heard of dark matter before I got engrossed in a PBS Nova documentary the other night, but I had no clue what it was. As I listened to the scientists describe the mystery of the force, the force that pulls and connects and fills in gaps in the universe, I discovered that they don't have a clue what dark matter is either.

One scientist, Marcelle Soares-Santos, said that she, along with other scientists, is "trying to figure out something that we have no idea what it is." I say the same thing about God. Good theologians likely would say the same thing about their work.

Maybe when it comes to God and people and the mysteries of the universe—I need to stop pretending I know anything. Maybe the only thing I am called to do is learn how to relate to the mystery. I suspect the proper gesture in this relationship is not interrupting with questions—it is probably better for me to lovingly listen or bow in submission.

The force that connects the universe is a mystery, and nobody knows what principles guide it. Although there is much that is clear and definable and principles that are certain, these truths coexist with that which we cannot see or identify.

I've been thinking, lately, that it could be the same with humanity, with our call to relationship. Whenever a person is defined, categorized and made into an "other," we are ignoring what is real about them. We are avoiding seeing their fullness, their hidden goodness.

What is it about our humanity that insists on stunting our openness to possibility and growth? Perhaps we can only feel confident when we are under the illusion that we know and understand. Perhaps sticking others into tidy containers is one way we try to control and navigate the mystery.

I don't remember where I heard it or where I read it, but it's been rattling around in my mind a lot lately that the healthiest and holiest people are the folks who are conscious of the power of paradox. These good ones can love those they disagree with and want goodness for those who have harmed them. They are the saints who can hold two contradictory truths together, who aren't threatened by inconsistencies.

I wonder how different our church and our world might be if we were taught from a young age that prayer is a type of communion with the mystery, that it is the practice of embracing opposing truths as they coexist. Opening ourselves to seeing every side and knowing we will forever be limited in our knowing is another way we can touch the cross of mystery; it is a way we get to put our fingers into Christ's side.

Back at the Mississippi River, I think of Jesus and our connection on Pentecost Sunday. His calming gesture assures me I don't need to know, that mystery ought to be a place where I am at home, at peace. His love invites me to move out of my head and to live fully from my heart. After all, my heart knows mystery is not a threat but an awesome place to pray.

June 8, 2018

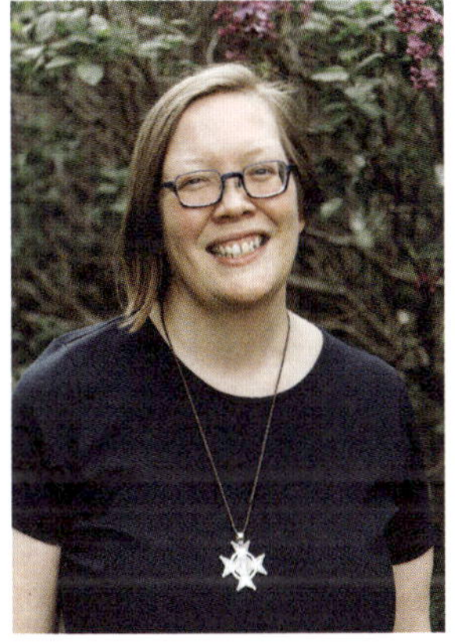

Julia Walsh is a Franciscan Sister of Perpetual Adoration who is part of The Fireplace Community in Chicago. She serves as a spiritual director and vocation minister, plus hosts the Messy Jesus Business podcast. A widely published spiritual writer, her work is found in places such as America, Geez, Global Sisters Report and St. Anthony Messenger.

Reflection

How does the Spirit invite you to abandon your preconceived, perhaps even entrenched, definitions including who you define God to be?

How are you called to relate to the mystery of paradox in your life, good or bad things that have happened, those who helped you or hurt you, things you appreciate or resent? How can you remain open to the mystery of paradox that helps us grow or even keeps us in communion with one another?

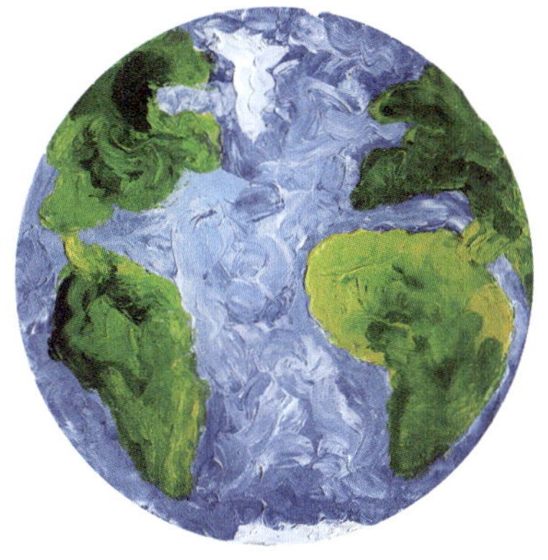

Growing in Grace

We are the midwives of new ways of living, therefore of thinking and worshiping and relating with everybody and with everything.

Magda Bennásar

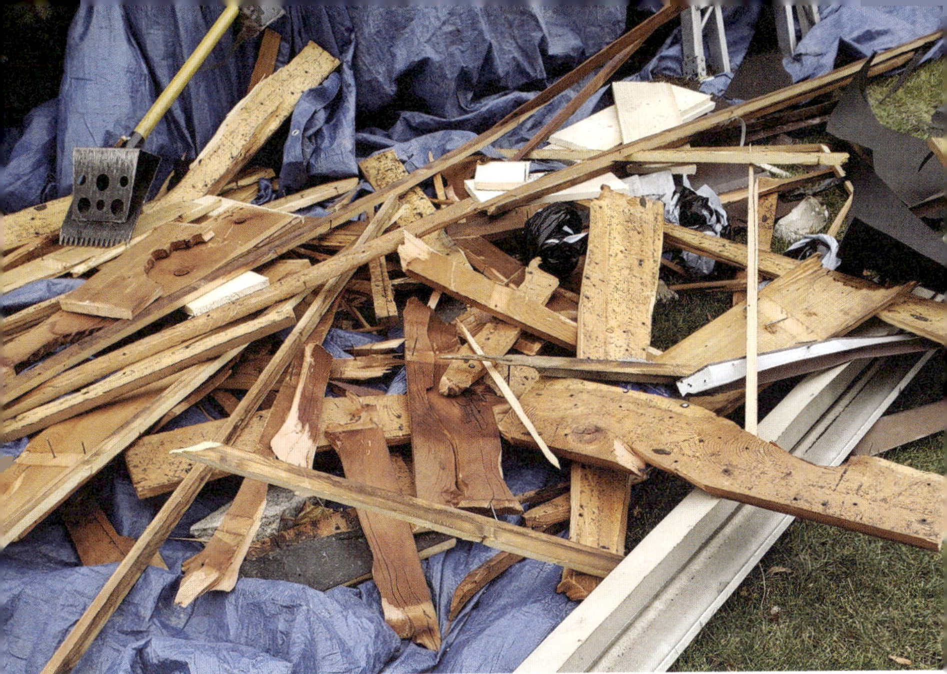

Pieces of the roof from Sr. Jane Marie Bradish's residence stand in a pile during a construction project.

(Courtesy of Jane Marie Bradish)

It's always construction season in our hearts

By Jane Marie Bradish

Where I live, the running joke is that we have two seasons: winter and construction. The length of each varies depending on the weather. Lately, every place I go, I meet construction.

The church I attend was having window work done; the stained glass needed serious attention. The windows were gradually removed, repaired and returned to their respective places. Every couple of weeks or so, scaffolding was moved around, and different areas of the church were taped off with red "caution" tape.

I've often joked that prayer/real God encounters should come with a warning sign of some kind. I never expected caution tape. My initial encounter with the taped-off areas of the church brought giggles. Let's be honest: Opening yourself to God means dramatic change—it is not for the faint of heart.

For the past few years our international motherhouse has been under construction as it is transformed into affordable housing for the neighborhood. It was a giant maze of noise and dust and constant detours, one I'm very grateful not to have lived through on a daily basis. Negotiating my way through when I came for choir rehearsals or liturgy was more than enough for me.

I was very conscious that the physical structure was being transformed, and with it our community. The building would no longer "be ours"; instead, the structural heart of our community would be opened in new and once-unforeseen ways. Our foundresses often spoke of responding to the needs of the times; offering "our home" to others is just such a response.

My place of ministry had a major utility failure, which resulted in—among other things—the concrete at our main entrance being torn up so the underground power lines could be repaired. It was a little unnerving to walk around barrels and across plywood labeled "hole" to get in and out of the building. And, of course, because this happened as the temperatures plunged, filling holes and repouring concrete will take a while. I say "hello" to the barrels each morning as I arrive; it seems a better approach than complaining about them.

And not to be left out, my residence needed minor roof repair. The front yard was piled with debris during the work. It was a quick repair, taking less than two days, but I found myself rattled seeing the volume of decayed pieces that needed replacement.

It seemed everywhere I went, every piece of my life was "under construction." Then, a single line of Scripture started haunting me. Seemingly out of nowhere, Ezekiel 36:26 popped into my consciousness. The passage has God promising a new heart in replacement of a heart of stone and that—once that happened—we would be God's peoples, and God would be ours.

Two phrases from a song I can't identify (Google failed me big time) are constant companions: "I will give you a new heart, a new spirit within" and "And you will be my people and I will be your God."

I'm humming them as I write. Belonging to God and being one of God's people—YES. Heart of stone . . . what?

It's easy to look at the stones of the world: violence, discrimination, human trafficking, pollution, poverty, mental and physical illness. The list could go on. But what was this passage trying to say to me? With a haunting Scripture passage and hymn lyrics running through every part of my being, it didn't take long to find pieces of my heart that can best be described as stony.

There are the things I just can't understand and make me angry. For example, why are people killing each other in random ways and times?

Elsewhere, children are being exploited globally. There's nothing wrong with not understanding or being angry, but if there is nothing but angst, there are stones.

There are stones called grudges, usually from when something didn't go "my way" (or a way I agree with and can support). It could be the position I wanted but didn't get, even if the end result is better. It could be the people who speak about me behind my back that I can't seem to ignore. It could be institutional policies that aren't changing fast enough for me.

There are stones I carry from premature, untimely or sudden deaths. Yes, I grieve and celebrate life and have good memories of shared time. But every once in a while, some seemingly insignificant event or memory creeps in and I find myself resenting the events and circumstances around death.

There are other stones, too personal to share publicly, that keep me from being the person God has called me to be. So that begs the question—what do I do? Let's go back to my construction encounters. In none of the cases was the construction simple; things had to be taken apart, repaired and/or replaced and put back together. Each project: windows, remodeling, power restoration and roofing—required money, planning, time and effort.

The same has to happen with all of us. God isn't going to just show up and "fix us." That's not how it works. We need to put time and effort into first identifying and then softening our stony hearts. I guess I have a project ahead of me.

April 17, 2023

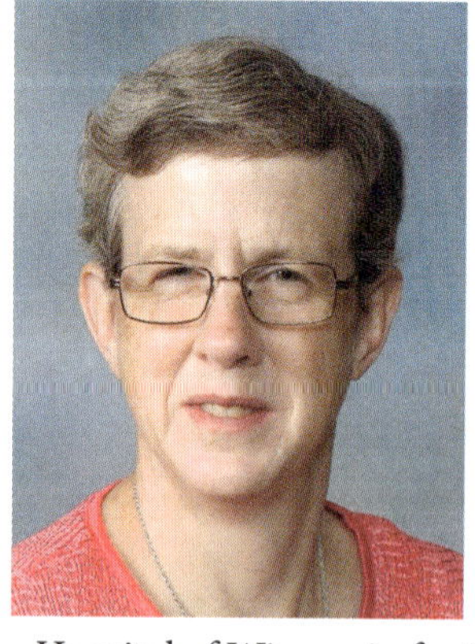

Jane Marie Bradish is a member of the School Sisters of St. Francis based in Milwaukee, Wisconsin. Her ministry has been in secondary education; she teaches theology and is the academic programmer for a large, urban, multicultural high school. She received the Project ADAM Karen Smith Award from Children's Hospital of Wisconsin for implementing comprehensive CPR-AED (cardiopulmonary resuscitation and automated external defibrillator) programs for the school community.

Reflection

Construction or even reconstruction does create a mess even as it creates order and newness; it can make familiar routes a quagmire of delays and unexpected, even dangerous barriers. Yet it is constantly necessary for growth. Where are you constructing and reconstructing in your life? What insights has it caused you to discover?

The author speaks of "stones"—in world issues, grudges, losses, injustices, etc. But God's Spirit comes as promised into hearts of stone and offers a new heart. Where have you found God has come to you with a new heart or even softened your stony heart? (Or where do you pray God will come?)

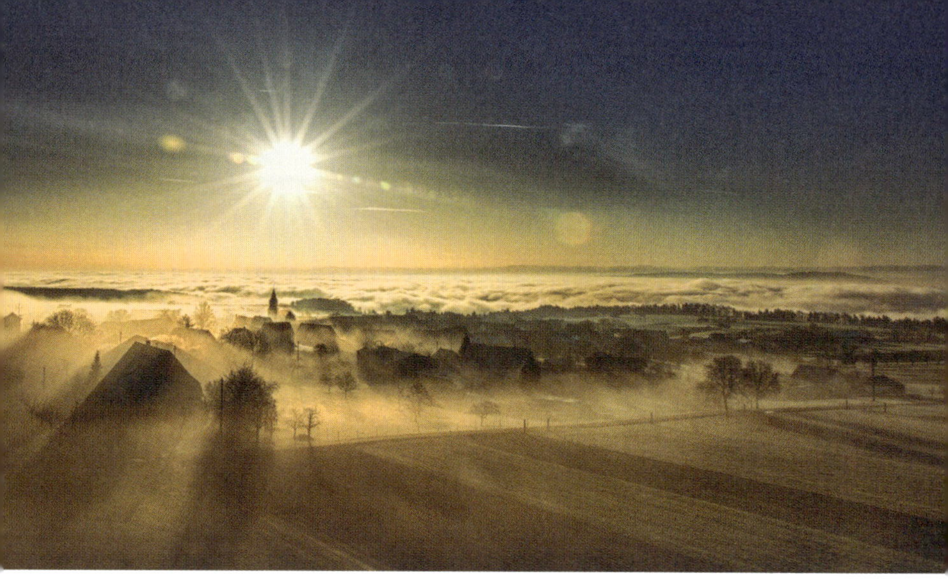

(Pixabay/winterseitler)

'Quotidiano' theology—the theology of everyday

By Mary John Mananzan

We have been living for over a year already in these pandemic times. It is at this time that we become very conscious of our daily routine—especially we religious who have a fixed daily schedule. Day in and day out we get up, we go to lauds, we attend holy Mass, we eat our breakfast, we go to work, we say our midday prayers, we take a nap, we return to work, we say our vespers, we do our one-hour lectio, we eat supper, we pray compline and prepare for bed. And since travels, visits, outside meetings and social gatherings do not happen at this time, there is hardly any interruption to our routine activities.

It is at this time that we should reflect on the theology of everyday life (or quotidiano). To me, it means that everyday life is holy, is sacred, is the actual juncture where God meets us, where we encounter God, where we experience God's love, God's grace, God's mercy and it is the venue of our own conversion, of our own transformation. We do not need an extraordinary event or a special moment of divine intervention, a sacred ritual, or even a special place for us to have an experience of God.

Where, but in our everyday life, did we experience a kind gesture from our superior; a co-sister who listened to us, gave us solace and comfort, or even made an extraordinary, generous gesture? But is it not also in our everyday life that we offended someone, scolded a lay partner in public, became impatient, became angry, became envious or jealous? Is it not in our everyday life that someone hurt us, betrayed our confidence, bore false witness against us, spread rumors about us, and the like? It is also in our everyday life that we are able to forgive and to be forgiven, to help and to be helped.

Is it not during our everyday life that we hear of a close friend, a relative, or a co-worker dying of COVID-19, making us experience this pandemic closer and closer to home? Before this, COVID-19 was an accepted reality but a far away reality. Now it has become a part of our everyday reality. So we start to do consciously what we automatically do every day: put on a facemask and maybe face shield, wash our hands thoroughly, take advantage of an alcohol dispenser to drench our hands thoroughly, practice physical distancing, and so on.

The realization of our mortality makes us appreciate life—not in the abstract but in our everyday lives. When we wake up in the morning, we realize that although God did not promise us a tomorrow, here we are awakening to a new day. After taking a shower, we are amazed at the refreshed feeling it gives us. As we are on our way to the chapel, we pass by a familiar garden, which we used to see with our peripheral vision. But now we stop.

We see the beauty of the gardenia we have seen every day, but now we pause to admire its velvet petals and breathe its unique fragrance. We look up at the blue sky and are amazed that there is no speck of cloud to be seen. We allow the warmth of the sun to bathe our face, hoping to absorb its vitamin D.

And yes—is it not in our everyday life that we get a sudden insight into ourselves or into a situation that is the beginning of our transformation, of a Damascus experience, a metanoia, a return to God's embrace? It is in our everyday life that we experience the consolation that rains down to water our arid spiritual life in the desert of our desolation.

Zen teachers, when asked by disciples what they should do to achieve "Buddhahood," reply that they should do just what they are doing: washing a plate, sweeping the floor—and in our context—writing on our computer, auditing a financial statement, preparing a community pantry, yes even viewing a Korean drama!

The most important attitude in the theology of everyday life is: mindfulness, or as Eckhart Tolle prefers to say: conscious awareness, meaning to live moment to moment, to focus in the here and now. Yes, because the past is no longer real because it is past, the future is not real because it has yet to be. So, the only reality is the here and now. When we spend our time feeling guilty about the past and being anxious about the future, we are missing the blessing of the now, which contains all opportunities, challenges and realizations. It is in the here and now that we will recognize God's visitation when it happens.

Now that I am 83, I realize that I have overshot the biblical length of life—"80, if you are strong" (Psalm 90:10)—and that every day is a "bonus." My prayer on awakening is:

"Lord, thank you for this beautiful day. Thank you that I am still alive and relatively healthy on this beautiful day. Help me to live this day with conscious awareness, compassion and joy. Amen."

November 16, 2021

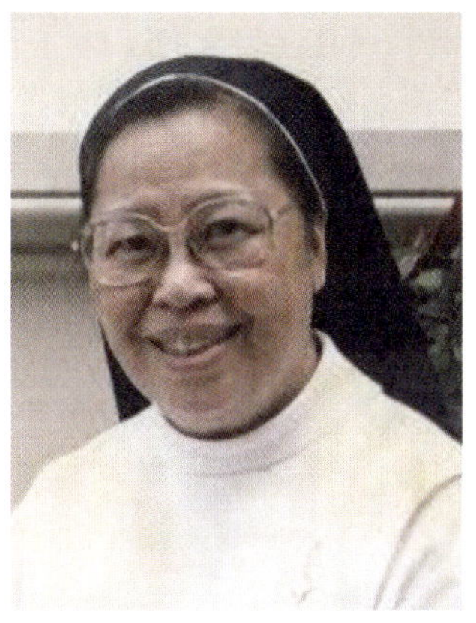

Mary John Mananzan is a Missionary Benedictine sister from the Philippines. A noted theologian and author, she has served as president of St. Scholastica's College, as prioress of the Missionary Benedictine Sisters in the Manila Priory, and as national chairperson of the Association of Major Religious Superiors of the Philippines. She is a political and feminist activist who helped develop an Asian feminist theology of liberation and works with a number of organizations that deal with gender issues and women's concerns. She is the founder and executive director of the Institute of Women's Studies at St. Scholastica's College and an executive chairperson for CyberGuardians Philippines. Currently, she ministers as superior of the community in St. Scholastica's Academy in Pampanga and as a member of the Priory Council.

Reflection

Even though big moments can shake us into awareness of God, it is everyday life that gives us an opportunity to encounter and experience God's love and grace. But to be conscious of each moment in that everyday life takes effort. How do you put that conscious awareness into practice?

Mindfulness to live in the present moment—in the here and now—and not the past or future takes energy so we can recognize God's visitation. Where have you experienced God's presence when you have fully been present in the here and now? If you could write a prayer of thanksgiving to mark your recognition and express your gratitude, what would you pray?

Mary of Magdala's profound connection to Jesus shows us the power of love

By Christine Schenk

Mid-July always reminds me that it is Mary of Magdala season. Over 20 years ago, I helped launch what would become an annual event hosted by FutureChurch designed to honor this preeminent "Apostle to the Apostles."

Inspired by the global women's marches, this year's theme is "Celebrating Feminism and Faith in Union." A special prayer service includes optional readings from feminist theologians such as Elizabeth Johnson, Miriam Therese Winter, Diana Hayes and Emily Maynard. Since Mary's feast lands on a Sunday, July 22, special resources offer ideas for honoring this great woman witness at Mass.

It has been gratifying to watch the Mary of Magdala celebrations explode in popularity. An amazing 250 to 400 events are held around the world every year. FutureChurch leaders Deborah Rose Milavec and Russ Petrus are reaping the rewards of their faithful perseverance.

Why has celebrating St. Mary of Magdala become such a hot ticket?

I suspect ordinary Catholics are attracted to the idea of helping correct an egregious wrong. Plus, there is something intriguing about the hiddenness of the women in Jesus' discipleship. After all, most of us are pretty much "hidden disciples" ourselves. We don't think of our Christian witness as anything special, even though it is what gives our lives meaning and drives our decision-making.

Could we be among those Pope Francis is talking about when he quotes St. Teresa Benedict of the Cross (Edith Stein) in *Gaudete et Exsultate*?

> The greatest figures of prophecy and sanctity step forth out of the darkest night. But for the most part, the formative stream of the mystical life remains invisible. Certainly, the most decisive turning points in world history are substantially co-determined by souls whom no history book ever mentions. And we will only find out about those souls to whom we owe the decisive turning points in our personal lives on the day when all that is hidden is revealed.

For the most part—at least until recently—Mary of Magdala's witness was all but invisible in Christian history. Even though her testimony is the lynchpin upon which the proclamation of the resurrection depends, for centuries, she was falsely remembered—at least in the West—as a forgiven prostitute.

Her prophetic witness emerges from what is surely the darkest moment in the lives of the earliest believers. She went to tell her brothers—despairing male disciples who probably figured Jesus' promise of a new reign of God was nothing but a pipe dream—and they did not believe her. Before belief could take hold, they needed their own experiences of the risen Christ.

Mary's deep love for the one who had healed her led her to the garden on that fateful morning. First, she discovers that the tomb is empty. And then she saw him. She saw the one who had not abandoned her in her time of trial. The one that she and her sister disciples could not abandon during his time of horrendous suffering and death.

And the rest, as they say, is history. Or is it herstory?

Some biblical scholars suspect that the empty tomb and resurrection narratives came down to us predominantly through female oral history. The popular memory of the women's experience at the tomb was so strong it could not be extinguished, even though early male writers minimized it out of concern for propriety. In Greco-Roman culture women were not permitted to be legal witnesses or to speak publicly.

This may be why Mary of Magdala and her companions are not mentioned by Paul, whose letters precede the Gospel accounts by several decades. But by the time the Gospels were written down, it was impossible to tell the story of the resurrection without including the women witnesses. The oral tradition about the empty tomb and Mary of Magdala's encounter with Jesus was too deeply entrenched in Christian memory to leave out.

Mary of Magdala's profound connection to Jesus in the garden recently came to mind as I watched the Disney film, "A Wrinkle in Time." I had loved Madeleine L'Engle's book and enjoyed the movie almost as much, even though the production was uneven at best.

I resonate with the story's focus on love as the binding force in the universe and its capacity to traverse the space-time continuum. Perhaps a bit like our Catholic communion of saints. Perhaps a bit like Jesus' ability to be present to Mary of Magdala, then to the other disciples, and now—to us!

L'Engle's tale contains other lovely Christian themes: Each person's inner light brings something uniquely important to creation; we can access divine power by loving and seeking the good and by realizing that acknowledging our faults contributes to victory over evil—for evil most certainly exists in L'Engle's narrative world as it does in our own.

In the story, teenager Meg Murry becomes a Jesus-figure, saving her younger brother, Charles Wallace, who has been possessed by "It," the dark enemy of all that is good. She saves her brother by loving him despite the evil invective and pain he spews. Her love persists in the face of grievous suffering. In the end, her love overcomes all dark powers, and her brother is returned to her, whole and healthy.

This is a powerful story. It increases my faith that the significant evils we face in our day can be overcome by our union with divine love. In the process, we must also acknowledge our faults—individually and corporately—because then their power over us is weakened.

I suspect there may be many "hidden mystics creating a decisive turning point in human history," in our world.

Perhaps, like Mary of Magdala and Jesus, we will create a new "wrinkle in time," when dark powers are overcome and all that is hidden is revealed.

July 17, 2018

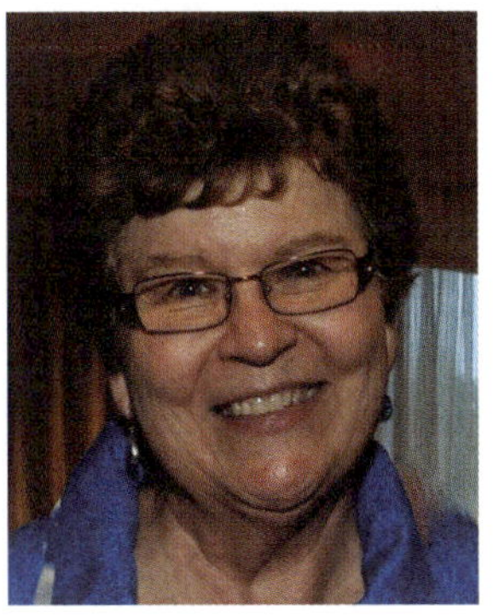

St. Joseph Sr. Christine Schenk, an NCR board member, served urban families for 18 years as a nurse midwife before co-founding FutureChurch, where she served for 23 years. Her books *Crispina and Her Sisters: Women and Authority in Early Christianity* (Fortress, 2017) and *To Speak the Truth in Love: A Biography of Therese Kane, RSM* (Orbis, 2019) received first place awards from the Catholic Press Association. She holds master's degrees in nursing and theology.

Reflection

Prophetic witness often does emerge in the darkest moment in our lives, as it did in the early community of believers. Yet it is often dismissed because it comes from a hidden mystic in an unexpected place—a woman, the young, an outcast, an enemy. Where are you being invited to listen and perhaps trust a hidden mystic, maybe even an inner one?

Many have found themselves at the tomb, a place of dashed hopes and emptiness and pain. Yet it is at the empty tomb that Mary of Magdala found new life in the God who had not abandoned her. He called her name and sent her on a mission. Where have you found an empty place, and what have you found there?

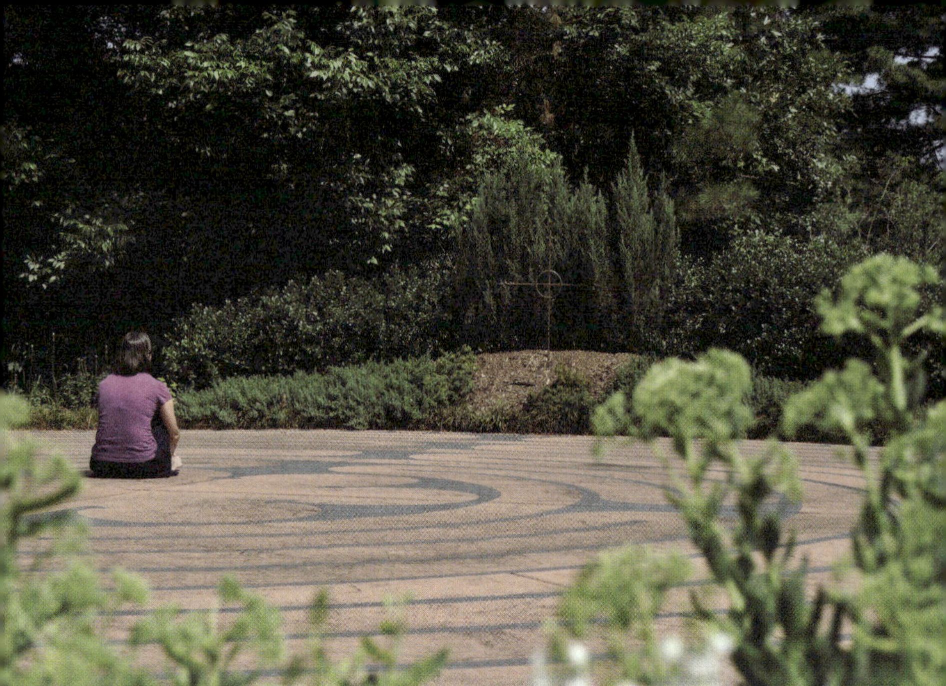

(Pixabay/ev3177)

Baptism works slowly and spirally

By Magda Bennásar

Baptism is a process. There is a special time for its ritual at the heart of the community. But the awareness of our deep identity may only come slowly and spirally.

It might come only slowly because it is too profound to be absorbed fast. Like a balm, it slides along the skin of our soul, permeating each pore, hydrating the dryness of our inner self, which is tired of seeking outside what abides within.

It is the water that opens our soul to the *Ruah*, the water that cleanses the dust from our eye, so we are able to comprehend, bit by bit—spirally—who we are.

Spirally, yes, since like any relationship, it has its different seasons: A day of winter may be followed by an experience of spring for a period of time, then back to winter. It depends on our personal and social reality and the emotions and life changes we experience—our personal and social pain, injustice, joy or renewal.

To enter into the spiral dynamism of the *Ruah* is a safe refuge. She understands processes and spirals, and if we remain quiet, she does her work.

It is in this movement of the Spirit in and through us that baptism, received ritually once, acquires its meaning again: "You are my child, in you I find pleasure." And the wheel of life starts to roll again, leaving the anger and the pain and the loneliness behind, and offering the water, the meaning and love needed, like air to breathe anew.

One of those deep breaths in the *Ruah*, filled with new, fresh air for me, happened a few years ago in Wicklow, Ireland. A small community of Dominican sisters offers an integrated sabbatical program on "the New Story." It is a 10-week immersion in the study and the experience of the beginning of every kind of life in its different forms; of inner and outer life, through the lenses of present-day science and diverse spiritualities, especially Celtic spirituality.

The place is called An Tairseach, which means "Threshold" in Gaelic. It houses the ecology and spirituality center whose mission is "to grow in awareness that the Earth is our own home and home to all living beings."

And it happened that the experience, generously provided by a grant from the sisters, was a threshold of a new baptism for me.

I was getting near the end of my rope with the patriarchal-clerical model, whose presence is still dominating our church in Spain. I needed to create a space within me and around me that was safe from its tentacles!

And while it is true that the power comes from within, it helps if you can get immersed for a while in the deep, warm waters of baptism. Those sisters and their program were, for me, the hands, mind and heart of the *Ruah*.

I did experience personally and in community an entrance, through their threshold, into a deeper comprehension of everything: science, mysticism, myself.

Now, a few years later, I experience that the gifts of "becoming"—priests, prophets and shepherds—given to us in our baptism have acquired a new meaning. I see my priesthood as a profound call to consecrate everything my hands and mind and heart touch: the planet within the universe in its multiple facets; the air, the water, the earth itself, the mountains, the forests, the animals; and foremost the suffering people—especially those in deep search of meaning—which is the kind of poverty and injustice I am called to address.

To be prophets is an amazing challenge for today's people of all ages. We are at a threshold as a civilization, and a new paradigm is emerging. We are the midwives of new ways of living, therefore of thinking and worshiping and relating with everybody and with everything.

This is not new to anyone anymore; what is new to me is that after having been touched by a new comprehension, my call to be prophetic takes a turn in the spiral of life, a turn from which there is no return. And that means a change of attitude about who I am and what I do with my mind's energy, my creativity, my religious vows.

How much better I understand now the "listening" to the cry of the Earth, far and beyond the obedience to somebody else's vision of . . .

Or how the sharing of everything I am and I have is acquiring a dimension that I never suspected I would experience: to collaborate with the planet, far and beyond the repressive guilt of never being poor enough.

The same wonderful sensation happens with my invitation to unconditional love—not to abstain from love, but rather to participate in a life of giving love, creativity, compassion and passion to care for and heal the Earth and its inhabitants.

Yes, I like to see the unfolding of the experiences that this new baptism has ignited in me. And I dare to say, that as a consequence, many people have been touched by it.

Thank you, sisters, caretakers of the Earth, for your new ways of consecrating life, of being prophets and excellent shepherds whose pastures are as green as those in Ireland.

April 15, 2020

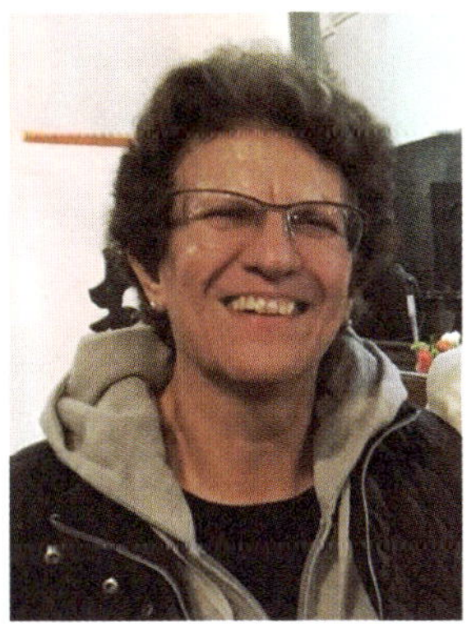

Maria Magdalena Bennásar (Magda) of the Sisters for Christian Community is from Spain. She has worked in teaching, conducting retreats and workshops, creating community and training lay leaders in Australia, the U.S. and Spain. Currently, she is working on eco-spirituality and searching for a space to create a center or collaborate with others both online and in person.

Reflection

The author offers many images of becoming fully who we are as God invites us at Baptism: Ruah; deep, warm water; wheel of life; breath of air; priest/prophet/shepherd; midwife; vertigo. Which resonate with your current spiritual journey? Do you have other images from your life?

A deeper comprehension of any dimension of God, creation or humanity can lead us more deeply into our own response to life. Where has that contemplation led you? In what ways does it relate especially to the Earth and its inhabitants?

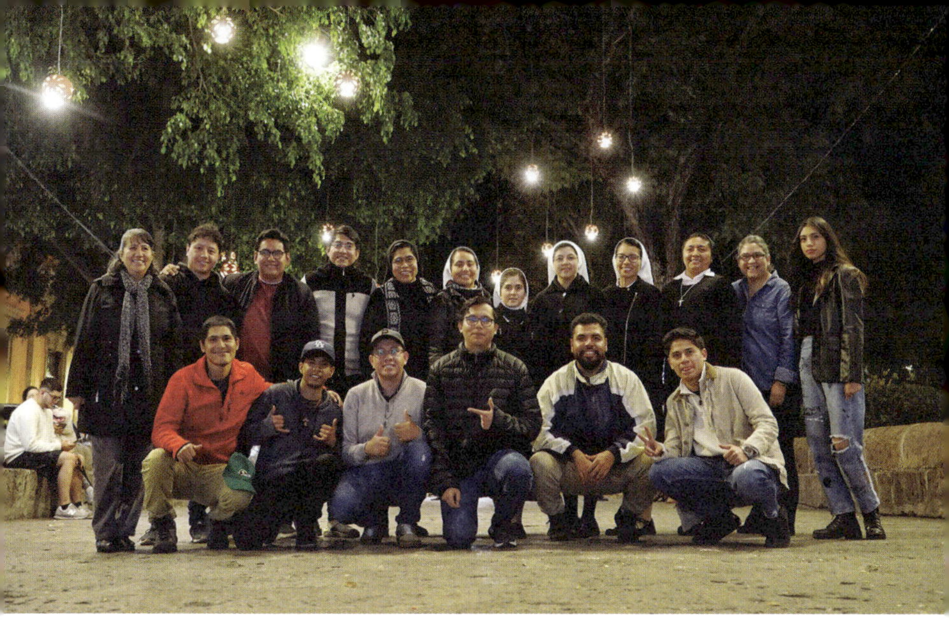

A group of young adults and members of the Verbum Dei Missionary Fraternity on a pilgrimage to the Sanctuary of Our Lady of Guadalupe in Morelia, Mexico.

(Courtesy of Asaid Castro)

We are all pilgrims. What footprints do you want to leave?

By Blanca Alicia Sánchez Olvera

This year, I had the privilege of accompanying children, young people, adults and members of the Verbum Dei Missionary Fraternity on a pilgrimage to the Sanctuary of Our Lady of Guadalupe in Morelia, Mexico. Though the original image of Our Lady is in the Basilica in Mexico City, the church in Morelia is widely acclaimed as one of the most beautiful in the country and is a frequent site of pilgrimage.

As we walked through downtown Morelia, I observed the faces of the people there. I saw faces full of hope, understanding, surprise and amazement. I sensed that they might wonder: How could this group of people have the audacity to go on a pilgrimage on a Sunday afternoon to a shrine? And, at the same time, I could see the smiles and welcoming looks of the people as we passed.

I felt they connected with us, allowing themselves to be touched by our songs and be flooded with joy. How could there be such a deep connection if we did not know each other? Deep down, we are all pilgrims; we are all on a journey searching for a goal, a dream or an ideal. As human beings, we are born with the capacity for exodus, for going out of ourselves to love, help, welcome and receive.

I felt a sense of solidarity with the people along the way, and with those who leave their countries searching for a better place to live. I believe humanity is one big caravan, constantly moving from one stage to the next, from one discovery to the next, and from one style to the next.

Indeed, all human beings are on the way, regardless of age, social status, race, language or nation. Human beings, from conception on, are open to change and growth and, at birth, go through the first great exodus that will accompany them until their last days.

We are walkers, and life is a path to walk, although sometimes obstacles like cold and darkness prevent us from moving forward.

How many people in this COVID-19 pandemic have lost the enthusiasm and joy for opening new routes of peace, dialogue and forgiveness? How many pilgrims have yet to find their goal or fulfill the hopes that led them to set out on the road?

I ask myself: What about me as a missionary? And what do we, in consecrated life, want to offer to all those who are tired of walking in their lives, who find themselves wounded, stretched and devoid of illusions along the way? What can we, as consecrated women, offer to the millions of people who continue to leave their homes in the hope of a new dawn?

I am excited, and I desire to live "on the way," knowing that I have not achieved everything, that I can continue to learn, that I can grow every day, and that I am called to respect and value the dignity of others.

What do I wish for this year? What routes do I want to take? I want to be constantly on the move, to build bridges to get closer to the marginalized and those who need to be heard and to have hope. Being a pilgrim is our personal seal; it is the mark we leave at every step that many can follow.

It is true that when we connect with this deep identity in our hearts, the call to set out on a journey is renewed—to live in constant exodus, to love, to forgive and to serve. As the Spanish poet Antonio Machado says, "*Caminante, no hay camino, se hace camino al andar*" ("Traveler, there is no path; the path is made by walking").

We are made to explore new territories, expand our horizons, and share the hopes and fears of others. We cannot cover our hearts with stainless steel on this path of life, because we have been called to live in solidarity, allowing ourselves to be touched by the suffering and pain of people we encounter.

Did not Jesus of Nazareth walk along the roads? He went from town to town, announcing peace. May this year be a year of exploring new paths and sharing our bread with others. We value the footprints that others have left so that we can move forward on the same path.

At the end of the pilgrimage to the shrine of Guadalupe, several people joined us with a grateful look as if to say, "Thank you, because I also wanted to walk."

After all, we are pilgrims; what we leave behind is our way of loving, being present, and reflecting on the person we are called to be.

And you, what footprints do you want to leave? What paths will you open? What crosses or baggage will you carry?

April 5, 2023

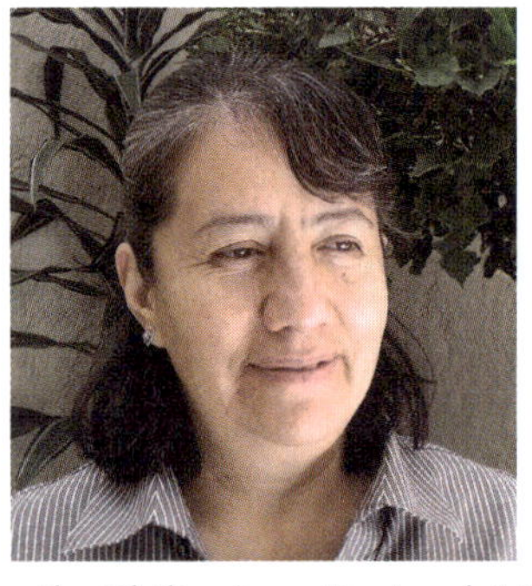

Blanca Alicia Sánchez Olvera is a sister of the Verbum Dei Missionary Fraternity in Mexico City. She received early formation and education in Guadalajara, Mexico, a licentiate in Rome, and other courses in the Philippines, Portugal, Mexico and London. A teacher of dogmatic theology and a spiritual director, she has worked in vocations, retreats and novitiate formation. She was a formator in the International Centre of Missionary formation in Spain and in novitiates in the Isle of Wight (the United Kingdom) and Cebu (the Philippines).

Reflection

There are many images of pilgrimage—being on a caravan or journey, exodus or moving from one place to the next, searchers, explorers, walkers on the way. In fact Jesus' disciples were sometimes referred to as followers on the Way. How do those images relate to how you have lived out your life?

The author says that being a pilgrim is leaving a mark, a footprint, "at every step" that others can follow. Reflecting on the questions in her last paragraph, how would you respond? What footprints do you want to leave?

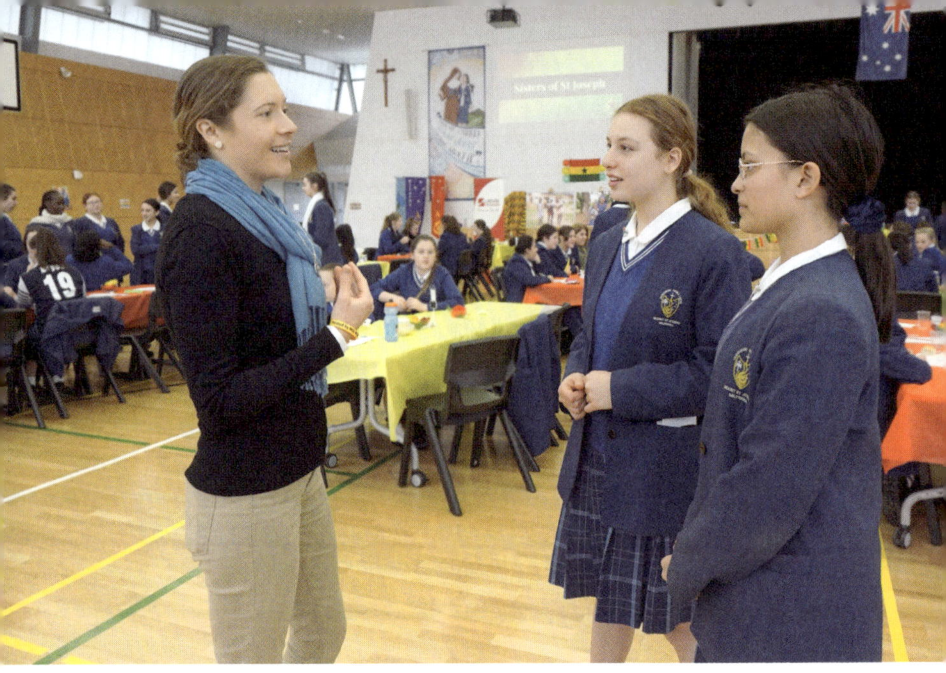

Sr. Jane Maisey with students of Mount St. Joseph High School in Milperra, Sydney, Australia in 2019. To Maisey, the following year, 2020, was the year of reverberant rhetorical "Are you serious?!" moments.

(Courtesy of Sr. Jane Maisey)

The gift and freedom in "I don't know"

By Jane Maisey

"Are you serious? I mean, c'mon? Really?"

Recently, I heard these words exclaimed from the lips of a frustrated teacher while she loomed over a photocopier at school. Her words, proclaimed with gusto, were like greyhounds bursting out of the gates—and they're off. . . .

When I heard her, I happened to be on my knees, trying to figure out how to load paper into Tray 7 (God only knows where that is). At first, I was startled, but then found myself empathizing with her frustration. I stood up to ask if she was OK, our eyes met, and before I knew it, we were both laughing and crying at the same time.

Her arms were flung out like rubber bands expanding, and suddenly, those arms snapped back—and I found myself wrapped up in love. As we embraced, rocking side to side, our teary eyes both welled up as our hearts contemplated joy and sadness. I felt her pain and she felt mine: We were, indeed, in it together.

It seems to me that 2020 was the year of reverberantly rhetorical "Are you serious?!" moments.

Watching from "Down Under," we have a unique take on the world. Australia, New Zealand and the Pacific Islands are far removed in physical distance from Asia, Europe, Africa and the Americas. If viewing world news is anything to go on, I understand that all countries have been affected differently. But I have also seen a new emergence of a constant for all. We have all lost our sense of certainty and we have all lost control in a new way. Gone are the days when we could plan in school or other ministries.

2020 was undoubtedly a year for the classic Merton Prayer: "My Lord God, I have no idea where I am going. I do not see the road ahead of me. I cannot know for certain where it will end." I wonder if Thomas Merton would have befriended the classic saying, "If you want to make God laugh, tell God your plans." Well, I hope you're having a good laugh, God, because I have a few words for you!

With the confusion and inability to plan, I have found myself saying "I don't know" a lot more. People often ask: When will you see your family in New Zealand? What will your school do for the end of year? What will you be doing next week? The response to all: "I don't know." And you know what? I'm finding that there is a freedom in not knowing.

I've come to see this time in many ways as a gift—the gift of not knowing. If my God/our God is truly all-loving, then this must be a gift of love we have all received. All the "I don't know" moments, seemingly packed full of emotions such as joy and grief, revolve around God's grace. My joy grows by welcoming "not knowing." If Jesus reminds me to let go and forgive seventy-seven times (Matt 18:21-22), then perhaps I also need to keep choosing to not know, not once, but infinitely seventy-seven times more?

Lately, I've also been asked by staff and students, "Where is God in all this?"

Oh boy, trying to know God's ways seems to me like trying to know how to herd cats—their destination is surely best left unknown! As we do know, there is much mystery to our faith, the surprising ways of God are not always our ways. As Isaiah reminds me: "For my thoughts are not your thoughts, nor are your ways my ways, says the Lord" (Isaiah 55:8). This feels like a time when I/we are being invited to live more and more into mystery, becoming more comfortable with not knowing, and most certainly not planning. As Joyce Rupp puts it, "The difference between confusion and 'don't know' is that confusion can only see one way out, and that way is blocked, while 'don't know' is open to miracles and insights."

In seeking ways to live with this new mysterious uncertainty, and perhaps even find some collective joy in it, we have adopted some new language as individuals and community at school. For example, we have picked up on the term already in use in the medical community: "Covid Brain." The way we use it, having Covid Brain does not mean you have the virus, but instead symptoms that include disbelief, inability to plan, forgetfulness, tears with simultaneous laughter, and general feelings of "C'mon . . . what . . . really!?" For example, when a teacher misplaces his/her/their keys for the fifth time, and sends an email to all staff, one could easily proclaim an explanation: "Covid Brain!" Thank God for the "calamity of community."

Amidst the uncertainty and many Covid Brain moments, a deeper awareness of one other constant has emerged—through all the surprises, tears and "I don't know" moments, God is with us 24/7. As I continue to run or walk in nature, it reminds me that our loving God is ever present, ever transforming and closer than I can imagine.

I've more deeply realized this year that I need to trust in the presence of God, while fallibly letting go into the "Are you serious?" mystery. It's not easy, but by choosing "I don't know" while trusting in God's constant transforming love, my vision has cleared to hear the birds chirping, see ducklings waddling, kangaroos pouncing, sun rising and sun setting—transforming, making all things new, in God's time, in God's ways.

This year was also special for our congregation. On October 17, 2010, our co-founder, St. Mary MacKillop, was canonized in Rome. Ten years on, she especially reminds us to renew our courage and trust more deeply in God through the surprises and uncertainty. She wrote to sisters in 1877, expressing her relationship with God: "He wants us to take fresh courage—to lean more on Him and less on ourselves." So, perhaps when you next load paper into your printer, feel a sense of "don't know," think about herding cats, or hear birds chirping, you might spare a thought for us Down Under. We may be far away in distance, but we are all connected through and to the sacred mystery. May our hearts remain united, leaning on God and collectively proclaiming with courage, "I don't know."

February 2, 2021

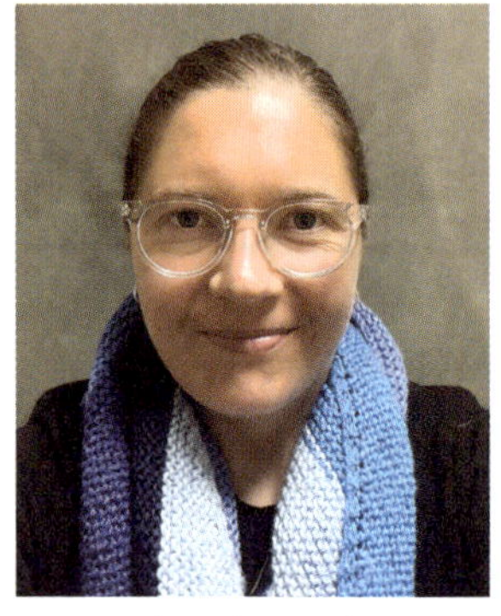

Jane Maisey is a Sister of St. Joseph of the Sacred Heart. Born and raised in New Zealand, she previously explored the world while working as a snowboard instructor. She has primarily worked as a graphic designer and illustrator since 1999, including running her own design business for several years. Currently, she is studying towards a degree in counseling. She is also developing artwork part-time—hoping to reveal beauty, goodness, truth and create connections with our God today. Find out more about her fallible leaps of faith via designjane.com.

Reflection

Perhaps the years of the COVID pandemic taught many of us to live in the world of "I don't know." But many times in our lives can bring a sense of uncertainty, even anxiety of not seeing clearly—a time of not knowing. Where is God's grace and presence in your times of unknowing? Have you found yourself open to new insights or even miracles?

The author recounts her school community's engagement in humor during their recent experiences (COVID Brain). Where have you found humor, laughter or joy in your moments of stress, difficulty or anxiety?

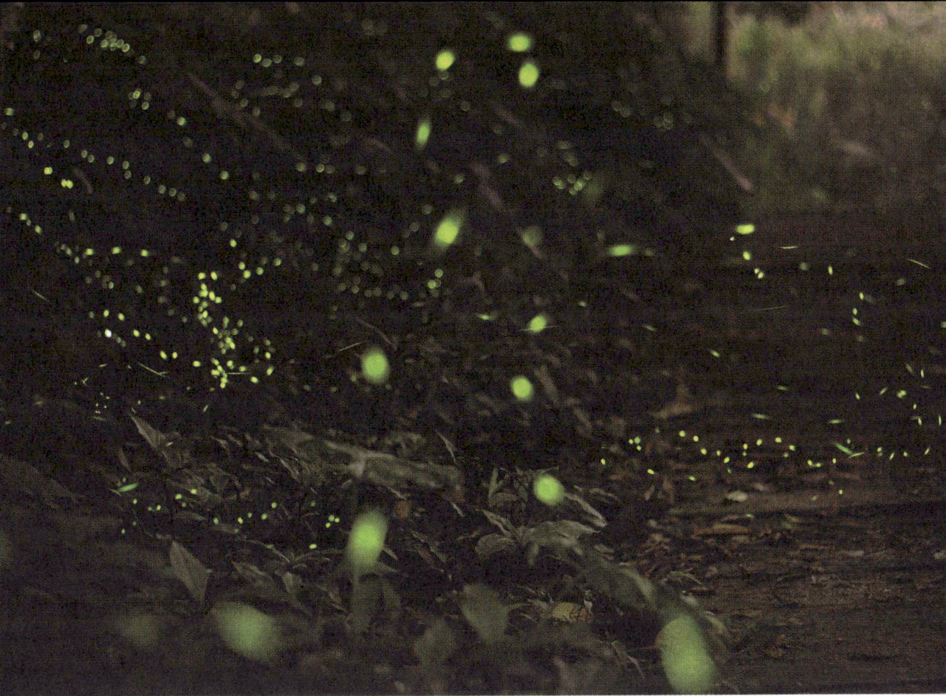

(Pixabay/Monika)

Uncovering my inner light, living in synchrony with God

By Corbin Hannah

This past June, I was able to witness the synchronous fireflies in the Great Smoky Mountains. As I delighted in the dance and light show, I started singing to the fireflies, "This little light of mine, I'm going to let it shine." I created verses just for these fireflies. This led me to reflect on my own light. Am I letting it shine? What is my light anyway?

Jesus said that we are the light of the world (Matthew 5:14). I like to imagine that the Great Light that is God shines through each soul-prism to create a unique spectrum of light that is us. He also said that it is silly to hide our light and that it is meant to shine and give light to others (Matthew 5:15). I believe Jesus said this because we too often hide our light. But why would we do this?

I, like many of you, had experiences growing up that led me to some conclusions about who I am, how I should look and act, whether others are trustworthy, etc. Some of the messages I heard were spoken. However, many were my young mind's attempt to make sense of the world and determine how to navigate it safely. This is a natural and good process we all go through. Some call it the development of the ego that helps us live in this material world. Thomas Merton called it the false self because many of the ideas and identities created are false and hide the truth of who we really are. They can hide our light.

I believe that the purpose of the spiritual journey is to re-member our true self, our light. This is what Jesus spoke of when he told us that we must lose ourselves (false self) to find ourselves (true self) (Mark 8:35). He warned us that we would profit nothing if we win in the eyes of the systems of the world and in the process lose our souls (Matthew 16:26). I imagine this is one reason Jesus went off alone to prayer – to remember who he was – to reconnect to his essence in God and his purpose.

What is the true self? Like any big truth, it is hard to define. Many great authors and mystics have written entire chapters and books to try to describe the true self. Richard Rohr's *Immortal Diamond* comes to mind, where he says that the true self is like the soul but bigger. At this point in my life, I would describe my true self as God within me, my divinity. My true self lives in oneness with the Source of All Being while also living within this body. This true self embodies the Fruits of the Spirit (Galatians 5:22-23). I am always my true self, but I can't always see it, blocked by all the untruths I believe about myself, others, and God.

On my own journey of self-discovery, I am slowly uncovering this light, remembering who I am in my essence. I get glimpses of connecting with my true self that feel like coming home, like peace and freedom. It also feels like love, ease, and flow. It is knowing that I am exactly who I am supposed to be and exactly where I am supposed to be. The path requires me to unlearn and take off the masks I wear to keep myself acceptable to others. These masks have helped me fit in and feel a sense of safety in my relationships, but they keep me from experiencing true belonging. I have learned that belonging is not something I need to find because it already exists within me. As Jesus put it, we are all children of God. Nothing can separate us from the love of God. It is always available to us, even when we cannot see or feel it.

This journey is not easy. The false self thinks it is protecting me – and in some ways, it has. It often throws fear and anxiety in my path. I have found that it is important to accept and love my ego, my human self. I think this is a huge point. It is not about denying my humanity but allowing my humanity and divinity to coexist in synchrony.

It is about love, our true essence. When I begin to love all the parts of me, I begin to touch and live from my inner Light. Those parts I have suppressed, denied, or hated because of the messages I heard from the outside world are only waiting to be seen and loved. And in this way, they can teach me as they transform into the light they always were.

I remember the freedom, lightness, and energy I felt when I chose to let go of some of the expectations I had internalized. Over many years I had heard messages about how I should look and dress. Daily I would spend significant time, energy, and emotion over whether my appearance would be acceptable to others. I was pretending to be someone or something that did not feel natural to me. I was suppressing my light. Once I realized what was happening and decided to express my inner self freely through my appearance, a huge weight was lifted, and energy was freed. I love the me that has emerged. This did not change others' expectations, but I freed my true self - my mix of human and divine - to shine even in the presence of judgment.

Many practices have helped me uncover my Light. These practices include mindfulness, meditation, centering prayer, spiritual guidance, companionship, therapy, and journaling. Anything that helps me see reality as it is, break free from the chains of judgment and expectations, and embrace the beautiful soul that I am is helpful in this journey.

The journey in is the journey out. Self-discovery is not a selfish, isolated journey. The journey inward ultimately leads us outward. This is one of the gifts of the social gospel of Jesus. It teaches us who we are and how to recognize and love that light in each other, in all of creation. When we realize that we are not separate, we desire to create a community where all know and can live from their true loving self. This is the Reign of God on Earth - Heaven on Earth - it starts with embracing all of me and letting my light shine!

May we remember who we are. Remember, we are the Beloved of God —we belong. Our light comes from the Greatest of Lights and is, at its essence, love. This is the good news!

August 4, 2023

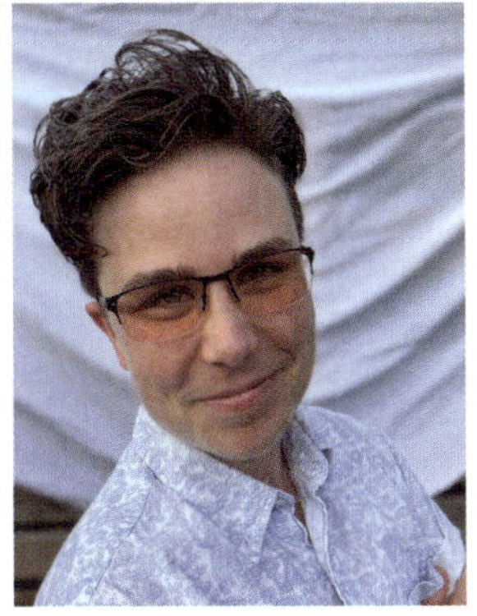

Corbin Hannah is a Sister of Providence of St. Mary-of-the-Woods, Indiana. Educated as a social worker with experience serving young adults experiencing homelessness, Corbin is currently writing and leading prayer and retreat opportunities while healing from a traumatic brain injury. Corbin is passionate about justice, connects with God through nature, and dreams of a world where everyone remembers that they are the light of the world.

Reflection

There are many images for light, in spiritual readings such as the Scriptures but also in daily imagery: light at the end of a tunnel, a light in the darkness, a lightbulb went off, etc. Consider the Scripture citations in this article along with your images for light or specific music that speaks to you of light's energy. How do those images animate your sense of yourself as a light of the world?

The author suggests that by learning to love oneself, we can then allow our "humanity and divinity to coexist in synchrony". She acknowledges the struggle it can be to deal with inner messages and outer judgments. What have you faced in your own life in your journey to not only feel loved by God but to also love yourself as God loves you?

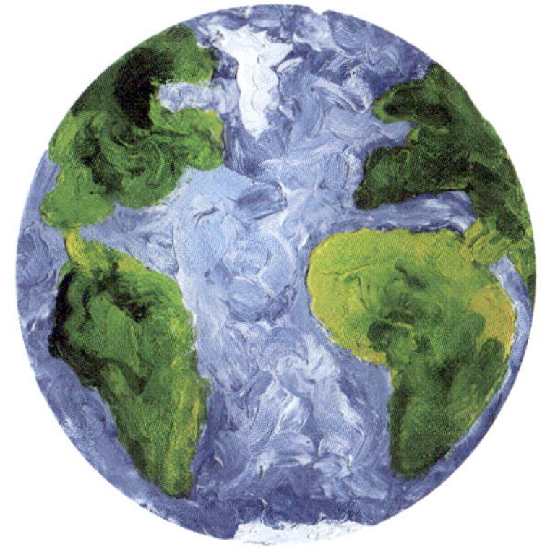

Gift of Community

Community life is a gift. It is a space to grow and practice charity, love and other virtues. Community life involves a relationship with other disciples of Jesus. We hold on to our belief that it is God who called each one of us to be together, and we responded.

Jennibeth Sabay

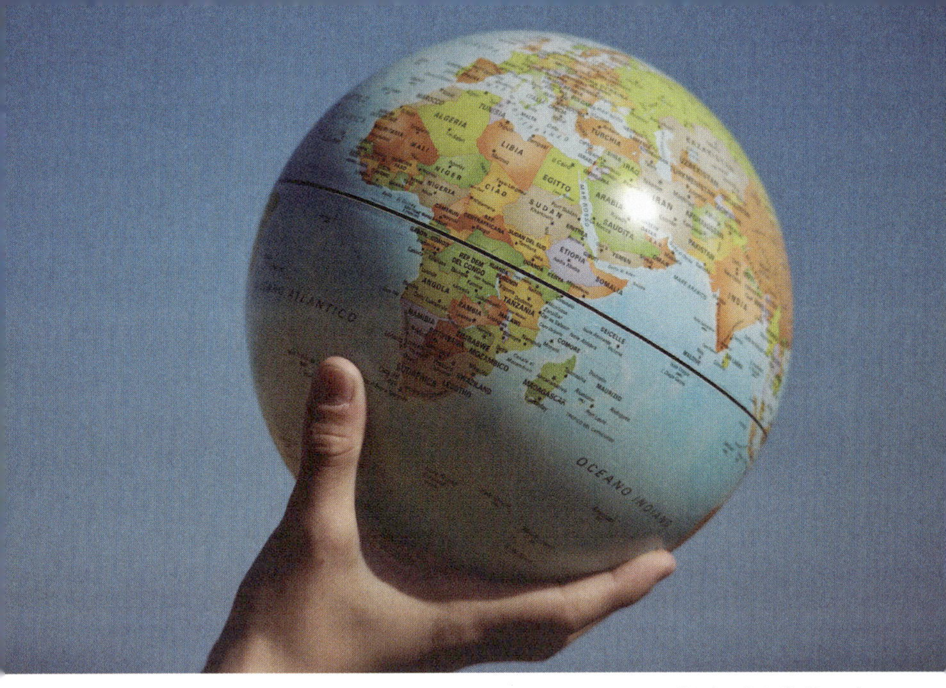

(Pixabay/Luisella Planeta)

The global sisterhood: Nowhere and everywhere

By Joan Chittister

It's a simple story. Some would say "simplistic." But it didn't feel like that to me the night it happened.

I arrived at my destination in Australia on the last flight of the day. The program wouldn't start until late the next afternoon so, travel worn as I was, I wasn't really worried about either the land travel to come or my lodgings. After all, the sisters who were hosting the workshop would meet me at the airport. I would be in bed somewhere within an hour.

Except that no one was waiting for me at the gate. There was no one looking for me in the baggage area either. No one at the arrivals door. No one parked outside on the curb.

A few stragglers were still milling around inside the atrium, but not many. There was no time to stand around hoping for the car that had not come.

This was one of those speaking tours where Group 1 dispatched the speaker to Group 2 at their expense and through their own channels. Translation: I had no names, no addresses, no telephone numbers to go by. And I had no backup plans either.

The ticket counters were all but closed by the time I got back inside to the bank of pay phones, for which I had no coins either. The telephone book seemed to be arranged in alphabetical order, but there were none of the usual categories: convents, churches, schools, hospitals, motherhouses.

A man at the next phone supplied the money and found a couple entries that read "Religious of the Whatever. . . ." With the night watchman hovering over my back to hurry me out of the place, I started down the list. No answer. No answer. No answer. I was getting desperate now out here in the middle of nowhere. And then, with the clock showing midnight, I got a very quiet, very sleepy hello. A kind voice. A nun's voice.

No, they didn't know me. No, they had not heard about the workshop. No, they had no idea who should have picked me up at the airport.

But then, the solution: Listen, Sister, we will have someone there to pick you up in 20 minutes – and we'll work out the whole problem tomorrow. Don't you worry.

Click, and it was all taken care of: the car, the house, the lodging. With strangers who were not strangers at all.

Indeed, the Global Sisterhood in action is an awesome thing. Nothing is too small for its attention. Nothing is too much for it to attempt.

But what exactly is "The Global Sisterhood?"

At one level, there is no such thing as a "Global Sisterhood." It does not exist at all. Women religious – "the sisters"– do not come together in one large umbrella organization anywhere. They do not live under any single Rule of Life. They do not own any kind of common property. They do not all do the same work. They do not all practice the same customs or even live the same schedule or wear the same common clothes.

But they do all come out of one heart.

They have all been formed by the Gospels; they all see themselves as followers of the one same Jesus. They are full of the zeal of discipleship that simply does not wane from one end of life to the other. And they recognize in the face of all the others a sisterhood of centuries. However many miles away, the same commitment to a life of spirituality, simplicity and sacrifice of the self for the sake of the poor makes them one. With the kind of people that Jesus called for in his Sermon on the Mount, they spend their entire lives.

For the very same kind of people Jesus attended to as he walked from Galilee to Jerusalem, they give themselves away. Like Jesus, they refuse to abandon the refugees that so many today call lepers. They, too, talk to women urging them on to be the best of themselves, no matter who reviles them. They raise outcasts out of the depth of their depressions. They contend to the end with those whose religion is more about legalism or pietism or ritual than it is of justice.

At this level, the Global Sisterhood has, for hundreds of years, been one of the strongest, clearest, truest institutions in the church. Everywhere these global sisters go they leave a footprint of care.

This common commitment binds them together as they go to those to whom Jesus went and do the work that Jesus did – healing, teaching, loving and raising people from the many deaths that weigh them down: poverty of soul, despair, disillusion, indigence, rejection, fear and powerlessness.

And so they recognize as their own every other one of their kind in the mission fields of foreign lands or in the midst of urban blight. They open the doors of their small houses and great monasteries everywhere to provide for those who, in that same spirit, are devoted to spiritual community building around the world.

The Global Sisterhood is an invisible network of impermeable steel forged out of mutual respect and the knowledge that when they themselves need something there will be another sister, other great communities, who will also be there for them, to help them up, to carry them on, to continue the work done for centuries by sisters who have gone before them.

We may not be present to one another physically, but we are together nevertheless. As communities everywhere were together in the Philippines to rebuild it at the time of the storms. As they were in Africa in the midst of civil wars. As they are to this day in the barrios and ghettos and inner cities around the world.

The challenges to the Global Sisterhood of distance and language, of paucity of resources and cultural differences are many. But the rewards that come from this felt oneness of heart and wholeness of spirit and common care for the people all of us serve everywhere are even more.

April 23, 2014

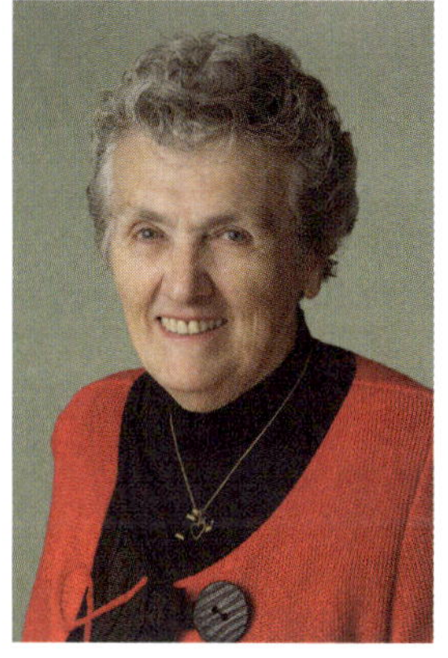

A Benedictine Sister of Erie, Pennsylvania, Joan Chittister is a best-selling author and well-known international lecturer on topics of justice, peace, human rights, women's issues and contemporary spirituality in the church and in society. She presently serves as the co-chair of the Global Peace Initiative of Women, a partner organization of the United Nations, facilitating a worldwide network of women peace builders, especially in the Middle East. Chittister has won 14 Catholic Press Association awards for her books. Chittister is the founder and executive director of Benetvision, a resource center for contemporary spirituality in Erie.

Reflection

The author experienced the care of sisters who did not know her, and she did not know them. Yet the hospitality she received gave witness to the ministry of Jesus to all those around him. Where have you experienced either a "sisterhood" or a community that took care of you when you were in need?

What is our personal challenge as we seek to care for those in need, whatever the need is, to leave our "footprint of care"?

EDITOR'S NOTE: This column was written especially for the launch of Global Sisters Report.

Intercultural community life is a gift of God

By Jennibeth Sabay

Growing up, I never desired to live in a foreign land or a different country. True enough, I haven't been in another country yet. However, I am living with people from different countries. Though I am in my own country, the Philippines, I am surrounded by people of different races and cultural backgrounds.

It has been seven years since I began living in an international religious community, two years of which were as a professed sister; currently, I am a member of a community of six sisters of five different nationalities: Pakistani, Vietnamese, Brazilian, Mexican and Filipino.

I didn't choose my community to which I was assigned. As with our families—we didn't choose them. Community members, like our families, are God's gift to us, and so are we to them.

Community life is a gift. It is a space to grow and practice charity, love and other virtues. Community life involves a relationship with other disciples of Jesus. We hold on to our belief that it is God who called each one of us to be together, and we responded. Our constitutions say that the spirit of faith makes us recognize in each sister a gift of God for us: that we are called to love one another as God loved them and loves them still.

One of the modules of our online intercongregational modular formation class for juniors is on community life and interculturality. In that one, Franciscan Fr. Prisco Cajes said that intercultural living is an intentional and explicitly a faith-based undertaking. It is a deliberate decision and a genuine commitment. It is unnatural, far from easy, but God's grace makes it possible.

Living in an international community has allowed me to discover similarities and differences of each person and their culture. We share the same faith in Jesus Christ, striving to live the Gospel values, trying to be more welcoming and accepting of one another.

However, it is a challenge too, for it is not easy to deal with different personalities and people of varied cultures. Clashing personalities, conflicts and arguments, attitude problems and misunderstandings are inevitable.

In my few years living in an intercultural community, I have encountered challenges and difficulties. One is the challenge of letting go of my biases and judgments. Community living entails awareness of one's cultural baggage that hinders community relationships. This baggage includes our personal biases—not only about cultures different from ours but also our judgment and fixed ideas.

The diverse languages of the community members also pose a challenge. I remember during my early years of formation, I felt upset when my sisters would speak their own language around me. The need to be sensitive to one another is important in community living.

Closed-mindedness, inability to accept differences, inflexibility, inability to listen, lack of charity, insensitivity and judgmental attitudes also hinder growth in community.

Community is not a finished product; instead, it is continuously built and sustained by each member. It takes the participation of every member to build loving relationships.

A community can be strengthened and sustained with prayer. The Vatican document "Fraternal Life in Community" says that communal prayer is "considered the foundation of all community life," contemplating God's mystery in significant moments as well as ordinary realities of our communities. It "reaches its full effectiveness when it is intimately linked to personal prayer." Common prayer and personal prayer are closely related and are complementary to each other.

In addition to prayer, communication—involving dialogue and listening—builds up bonds in community. Without effective communication, a community will not survive.

In dialogue, members get to know one another on a deep level. Listening is not just being quiet but being attentive and present to the other person. Conflicts arise when people fail to listen to one another.

I have more reasons to be thankful for my experience of community life. Here are three:

First, it strengthened my faith in God and made me more appreciative of God's work. I am still amazed at how we are able to live together despite differences. It is only God's grace that makes it possible.

Second, it provided me with a space for growth. The sisters in my community taught me lessons. I also learned more about myself and areas I need to improve, as I related to my community members. Learning is a lifelong process and is possible only in relation with others.

Finally, it made me experience God's love, care and mercy. The simple gestures, affection and words of encouragement from my sisters in community strengthen and inspire me in challenging times. The community accepts me as I am with all my weaknesses and limitations.

Community life has not been spared from the effects of the COVID-19 pandemic. However, this pandemic gave our community more time to be together. Because of the health restrictions, we are mostly in the house, especially during lockdown time. This pandemic challenged us to be more considerate, sensitive and caring of one another.

I experienced the love and care of my community when I actually got the COVID-19 infection, and the sisters in my community took good care of me, providing everything I needed. They were instrumental to my recovery and healing.

Community life is indeed a gift. It has challenges and difficulties but it is sustained by the commitment and deliberate choice of each member, and above all, with God's grace. Prayer and communication strengthen the bond of community. And it is in community that we support and love one another "in God and for God," as our foundress St. Emilie de Villeneuve would say.

June 23, 2021

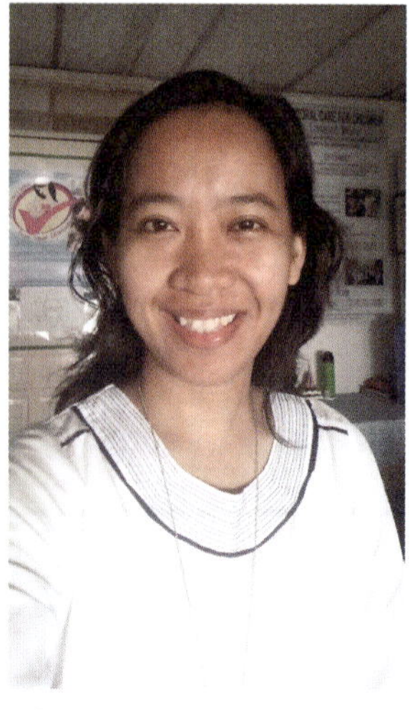

Jennibeth Sabay is a junior sister of the Sisters of Our Lady of the Immaculate Conception of Castres, a missionary congregation committed to the poorest of the poor. Before entering the novitiate in 2016, she was a public health nurse at Cebu Provincial Health Office in the Philippines. Currently, she serves at her congregation's formation house for postulants and novices and assists in the local parish with the lectors and commentators ministry. She also assists at Pastoral Care for Children-Philippines, a program for pregnant women and children.

Reflection

All the things the author names that hinder growth in an intentional community (closed-mindedness, inability to accept differences, inflexibility, inability to listen, lack of charity, insensitivity and judgmental attitudes) are also true in families or close relationships. Which things on her list are the hardest for you to practice with others in your life?

Can you make a list of the things that you are thankful for because you have been closely connected to others, either in community or family life?

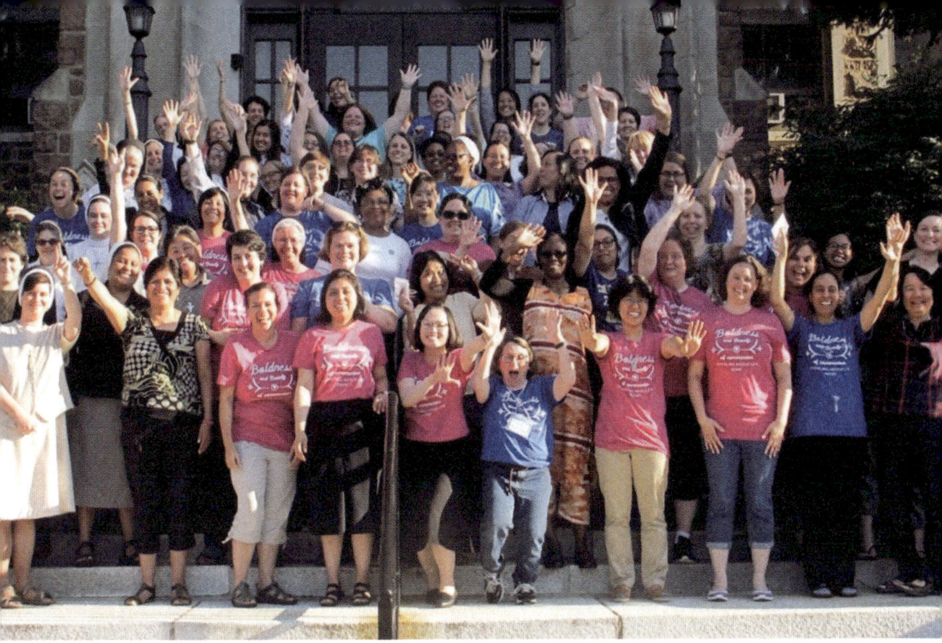

Sisters gathered in person for the 2019 Giving Voice national gathering in St. Louis.

(Courtesy of Giving Voice)

The future of religious life means real work on racism and a focus on vocation, formation

By Mūmbi Kīgūtha

I recently participated in the national gathering of the U.S. Leadership Conference of Women Religious (LCWR) as a member of Giving Voice, an organization of younger women religious. In recent years, LCWR has welcomed a few Giving Voice members to participate in the table discussions—this is how I ended up attending the virtual gathering.

I was very moved in particular by the presidential address given by Congregation of St. Joseph Sr. Jayne Helmlinger; I have reflected on it often since then, in light of my own vantage point but also my hope for the future of religious life. Sister Jayne's address had an overarching theme of vulnerability that she explored under four main sections, but I will collate them into two.

Racism and interculturality

We can no longer ignore the magnitude of racism—not only in this nation but globally—as events over the past few months have continued to lay bare this virulent sin. Racism is an extremely difficult subject to tackle; from what I have discovered through personal experience, this is perhaps the worst thing you could infer about a person. However, the walk of discipleship that we took upon ourselves at baptism and recommitted ourselves to as vowed religious has never been an easy one. Racism exists in our congregational histories, in some of our policies and in our communities.

One hallmark of current formation gatherings and seminars is the topic of interculturality. I doubt that there is any newer member in the past 10 years who hasn't attended a seminar or talk on this topic. However, interculturality within our communities is an impossibility until racism is addressed. When many newer members in religious communities continue to be the first Black, Indigenous and People of Color members (BIPOC), the impetus lies with the predominantly white older members to unpack their complicity with racism but also to learn about interculturality in order to create a hospitable and safe environment for newer members.

Teaching the diverse and newer minority group of members about interculturality does not result in any real change in their lives because they are also the group with the least power in congregational dynamics. Despite great strides in leadership, formation and discernment styles over the years, power—whether positional or inferred—is still a function of religious life today.

This power weighs heavily on newer BIPOC members in congregations, especially when viewed in relation to their previous experiences and encounters with white power in their lives. It cannot be and should not be the role of Black and Brown members to educate others on their prejudices and biases: That burden lies with the rest of the congregational members who in the U.S. context tend to be predominantly white. This (even more so when new members are calling out such bias) may result in negative repercussions for the new members—which I am sad to say, is a real consequence that many other newer members have shared with me at different times.

Even as we invite facilitators to educate us on anti-racism work and interculturality, we have to create sacred spaces where newer BIPOC members can speak honestly of the racism, both overt and subtle, that they have encountered in their time with our communities because our first responsibility lies with them even as we look to tackle structural and systemic racism in society. However, an emphasis needs to be placed on the safety of those members when they do share their stories because they are extremely vulnerable.

Religious life today, tomorrow and into the future

The religious life of tomorrow is already here with us. The newer members amongst us will be thrust into leadership positions within a very short time, by virtue of congregational demographics but also because many newer members do come in with life and leadership experience already. It is to this that we need to pay urgent attention now so that they, in the coming days, will have the ability and skills to continue to hold space for the endless possibilities of an unknown future. COVID-19 has demonstrated just how unpredictable the future might be; we can make plans and speculate, but that would be preempting the Spirit. Perhaps acquiring flexibility and agility is what the "now" and "next" require. Just as social distancing forcibly thrusted us into more creativity about how to meet and socialize, it also demonstrated that endless possibilities are possible if we are open to them.

What are the needs of the much fewer and newer, younger members and those of our majority older members? How can we ensure that both are met? I have been in many forums that are trying to discern what is next in religious life, but my personal belief is that vocation and formation work have to be prioritized in religious life in order to prepare for that "next."

What does the world demand of religious women at this point in time? Theological education, yes, but also perhaps a second or third language. A different cultural experience as the world becomes a global village, so that one can experience the vulnerability of being the other, the minority. What skills do those journeying with newer members need in order to prepare them for a future that is unknown within the church and greater society?

We also need to trust the vision in newer members and the dreams that God the dream maker has placed within their hearts. Religious life has always been about taking risks: Our histories and achievements stand as a testament to the change and good that is possible when that happens. Just as many congregations entered into a time of experimentation after Vatican II, allowing members to explore new ways of doing mission and being in new ministerial settings—the time we are in is asking for the same. It is imperative that religious congregations encourage and support newer members in experimenting with new ways of responding to God's call.

They need to explore the road less traveled, which demands greater intentionality in order to fan the embers for mission that lies in the hearts of newer members. The familiar needs of the world continue to grow as new ones emerge. Just as religious women originally responded to the health and education needs of the 19th and 20th centuries—transforming themselves with each passing era—we find ourselves at the cusp of a new era precipitated by changing demographics in our religious communities and an extraordinarily dynamic world with previously unseen levels of suffering. And we need to act. We need to start living the future now, and we need to do so with a sense of urgency.

September 11, 2020

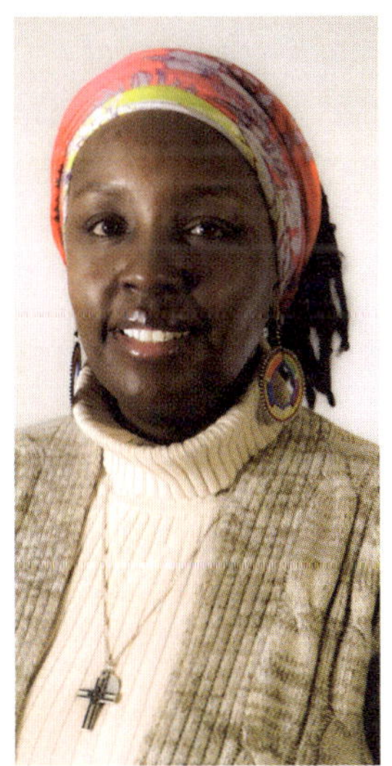

Sr. Mūmbi Kīgūtha, a member of the Sisters of the Precious Blood - Ohio, was born and raised in Kenya. She has worked with diverse vulnerable populations, including assignments with various U.N. agencies. Currently, she ministers in Silver Spring, MD, as the president of Friends in Solidarity, a Catholic non-profit supporting capacity building in South Sudan.

In addition to a Master of Business Administration in marketing, Sr. Mūmbi has a graduate degree in justice ministry and a certificate in pastoral ministry from Catholic Theological Union, a practitioner diploma in executive coaching, and training in the circle process as a tool for dialogue.

Reflection

Entering into real dialogue about deep-seated issues requires creating safe spaces where people can speak honestly even though it may surface feelings of shame, indignation or denial. Where are you being called to either speak honestly or listen carefully to others who may offer an experience other than your own? What can you do to assist communities of all types to listen with respect or speak with candor so that hard conversations can continue?

Members of religious communities are not the only ones who face the need to consider an unfamiliar future. All of us face an unknown and unpredictable future and yet are called to be dreamers who will find ways to transform the world. In the communities you find yourself living or serving in, where are you called to trust the Spirit of God and to take risks to be of service?

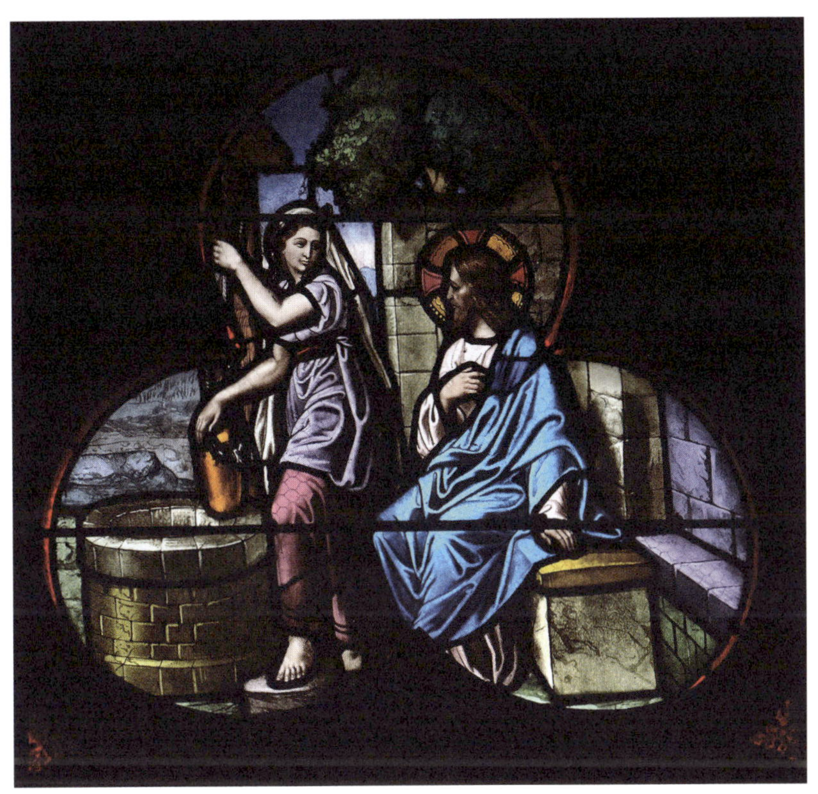

(Pixabay/12019)

It's traditions, not religious life

By Linda Romey

It is an oversimplification to say that religious life will "look different" in the future. More accurate would be to say that it will *be* different. Cosmetic alterations can make us "look different." To *be* different is more than skin deep.

How much of the talk about the future of religious life is really about the future of our religious traditions, not the life itself?

When we see associates as our hope for the future or talk about turning our ministries over to them, our topic is no longer the continuance of currently-lived religious life. Is it more accurate to say that the most common, contemporary expression of our *traditions* (i.e. vowed religious life via institutional living tied to the church/church hierarchy) is no longer the only way to live these traditions? The reality is that we are expanding the ways we live the traditions, but our language hasn't caught up yet. We have to be bolder, more prophetic, in naming them as ways of living religious life.

In her recent interview with Oprah Winfrey, Benedictine Sr. Joan Chittister told Oprah that it is the *healing* Jesus we follow most easily. The Jesus who fed crowds and healed the sick and forgave sinners. But, she said, our challenge is to follow the *prophetic* Jesus. The Jesus who threatened the status quo, demanded that systems designed to keep the poor poor and to hold women down be changed. The Jesus who refused to defend power and greed and sexism and war. The Jesus who spoke the prophetic message so clearly that he was crucified for it.

Jesus also told us not to go it alone. He called us to tend to each other as well as all others. He called women as well as men not only to follow but to lead (2,000 years of patriarchal theology notwithstanding). He called some, though not all, to leave everything for the sake of his work. He called everyone to care for the common good: to love others, to show mercy, to forgive, even our enemies.

Human beings long for connection—at some level we know that we can each be a better "me" together than when we are alone. And something in our very nature draws us to the good, to the divine, however we conceive of it and whatever we name it. Combine the longing for connection and the pull towards the good with the call to follow Jesus, and you have the makings of

Christian community. Add prophetic and charismatic leaders of any era with a vision of following Jesus in a specific way, and you have the foundation of the traditions underlying our religious communities.

But we have to stop seeing what we have been trained to see over decades and see what really is: the prophetic moment we are living now as our traditions grow in as yet unrecognized ways. If we can stop focusing on adapting to changing demographics and embrace the different ways of living our traditions that are emerging, we can then deal in creative ways with questions like, Who will fill our empty buildings now? Who is called to do good works today? Who will carry our tradition into the future?

We can be the conveners. We can host the conversations, invite the questions, gather and engage seekers across lifestyles, commitments and generations to live our traditions in diverse ways. We are still vowed, we've still given our life to these traditions, facts which are not diminished by broadening or shifting definitions or even coining new terminology. Vowed members will continue to be as important to the lifeblood of the traditions as non-vowed members are coming to be.

The traditions that became religious communities were not born in isolation; many components came together to create each of them:

- the physical and spiritual suffering of people and the Earth
- human longing for connection, for community
- the desire for God, for goodness, truth and beauty
- a vision for a better world
- the source of wisdom, the voice of the prophet (Jesus, Buddha, Mohammed, the Goddess)

The initial spark of each specific tradition often came from a single visionary and eventually vowed religious women grew and developed the traditions—but we will never come to the point of exhausting the interpretation of any living tradition.

My own thinking has shifted. I now see us in a time of expansion of the traditions rather than an evolution of religious life. By clinging to a single model, we stop expansion and we stunt growth. Religious life now is vowed, yes. It is canonical. It is communal living among unrelated adults, often with shared finances. But that is only one way. Can we expand our vision and see how else it can be lived, is already being lived? Expanding our vision will require not only expanding experience but also expanding the language we use to describe what is becoming. What do we call non-vowed, non-canonical, non-financially dependent models of living our traditions? How do these different ways relate, how do we share experiences, what makes us different facets of a single lived tradition?

And how will vowed members *be* different? With less institutional focus, we will be nimbler in response to changing needs and circumstances. We can excise whatever remnants remain of authority models that suited large-scale institutional life and that attempted to mold women into one mind as a labor force for the church. Our relationships with those who share our traditions will continue to be an important asset in the educational institutions and service agencies we founded but no longer run; we're not "turning over our ministries," we're expanding our base.

Jesus and the Gospel are still the core. And around that core are vowed members who give their lives to the living traditions and to each other. And married couples and families who live the tradition even as they give their lives to their spouses and children. And those who love the tradition, find meaning in it, integrate it into their lives. For some, it will be a singular, lifetime commitment. But not for all, and that is OK.

This narrative isn't diminishment and replacement but expansion and cross-fertilization. There are communities already experimenting with new models, new living arrangements, new leadership models, virtual communities. We must be creative with structures and governance models, funding and financing. There will be legal issues to resolve. But unless human ingenuity and creativity have expired, this won't be a problem; religious women have always been resourceful in meeting whatever challenges and needs they face.

The increasing number of associates and oblates gives testimony to the longing for community and connection and the desire to ease the burden of our suffering sisters and brothers and of our Earth. We see those same desires in seekers like Nuns & Nones and in movements calling for social change like #MeToo, #MarjoryStonemanDouglasHigh, #BlackLivesMatter.

We must find the disconnect between convents and monasteries that are emptying while streets and social media and schools of theology and divinity are filling with seekers and social justice activists of all ages, many of whom are inspired by the gospel of Jesus, working for the same new world as vowed religious women. Our task is to find intersections where we can learn from each other, discover the spaces—physical as well as virtual—where we can support each other and build the community to which Jesus calls us.

If we realize that our traditions are bigger than any one way, that the essence remains even while the form is changing, we will find our way. We will BE what is needed now.

September 4, 2019

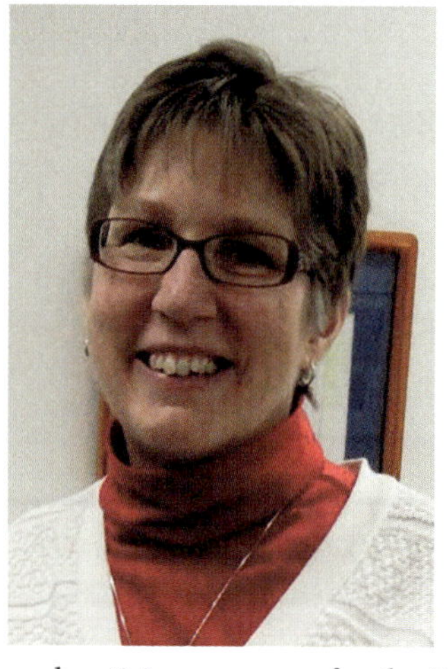

Linda Romey is a Benedictine Sister of Erie, Pennsylvania. She previously worked for seven years in Colombia, partially under the aegis of the Denver Archdiocese. A former marketing and advertising manager for the National Catholic Reporter Publishing Company, she holds a bachelor's degree in theology and an MBA. She is the community's communications and development coordinator and serves on the community's Monastic Council.

Reflection

The author suggests that the church, the community, needs to be aware of and live in the prophetic moment that is now and in that way our traditions can grow in as yet unrecognized ways. What would prophetic living look like to you? Where does the world need the prophetic voice of the followers of Jesus?

There are shifts in many religious communities of both men and women; many have welcomed others to join their work in a multitude of ways. If you are not connected to a specific religious community or charism, is there one group whose mission attracts or draws you to its ministry? What speaks to you from that mission? If you are connected to a specific one, what attracts you to that mission? In either place, where does transformation for new life begin?

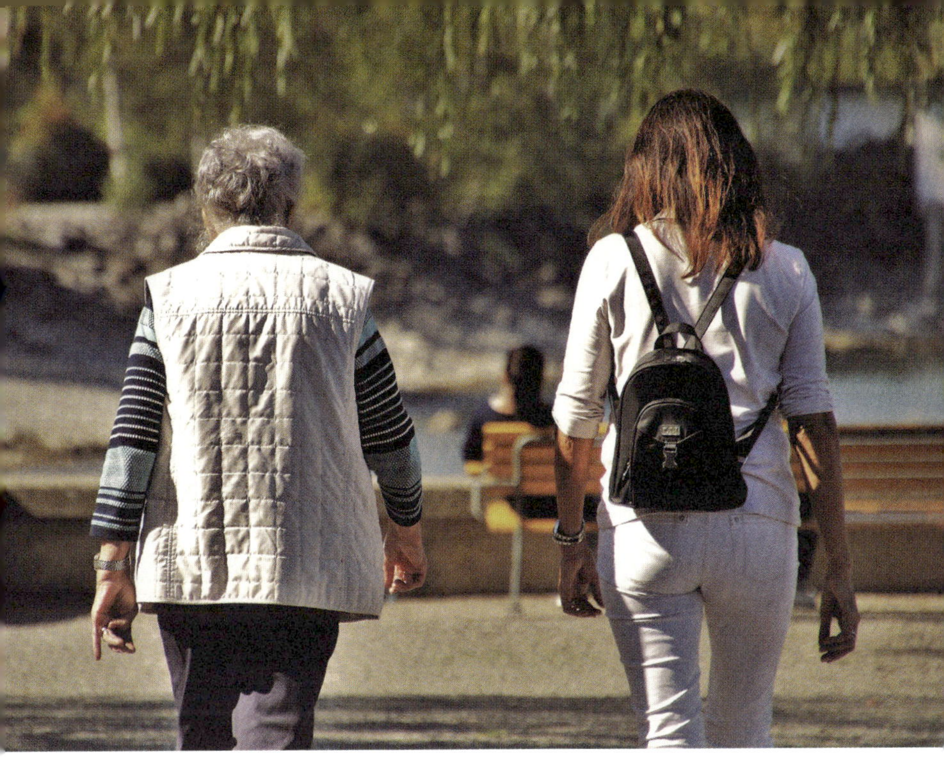

(Pixabay/Julita)

A vow of listening to each other

By Jennifer Wilson

Religious women take vows of poverty, chastity and obedience. My congregation, the Sisters of Mercy, also takes a fourth vow of service. I recently heard a sister say that the vow of obedience is the "listening" vow, and I found myself reflecting on this. The vow of obedience is the one that is often hardest for me to explain when someone asks about it.

On their website the United States Conference of Catholic Bishops explains obedience like this:

> The role of the community is integral to the obedience professed by a woman religious. Far from being a "blind

> obedience" in which one simply does what she is told, the obedience of a disciple stretches her to take an active role in sifting through the various influences and calls in her life. Together with the community, she looks reverently at her gifts and talents as well as the needs of the world and strives to know how God is calling her to respond. Truly, the grace of community in this process is to have an extra set of ears to hear God's call and invitation in the broader context.

This way of explaining obedience has evolved over time and has changed, especially after Vatican II. I have heard that sisters who experienced religious life before Vatican II often had to listen and respond without having their voices heard.

All of this has me reflecting on how I and others listen to each other. There are so many obstacles in our society that keep us from listening. I find that I often do more than one thing at a time. If I am listening to something on YouTube, I am glancing at my phone or reading a text. Sometimes the temptation in Zoom meetings is to do something else. I know that this keeps me from truly listening and yet I still do it. I wonder what effect this has on how I processed the information.

Did not being fully attentive change how I acted on what I heard or didn't hear while I was responding to a text or another distraction? I see my friends interacting with their families in the same way at times. How many times do they miss what their children or husband just said because of a text or something on their phone?

I get irritated when someone looks at their phone while I am talking to them—however, I have probably done the same thing. I definitely stop listening when I hear my phone ding. At that exact moment I have this urge to check what is not as important as the person I am talking to. I wish I could solve this for myself and for others, but all I can do is be aware of it and try to truly listen to whatever is happening at that moment.

When I go back and think about the vow of obedience as the listening vow, what comes to mind is red cards. When the Sisters of Mercy are voting on something at meetings or we want to take a "test vote" to see which way the group sentiment is leaning, we use a system of red, yellow and green cards. Green means you agree, yellow means you have some reservations and red means you are not able to agree with the decision.

When this was new to me, it always caused me to gasp when there were no red cards. How could I be in a room with more than 300 women, and no one has up a red card? It has to do with deep listening. We have by that point discussed the issue and really listened to each other. Through that listening we are willing to say "yes" even if we are not totally convinced because we see it as being good for the whole. To me, this is the vow of obedience being lived out in our life together as sisters.

Some readers might take a vow of obedience, and others might not: However, we are all called by God to listen to each other in a way that honors the image and likeness of God in each person. The listening vow of obedience has reminded me to use in small ways what I have learned from when we have big decisions:

- To listen to what the sister I live with is really saying and to be attentive and ask questions.
- To try not to be distracted by technology and the "to do" list in my head.
- To truly try to be present in each moment.

This leads all of us to ask: when are the times we are not listening to others because something else is getting in the way?

We should try to listen and remember that the person we are listening to is created in the image and likeness of God and deserves our attention.

September 16, 2022

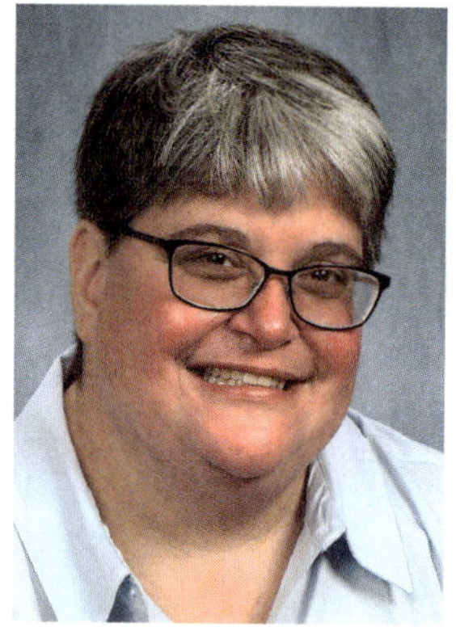

Jennifer Wilson is a member of the Sisters of Mercy of the Americas. Before entering the congregation, she completed two years as a Mercy Volunteer Corps member in Guyana, South America. Her graduate degree is in education and special education. She has worked with homeless women and children as a social worker and presently is a theology teacher and the diversity, inclusion and equity coordinator at Mount Mercy Academy in Buffalo, New York.

Reflection

Can you recall a time you have felt the respect or even reverence from another person who truly listened to you? What was that experience like?

What distracts you from the gift and practice of deep listening to other persons? Can you commit to a period of time and try to put aside that particular distraction to discover how your listening or interactions might change?

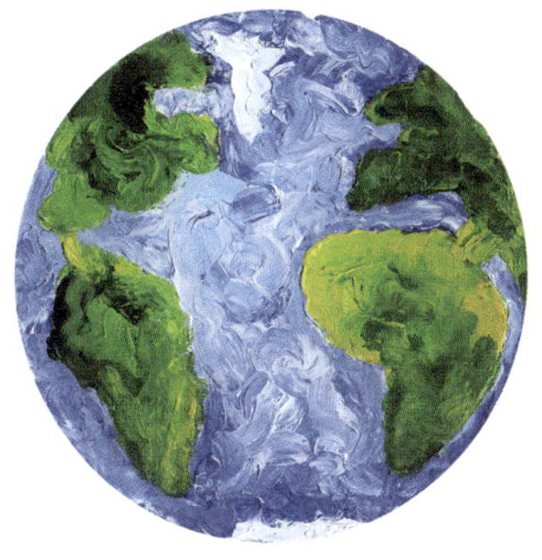

Care for Creation

The good news is that there is a growing number of people around the globe, aware and committed to the care of Earth—not only by planting trees but promoting concrete actions rooted on ethical, eco-friendly and sustainable lifestyles.

Celine Paramundayil

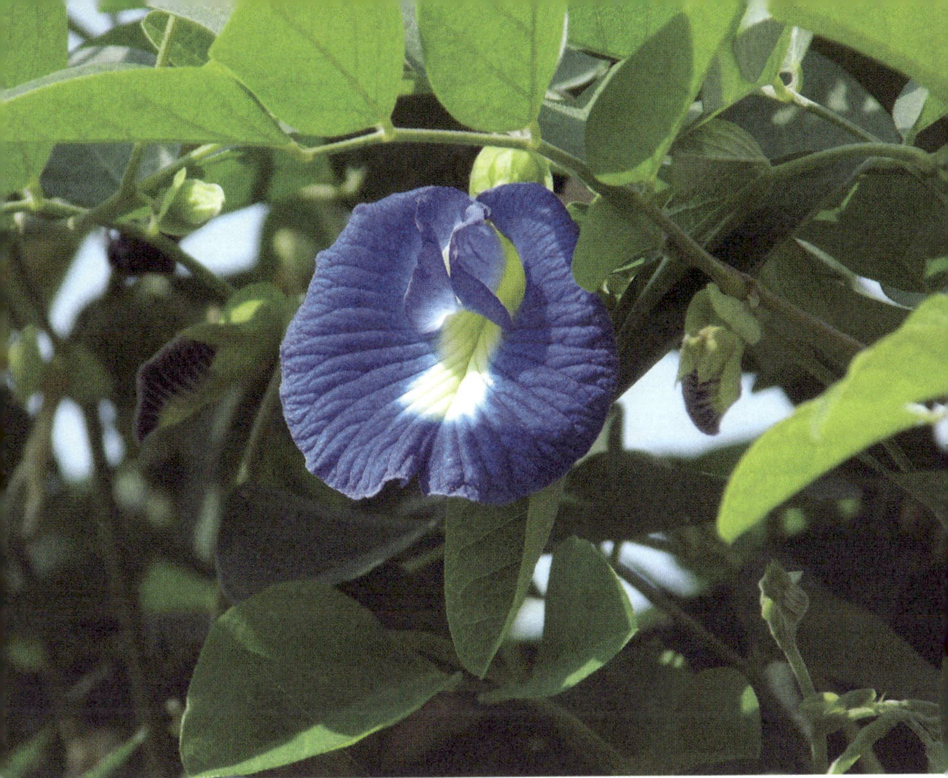

(Pixabay/632240)

The miracle of the butterfly pea plant

By Lissy Maruthanakuzhy

Recently one early morning, I allowed myself to visit the little garden adjoining our convent. There was a reason. I had a favorite butterfly pea plant growing there.

I had learned from my parents and grandparents, who walked through our fields in the morning hours, that visiting plants helps them grow better. They, too, waited for love and affection. "Like little children, they feel happy when we visit them, caress them," my mother told me one day.

Later, I learned that visiting plants nurtures me, too. During a retreat, the director told me, "Get friendly with a tree in the garden. Talk to it as a friend, spend time with it, caressing its leaves, trunk, shoots." In fact, that was a healing process for me.

The butterfly pea plant was in bloom and attracted me. It looked splendid in a pot in the corner of the garden; I had placed it there on purpose so it would be in the sunlight and not disturbed in its growth and expansion.

When I moved the large pot to this location—with some help—I was not sure what the future of this thriving plant would be. Would it fall off in the wind because I did not find a strong support for its expansion?

On this day when I saw it in bloom, I jumped with joy. The bloom looked like a decoration on the plant. I smiled, touched it, arranged its new stems, and stood silently beside it, enjoying its beauty.

I thought of God who waits for surprises from me—surprises of my doing his will, surprises of my walking the way he had marked for me.

I thought of how he allows me to experience the inconveniences and inclement weathers of life to strengthen me physically, emotionally, spiritually.

The plant before me spoke to me now of many things regarding how God directs our lives.

To begin with, I had brought a few seeds from a plant I saw growing in the wild. Being informed of its medical benefits, I decided to plant them in our garden. I spread the seeds in two places. One spot was under a tree. It grew and was extending its tendrils for support when it was plucked out. Of course, it was pulled up by someone who did not recognize its benefits, and who did not know that I had domesticated it!

I was upset, of course.

But I had also planted some of the seeds in a flower pot, which showed no signs of growth even after two months. I knew they were there, under the mud, and I had to keep them safe. I planted a ladyfinger plant, which quickly grew and produced fruit. It was actually protecting the seeds in the pot.

For some reason, I did not visit them for a long time.

One morning, I was surprised to see a pair of two-inch tall plants at the side of the ladyfinger plant.

I was immensely happy of course. The butterfly pea plant was alive and growing. I found a support for its tender creeper stems, and at this point I moved it to the wall to get more support.

It had grown and spread quite a bit, when one day the support system collapsed. But an amazing thing became visible. The creeping stems were supporting themselves by entwining. They found support within. With the little support I provided, they could now manage. They were establishing themselves well to withstand nature.

And now they were in bloom. "Bloom where you are planted." The saying flashed through my mind.

I felt something within me whispering: Find strength within yourself. You have the ability to discover new ways and means to help yourself and others, to support yourself and expand your mission. The seeds of faith, love and hope are your strength; they are within you; draw strength from them. The strength within you is the Spirit of God.

As St. Paul wrote to the Corinthians, "My words and preaching were not brilliant or clever to win listeners. It was rather a demonstration of spirit and power . . . not of human wisdom, but of God's power" (1 Corinthians 2:2-5).

Anthony Robbins, an American writer, says, "People don't usually lack resources; they lack control over their resources."

Here was a plant proving this.

I recalled the days when I faced inconveniences at various stages of my life: when I resented being moved from my comfortable office or convent, separated physically from friends, left to complete a work all by myself, when I had to find new ways to do my mission outreach.

It was not by chance; it all had a purpose. Purpose to strengthen my will, my heart and my spirit.

There is a saying: "The secret of success is making your vocation a vacation." Doing even cumbersome work with joy makes it enjoyable and brings forth much fruit.

The butterfly pea flower gently nodded in the gentle breeze that caressed the plant. It had no complaint when I moved it from place to place. It continued to grow in the sunlight of God's presence.

Yes, I had received a message from God, through God's tiny creation.

God has a plan in all that happens in my life. How true is what Anton Chekhov says, "Man is what he believes."

God wants me to grow to full stature, in the way he has planned for me, and he clears the way for me. Sends the light step by step. Only when I dare to step ahead, I can see that he walks before me. The way is clear, the lights are shining.

Blessed James Alberione once said, "God does not send all the light at once. He sends light for one step at a time." He said it from experience as he followed the promptings of God to launch into new activities even when physically no resources were in view.

We recently celebrated his 50th heavenly birthday in November, and now I can better understand what he said. He had experienced the light coming from God slowly but steadily. He was diagnosed with tuberculosis when the religious congregations he founded were still developing. He had begun publications and periodicals and found he was almost bankrupt. When he found himself empty-handed, he would lock himself in a room and spend time in close union with God. He trusted in God's assurance: "Do not be afraid, I am with you" (Isaiah 41:10).

In my heart, I am filled with joy. I can see the light as I take baby steps to newness, to challenging situations, to vistas in my mission.

I know I am in the loving presence of my great God. I trust in his promised presence.

He is always showing me new opportunities of growth, new systems of support.

This time he chose the butterfly pea plant.

January 12, 2022

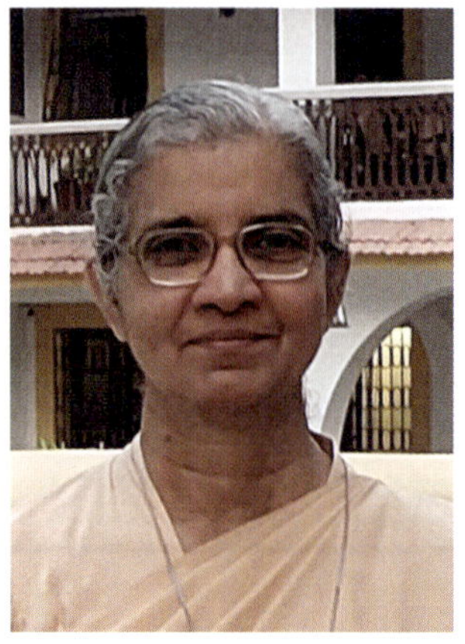

Lissy Maruthanakuzhy is a member of the Congregation of the Daughters of St. Paul, founded in Italy by Blessed James Alberione in 1915, and is committed to proclaiming Christ through social communications. She is a former editor of Pauline Publications in Mumbai. She was a correspondent for South Asian Religious News and Union of Catholic Asian News before becoming a correspondent of Matters India. She also contributes to local periodicals.

Reflection

Is there something in nature that has drawn you to its presence or life? What emotions were evoked in you as you contemplated life within another living thing? What ponderings stir within you as you contemplate all natural life?

Seeds, seedlings, stars, mountains—so much of the created world surprises us with glimpses of life, grace, beauty. Yet all rely on the others for unity, support, fulfillment. What part of God's creation fills you with joy and wonder and, in doing so, allows you to grow closer to the Creator?

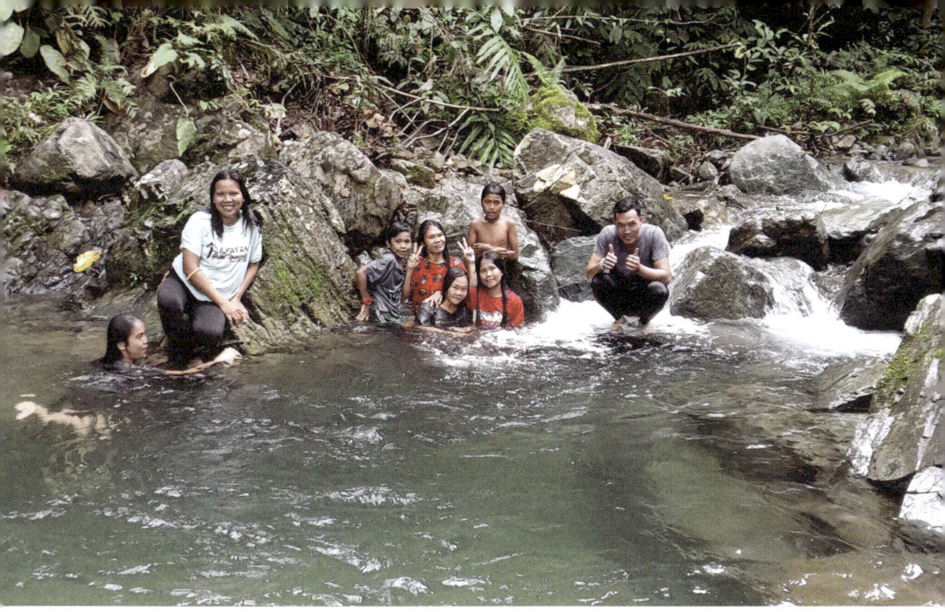

The author and her companions stopped for a quick swim in the river stream pictured in this photo, located near the road of a mountain village in Nanga Nangan, Philippines.

(Courtesy of Marjorie Guingona)

A quick splash in water becomes an unstoppable blessing

By Marjorie Guingona

"Then the angel showed me the river of life-giving water, sparkling like crystal, flowing from the throne of God and of the Lamb. . . . The Spirit and the bride say, 'Come.' Let the hearer say, 'Come.' Let the one who thirsts come forward, and the one who wants it receive the gift of life-giving water" (Revelations 22:1;17).

Yes, I can still feel it, the refreshing cool water that unforgettable Sunday of Jan. 22 tingling my tired and aching body in the flowing stream by the roadside. For one moment in time, I felt a deep sense of connection with the crystal-clear spring water cascading down from the rocks, spilling over my head, down to my face and shoulders. This vital source of life that quenches our thirst and slakes our longing for something more than a mere commodity for our daily existence, or a profitable source of revenue in our market-driven world.

On that seemingly ordinary Sunday, the community walked—accompanying Deacon Ariel on his way back to Pagadian City after our chapel liturgical celebration—along the muddy road of the mountain village in Nanga Nangan, Philippines. We were surprised to be blessed with nature's gift, which invited us to take a break and enjoy the moment. The mere sight and sound of the fresh gurgling river made us splash into the water with childlike joy and wonder. For one moment in time, I saw water with new eyes: it shimmered with spiritual radiance as the sunlight dappled it with light and shadows through the verdant tree branches swaying gently with the silent breeze.

Suddenly I became acutely aware that I am a water being and a spiritual being at the same time. Since some 60% of the human adult body is made up of water, without consuming adequate water every day we cannot survive. That is more than enough reason why water is an essential part of our nature as human beings—for this element embodies strength, clarity and persistence.

The refreshing power of water certainly has a healing effect that revitalizes our depleted energy, purifies our negativities and renews our soul to wholeness as it moves around and through obstacles set in its path with grace, and cascades into the unknown with force and persistence.

In short, our splash in the unstoppable grace flowing down gave me a renewed sense of inner peace and harmony with all of creation, a feeling of coming home to my true self. I also felt a deeper sense of awe and gratitude for being in communion with our Indigenous brothers and sisters, the Subanens.

The word Subanen means "river dweller" from the root word "*suba*," meaning river. Like many Indigenous peoples the world over, the Subanens live simply, sustainably and in harmony with nature. They share a deep connection with the natural world, honoring its seasons and cycles, and respecting the treasures creation showers on them—consuming minimally and when necessary, and ensuring that the flow of energy and natural order is conserved in everything they do.

It made me recall the movie "Avatar: The Way of Water," which I had the rare opportunity to watch on the big screen while in Manila. The movie reintroduces the innocent Na'vi indigenous tribe from the land of Pandora, who lived in peaceful coexistence with the lush flora and fauna of their beautiful ecosystem. It contrasts them with the "sky people," whose insatiable greed exploits the rich natural resources at the expense of the environment, threatening the precious biodiversity and displacing communities most vulnerable to their destructive invasion.

It may not be a real-life story, but it carries with it an urgent environmental message from the world of Pandora that far exceeds even this awe-inspiring film. Even more admirable to discover is that the director, James Cameron, is a staunch environmentalist. It is no wonder that he produced "Avatar" with an eco-conscious message, in order to "[rekindle] in us an awareness of our innate connection to nature, and to each other, which [for him] is primordial." It should shake us from our apathy and inspire us to apply Pandora's principles to life on Earth, and take action to protect our one and only planet in order to mitigate the impact of climate change and global warming.

I believe St. Francis of Assisi would say when water is not seen as ministering to us humans and all life, when it is not seen as our sister, or as representative of Spirit or of God, or of cosmic presence, it dies. We lose our identities as water-beings and creatures of spirit.

The ancient poets who wrote the Genesis narrative expressed from the outset the cosmic origin of water: "In the beginning when God created the heavens and the earth—and the earth was a formless void and darkness covered the face of the deep, while a wind from God swept over the face of the waters."

I have therefore come to value this essential element all the more, especially aware that about 71% of Earth's surface is water but less than 1% is fresh water in rivers and lakes. A 2006 report in the journal *Science* projected that edible ocean fish may decline by 90% by 2048.

What is even more worrisome: since much of our water now is polluted, including sacred rivers such as the Ganges and Jordan, future wars may be fought over water.

According to Water.org, in the Philippines, the water crisis is heartbreaking; some 3 million people living in Manila rely on unsafe and unsustainable water sources and about 7 million lack access to improved sanitation. Despite its growing economy, the Philippines and its growing cities face "significant challenges in terms of water and sanitation access."

My heightened awareness now of being a water and spiritual being is a call to a deeper union, to a marriage—so to speak—with water. We have a choice about our relationship with water. I am reminded of the Samaritan woman's life-changing encounter with Jesus at the well (John 4). She chose to leave her empty jar in a rush to spread the good news of the living water found in the person of Jesus. Moreover, Jesus himself humbly chose to be baptized by his cousin John at the River Jordan with the living water, for all to see the need to be cleansed from our sins and begin life anew in Christ (Luke 3:16).

That momentary splash was an unstoppable blessing, which opened up a crack in my dry well of emptiness and fatigue to a wonderful awareness of water and renewed responsibility to care for the Earth. I felt invited to journey with our Indigenous peoples, for we are water and spiritual beings called to evangelize and tell the great news of Jesus, the fountain of life-giving water (John 4:14). Likewise, we are called each day to celebrate with awe and gratitude the boundless love of God for us, coursing our way through the water running from our faucets and from the rivers and streams of life constantly flowing.

March 22, 2023

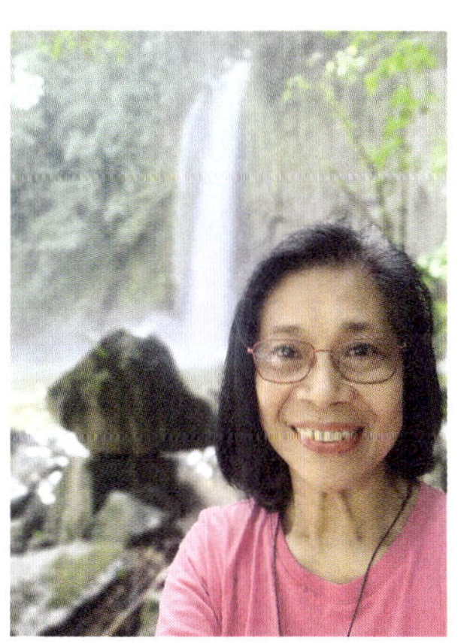

Guardian Angel Sr. Marjorie Guingona is from Butuan City, Philippines. After her initial formation in Madrid, Spain, she ministered in Mexico, Nicaragua and Los Angeles. Since 2020, the year of her silver jubilee, she has worked with the Subanen Indigenous peoples in the Diocese of Pagadian, Philippines. She has an academic background in religious education and pastoral ministry and has written several books.

Reflection

There are many ways to experience water—refreshment for thirst, rain on crops, whirling snowflakes, trickling creeks, mighty rivers, even the absence of water can remind us of its power and energy. When have you been aware of the gift of water? Where have you expressed your gratitude?

While we may experience enough water to supply our needs, many do not have enough for sustenance. How does the Creator call you to be responsible stewards and to work for the equity of this blessed resource?

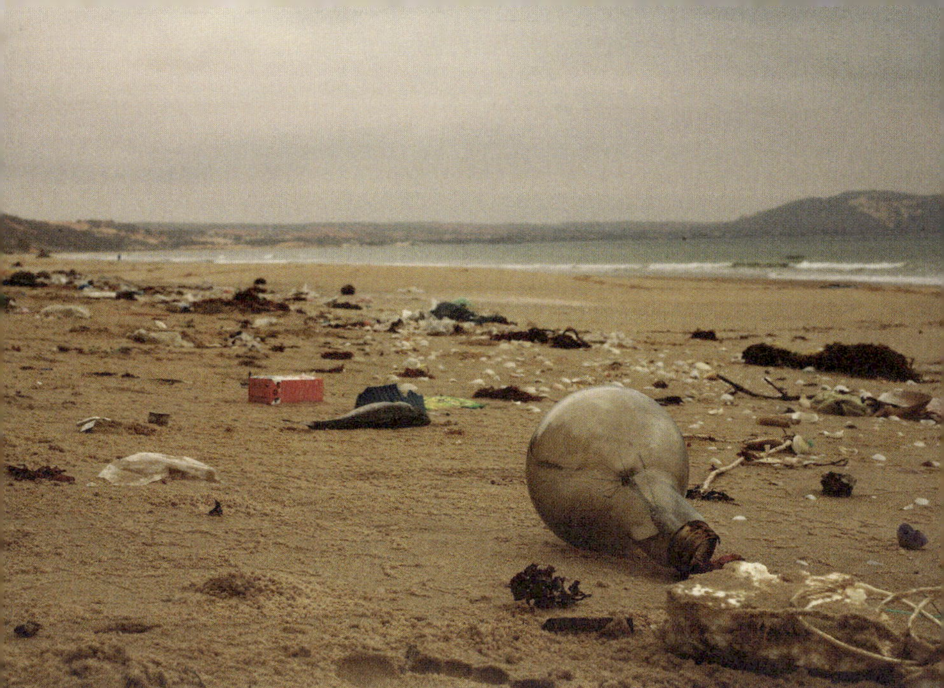

Plastic pollution on a beach. (Pixabay/Sergei Tokmakov)

Option for life requires a paradigm shift to care for creation

By Celine Paramundayil

The 1980s seemed to be the peak of talk about "preferential option for the poor," influenced by liberation theology which focused on the injustices lived by the poor. Peruvian Dominican Fr. Gustavo Gutiérrez was one of its founders, and religious everywhere embraced it—some even moving from their comfort zones to the barrios, slums and rural villages to live the Gospel in solidarity with the poor.

In the 1990s, I heard the late Jesuit Fr. K.M. Matthew—then a botany professor at St. Joseph's College in Trichy, India—say: "Option for life is bigger than option for the poor." He had done a considerable amount of work in the field of nature conservation.

Over the years the ecological crisis has become a serious threat to life on Earth. An article I read in the *New Leader*, by Jesuit Fr. S.M. John Kennedy, an environmentalist and former secretary-general of the United Nations Conference on Environment and Development, quoted Maurice Strong as saying, "The threat to earth's eco-system and our environmental security are like cancer, spreading quietly and pervasively through the body of our society, which by the time the effects become acute, will be too late to cure." The U.N. Intergovernmental Panel on Climate Change has reminded companies and governments that we have a truly short window of time to avert the looming climate crisis facing the world.

It is a paradox that extreme weather conditions disproportionately affect those in the poor countries, who contribute the least. Due to the high population of China and India, the West blames them as the polluters of the world—while the individual pollution rate is far behind those in the rich countries. The poor and marginalized around the world are first hit by climate change. Pope Francis talked about the historical "ecological debt" rich countries owe to the poor.

In 2014, in New York City I participated in a massive climate rally of over 400,000 participants. There were placards representing various organizations, religious congregations, and others, but Catholics were scattered. Feeling the need to unite after that, the Global Catholic Climate Movement was born, and later rebranded itself as the Laudato Si' Movement. The Global Catholic Climate Movement organized many activities, including the online training for Laudato Si' animators to spread awareness and action.

In 2015, the world welcomed some favorable changes: for instance, the outcome document of the Paris Agreement of the U.N. climate change conference, where the countries agreed that each would reduce greenhouse gas emissions and adapt to climate change. Pope Francis visited the U.N., where they loved his encyclical "*Laudato Si', on Care for Our Common Home*"—addressed to all people of goodwill, in response to the current environmental and social crisis.

It played a role in the development of the U.N. 2030 Agenda with its 17 sustainable development goals. During the negotiations we attended, Macharia Kamau, the ambassador from Kenya and one of the facilitators, raised the book *Laudato Si'* and told the General Assembly members and the entire U.N. family: "This is a must-read book; I am not a Catholic, but all should read it." He told the Vatican ambassador to thank the pope, saying that we had felt the pope's support all through the process. That was a proud moment for us Catholic religious nongovernmental organizations at the U.N.!

Pope Francis officially launched the Laudato Si' Action Platform, on the World Day of the Poor, Nov. 14, 2021. Vatican News described it as "an online hub that collects, directs, and coordinates global and local initiatives inspired by the encyclical on care for creation." The Laudato Si' Action Platform is coordinated from the Vatican Dicastery for Promoting Integral Human Development, formed in 2017. (Dicastery is a lay term that replaces "Vatican office" or council, which is a welcome gesture from Pope Francis.)

In addition to the call to people of goodwill, the pope particularly invites dioceses, parishes, religious communities, schools, and other "sectors" to actively get involved. The seven sectors are to achieve the seven goals of the Laudato Si' Action Platform in seven years.

Many others are joining the Laudato Si' Action Platform and there are international working groups under each of the seven sectors to promote the platform. The process begins with understanding the principles developed in the document and expanding our vision by having conversations and listening to each other about the issues.

Pope Francis says that the cry of the poor and cry of the earth are not two separate crises but one. Humanity has made incredible progress in science and technology, but this has not been matched by moral, ethical and spiritual growth. We need a paradigm shift. Paradigm changes (from long-established sets of concepts or thought patterns) require conversion of mind and heart that involve changes of attitudes, values, reordering priorities, and finding new ways of doing things.

In our faith, the awareness of ecological sin needs to be included. Kennedy also gave the following as essential elements for a shift in a climate paradigm:

- *Consciousness*: Growing in awareness about the implications of the environmental crisis and unethical practices;
- *Conversion*: Sincere awareness about the crisis will lead to a genuine conversion and change of lifestyle, using nature's finite resources in a sustainable way that respects planetary boundaries;
- *Conviction*: With conversion follows the conviction that immediate and committed actions are needed to restore the health of the planet;
- *Concrete Actions*: Conviction needs to be reflected in concrete actions at the individual, communal, social and institutional levels.

We can illustrate those four steps with an example: at the University of Bergen (Norway), scientists were horrified by what they discovered inside the stomach of a sick and dying whale. According to the Associated Press, they were shocked to see masses of plastic waste and about 30 plastic bags. They concluded that the whale probably beached due to the plastic in its stomach.

This awareness gives us the *consciousness* that our actions have consequences, with the message: "It should never happen again." That should lead us to a *conversion*, and the *conviction* for *concrete actions*: Reduce waste and use of plastic; reuse, recycle, and replace plastic with biodegradable materials like paper and cloth whenever possible; and refuse to accumulate unneeded stuff.

Option for life calls for a mass movement beyond the option for the poor, and that invitation is to you and me for micro solutions in our daily lives, while leaders of the national and global forum must find macro solutions. God, who created humans and other earthlings, invites us to sit around the table of creation each taking our rightful place, with humans no more at the center!

The good news is that there is a growing number of people around the globe, aware and committed to the care of Earth—not only by planting trees but promoting concrete actions rooted on ethical, eco-friendly and sustainable lifestyles.

Together with our visionary leader Pope Francis, let us join the Laudato Si' Action Platform and pray with the patron saint for nature, Francis of Assisi, "*Laudato Si' mi Signore*!—Praise be to you, my Lord!"

November 3, 2022

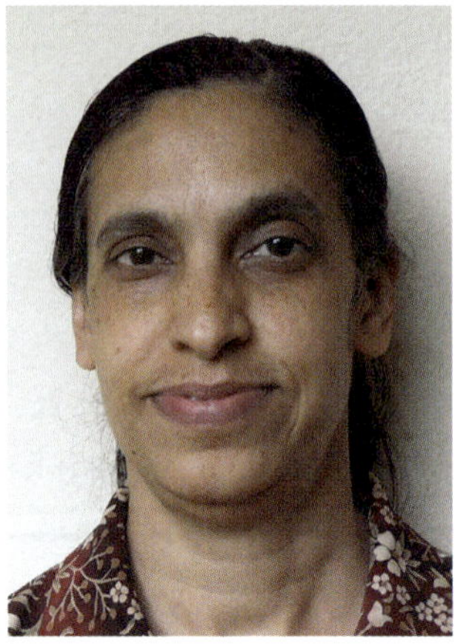

Celine Paramundayil is a Medical Mission Sister from Kerala, India, who represented the global Medical Mission Sisters at the United Nations for 10 years. She has been a trained Laudato Si' animator since 2017 and organized programs both in the United States and India. She currently lives in Kerala and works at Ayushya, the Medical Mission Sisters' Center for Healing and Integration, where she focuses on the integrated growth of adolescents.

Reflection

Where are you on the four listed steps or essential elements that could foster a climate paradigm shift? Which do you find the hardest to be attentive to in daily life?

In Laudato Si', *Pope Francis writes: "A great cultural, spiritual and educational challenge stands before us, and it will demand that we set out on the long path of renewal" (#202). What is your commitment to the ethics of care for creation set forth by Pope Francis? (A reading of* Laudato Si' *might be a helpful exploration.)*

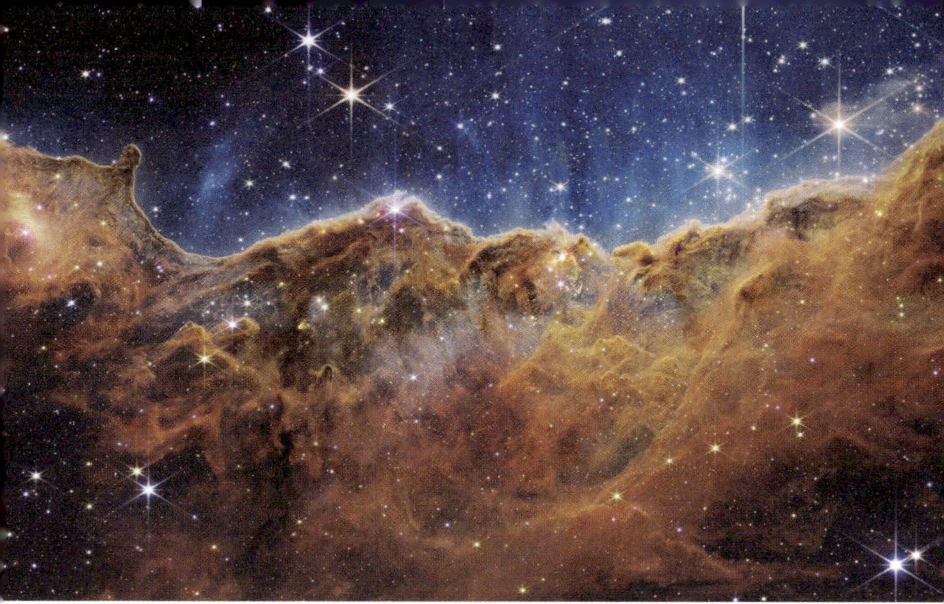

NASA's James Webb Space Telescope captured this image July 12, 2022, showing what NASA describes as "the edge of a nearby, young, star-forming region called NGC 3324 in the Carina Nebula."

(Flickr/ NASA's James Webb Space Telescope)

The wonder of outer space

By Kathryn Press

When I was 10 years old, my family embarked on a "pilgrimage" to a space launch. My sister and I piled into the back of the minivan, surrounded by books and cassette tapes to keep us entertained while we were awake. A flask of coffee and my mom as navigator assistant supported my dad on the seven-hour drive from Georgia to Cape Canaveral, Florida. It took us four attempts before we actually saw a rocket send five human beings into space.

Time has a way of reshaping memories. Truthfully, I remember very little of the space shuttle launch itself. Instead, I remember the time spent together with family—thanks in large part to photographs. For me, the trip was a catalyst in my love for outer space. Maybe it was also something we were studying in school. Perhaps it was because I was reading Madeleine L'Engle's *A Wrinkle in Time*. The seeds were planted. The vast world of the cosmos captured my heart.

Fast-forward 15 years. I'm a novice sister—and a novice teacher—tasked with teaching third grade science. Having studied humanities during college (and generally avoiding anything beyond the required Biology 101), I surprised myself with how much I enjoyed teaching science, especially our unit on space. A few years later, when I found myself teaching science again, this time to fifth graders, I was elated. For our combined English language arts/science unit, we read *George's Secret Key to the Universe* by Lucy and Stephen Hawking. This later turned into a biography unit on Hawking following his death in 2018. We watched YouTube interviews with astronauts on the International Space Station. Pluto as a planet or dwarf planet became a hot topic in our classroom.

On my own time, I listened to the "Naked Astronomy" podcast from The Naked Scientists. This went beyond preparation for my students, even if that had been my initial motivation. There was something simultaneously delightful and pleasantly frustrating when I challenged myself to learn about the Kuiper Belt, Mars rover, and the weather patterns on the surface of our sun. As an added bonus, my podcast listening gave me new topics to discuss and share with my family. Science, and space in particular, became a new, common interest and language for all of us.

Given my well-established pattern for liking all things galactical, it shouldn't come as a surprise that I immediately began drooling over the James Webb Space Telescope images when they arrived in my inbox earlier this summer as part of a family email chain. I found them so striking that they became a primary focus for me during my annual retreat. Echoes of the

Psalms came to mind when zooming in on the details of the images of cosmic cliffs.

"By the LORD's word the heavens were made;
by the breath of his mouth all their host."

—Psalm 33:6, New American Bible

"When I see your heavens, the work of your fingers,
the moon and stars that you set in place. . . ."

—Psalm 8:4, New American Bible

"I look up at your macro-skies, dark and enormous,
your handmade sky-jewelry,
Moon and stars mounted in their settings.
Then I look at my micro-self and wonder,
Why do you bother with us?
Why take a second look our way?"

—Psalm 8:3-4, The Message

"He numbers the stars, and gives to all of them their names."

—Psalm 147:4, New American Bible

"Where can I go from your spirit?
From your presence, where can I flee?
If I ascend to the heavens, you are there. . . .
If I say, 'Surely darkness shall hide me, and night shall be my light'—
Darkness is not dark for you,
and night shines as the day.
Darkness and light are but one."

—Psalm 139:7-12, New American Bible

Even our Christmas songs draw our focus to the heavens:
A star, a star, dancing in the night / With a tail as big as a kite / With a tail as big as a kite.

Perhaps it's the darkness of life in the Northern Hemisphere. Maybe it's my recent discovery of Dark Sky Parks (and that there are two near me!), but I've been turning my attention back to the night sky once again. For me, it's not about either science or faith. It's always been both. Science is a vehicle leading me to study and contemplation. Sometimes faith gives me the language to describe this experience. But more than that, my faith, especially the practice of *lectio divina*, provides a way for me to sit before an image of a deep field and pray.

The best word to describe this both/and practice is *wonder*. As Sofia Cavalletti described it:

> The particularity of wonder is that we find activity and contemplation inseparably blended within it. . . . Wonder is a very serious thing that, rather than leading us away from reality, can arise only from an attentive observation of reality. An education to wonder is one that helps us go always deeper into reality.

Science and faith always have something new to teach us. God delights in us as we make such discoveries. Wonder waits around every corner. So, having arrived at the start of a new year, I ask: What are you wondering about? What new area of study can you dive deeper into? How will you dance with action and contemplation given the reality before you?

January 26, 2023

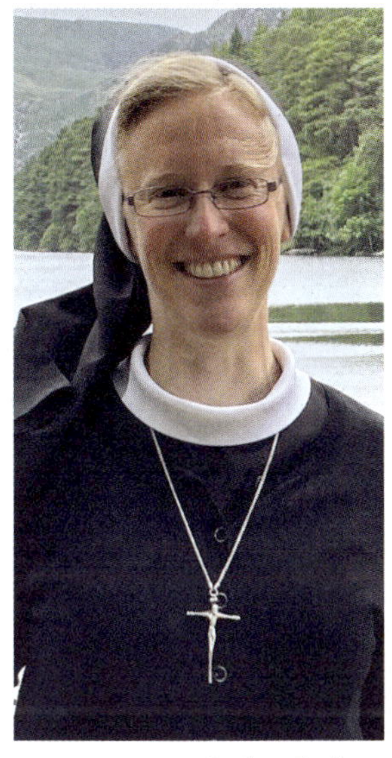

Kathryn Press is an Apostle of the Sacred Heart of Jesus from Georgia. She professed her final vows in 2018. With a Master of Divinity and a background in religious studies, she has taught every grade from pre-K through high school. After opening a convent in Ireland, she taught in New York City for three years before returning to Ireland in September 2020 to work in evangelization and parish ministry.

Reflection

What has brought you to wonder or even delight about the universe? Can you use the psalms that the author quotes to reflect on the wonder of God's creation? How are we called to care for this gift?

Can you find a place in the physical world to go to and reflect (even if you do it through a photograph or digitally) and contemplate the questions in the author's final paragraph? What are you wondering about . . . ?

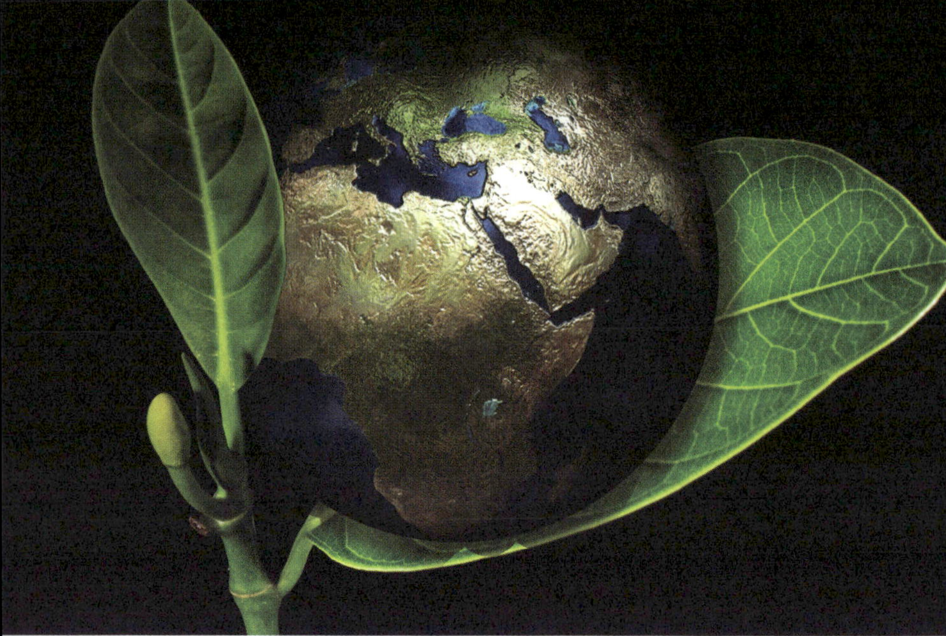

The more we destroy people and nature, the more we contribute to all kinds of disruptions in our world today: wars, pandemics, violence, drought, floods.

(Pixabay/Gerd Altmann)

Moving from a throwaway culture to nurturing and caring for God's gift

By Mercy Shumbamhini

As we celebrated Earth Day one year, I was reflecting on my pastoral journey with Sr. Theresa, a young religious from another congregation who was referred to me for counseling. She grappled with our "throwing away" culture in a way that illustrates the plight of us all trapped in similar situations. Even if it appears as if everything is well, the disruption in our world today tells us otherwise.

I have been inspired and amazed at Sr. Theresa's alternative/new story—a new story of our place within the natural world. An alternative story that promotes a new way of thinking about human beings, life, society and our relationship with nature. A new story of hope, a story of healing, a story of connecting with nature. I think sharing her story can cultivate respect and connection to the Earth.

Pastoral care should also involve ecological care because we are connected to one another through our ecological positioning. We have abandoned and mistreated our Earth, just like we have mistreated and neglected the fragile, the poor and the marginalized people in our society. I believe that injustice done to nature is injustice done to humanity; the destruction and brokenness of nature is humanity's destruction and brokenness, too.

We must work with nature, not against it. War against nature is inevitably a war against ourselves. The more we destroy people and nature, the more we contribute to all kinds of disruptions in our world today: wars, pandemics, violence, drought, floods. Breaking our relationship with nature will result in our own destruction. Arthur Dahl says this breakdown in our relationship with nature has not only led to serious environmental problems, but is precipitating psychological, social, economic and even spiritual problems for many today. Humanity's broken relationship with nature comes at a cost. Therefore, in order to reduce the risk of future epidemics in our world today, we need to heal our broken relationship with ourselves and nature.

During our pastoral conversations with Sr. Theresa, she became aware that humanity and nature are not separate. Resonating with what Pope Francis said in "*Laudato Si'*, on Care for Our Common Home" "We are part of nature, included in it and thus in constant interaction with it"—she sees the Earth not as a dead rock with resources to exploit, but as a living system that needs to live like each one of us. She explained:

> I can see that our lifestyles of greediness and selfishness lead our life to go distantly far away from God and God's creation; in this way, we destroy the healthy relationship between human beings' life and life of the planet and all creatures living in it. And as a result, this affects the environment of the world, especially the poor.
>
> We have to conserve, protect and restore the health of the earth's ecosystems. I also see that we have to select technologies that sustain the natural environment by becoming coworkers with non-human nature, not dominators over it. But we must also remember that whatever harm we do to our planet, we are harming ourselves too. I see that there are a lot of behaviors I have been doing myself—throwing food away, leaving electrical gadgets on, leaving my light to burn the whole night, wasting water, leaving soap in water. I want to mend this relationship with the earth.
>
> In caring for the earth, I also deepen my relationship with God, with nature and with other people, making my faith more alive and relevant, in and to a broken world. We benefit a lot from the earth, for she provides for our day-to-day survival, including the air we breathe, the food we eat and the water we drink. Therefore, if we take great care of her, we can greatly improve our quality of life. We must embrace a just and healthy attitude towards our environment, an attitude that values nature as the foundation for a just and healthy society.

Indeed, Sr. Theresa has started to apply the 3Rs—reduce, reuse and recycle—in her daily routine. She has changed her lifestyle by avoiding the use of plastic and paper, reducing water consumption, separating refuse, cooking only what can reasonably be consumed, showing care for other living beings, using public transport, planting trees and flowers, and turning off unnecessary lights, for example.

We are connected to one another, and each one of us is connected to nature. St. Hildegard of Bingen explained that we are not separate from nature, but an intimate part of it. She saw that each creature reflects something of God and has a message to convey to us. St. Hildegard invites each one of us not to injure, hurt or destroy the Earth that nourishes and sustains humanity.

From this I see all creation as a revelation of God's glory and beauty. The natural world itself—in its immensity, its beauty and splendor, its awesomeness and wonder—can offer an overpowering sense of connection to something beyond our imagination.

Fr. Thomas Berry says that it is very important to listen to the voices of Earth. We have to listen to the stars in the heavens and the sun and the moon, to the mountains and the plains, to the forests and rivers and seas that surround us, to the meadows and the flowering grasses, to the songbirds and the insects and to their music. This will activate our inner spiritual life and bring inner peace and serenity.

The presence of God in all creation is a precious and loving gift to each one of us, and I can only respond to God with gratitude. How beautiful to see God in everything around us, and as St. Ignatius of Loyola puts it, finding God in all things. With the beauty of flowers, I see the beauty of God. With the immensity of a sea, I comprehend God's infinity! With the light of the sun, I experience God's glory and love. Nature always soothes my heart and soul, puts me in a place of reverence. The colors, shapes—all these are a gift reminding me there is never an end to the mysteries all around me. With this awareness, I understand better the need to care for and protect our planet.

Therefore, if we nurture nature as she nurtures us, it means we must care for each other as brothers and sisters woven together by the love God has for all creation. It means also we must care for—as St. Francis of Assisi would say—our sister water, sister moon and our brothers the trees.

In this way we are caring for our future generations. Our children deserve clean air and a healthy environment. Let us stop harming our future generations! Let us give them the chance to experience God's beauty and glory.

We need to change our lifestyle and attitudes and replace our current philosophies of domination of nature with ecosystemic philosophies of partnership and boundedness with nature. And by promoting and protecting every life, we will be creating an inclusive, just, peaceful and loving society for all.

April 22, 2021

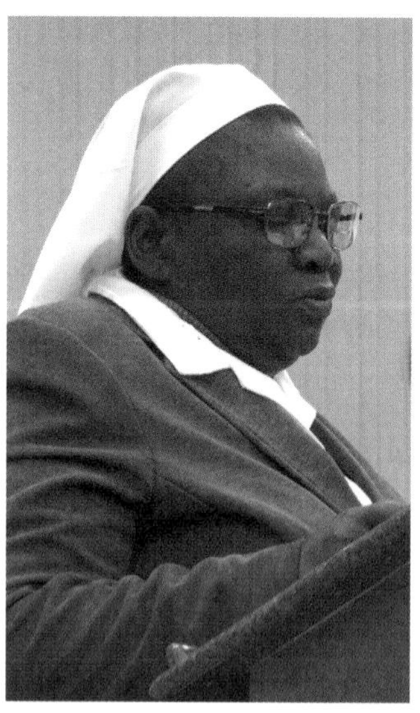

Sr. Mercy Shumbamhini is a member of the Congregation of Jesus in Zimbabwe. She is a registered professional clinical social worker, theologian, spiritual director, safeguarding consultant, narrative therapist, researcher and writer with an extensive background in leadership and project management. She has served in leadership for her congregation and is the former president of the Conference of Major Superiors in Zimbabwe. She currently serves as mission developmental director of her congregation in Zimbabwe. She sits on a number of boards and lectures at the university level, and she has been an external examiner for the University of South Africa.

Reflection

Reflect on your own habits when it comes to using resources (water, air, etc.) from the Earth. How responsibly do you use these resources? How might you be called to mend your relationship with the Earth?

Imagine yourself in an intimate relationship with nature and all living systems of the Earth. Consider your connection to all of it as a revelation of God's glory and beauty. Given your reflection, what part do you want to play in this legacy of God's gift for all future generations?

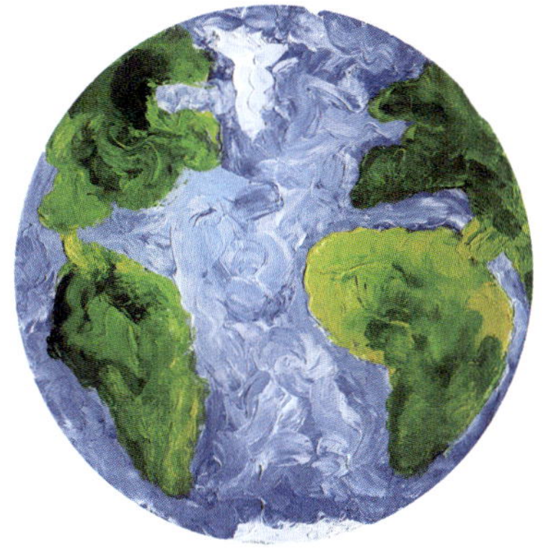

Grief and Healing

Love makes us something; it makes us alive and draws us into the dynamism of life, sustaining life's flow despite many layers of sufferings and disappointments. The person who cannot love cannot suffer, for she or he is without grief, without feeling, and indifferent.

Ilia Delio

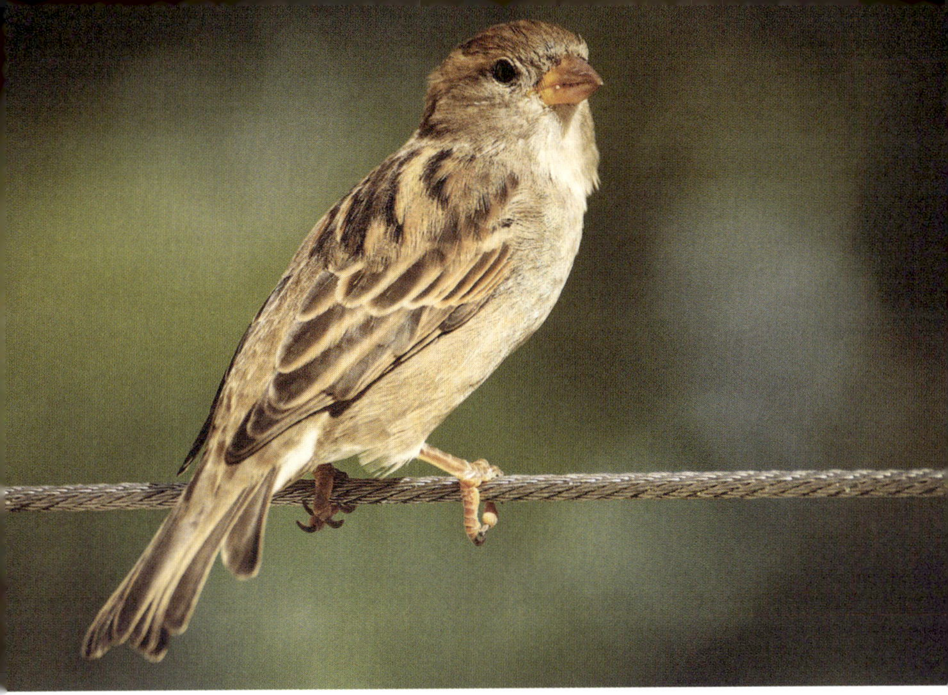

(Pixabay/165106)

A bedroom liturgy with my dying brother

By Joan Sauro

Here is the church—a small bedroom.

Here is the altar—a bed with five pillows propped.

Here is the offering—my brother Joseph sunk in the pillows. He is reduced to skin and bones. His brown eyes are alert.

Here is the celebrant, a kind priest friend. He and a church full of priests have just concelebrated Mass for a revered monsignor in august surroundings, after which the priest raced to be with us in an ordinary bedroom.

Here is the congregation—my brother's wife, his two sisters and a dear friend. Four women at a tomb, so it seems.

The celebrant stands in a bedroom and prays reverently. Non-stop. Without book or notes, he prays over my wide-eyed brother. Now and then comes "Amen" from the four women.

The priest takes a single Communion host out of a pyx, breaks the host in half, and offers it to my brother. Sunk in his pillows, he nods yes. And so my brother receives viaticum, holy Communion for the sick.

There remains a half host for four women. When the priest offers the sacrament to my sister-in-law, she whispers, "I'm not Catholic."

The priest answers, "Doesn't matter," and she makes her first Communion with her dying husband in their bedroom.

After the sacrament, my brother revives. For two weeks, he wheels himself out to the living room while birds in a nest sing outside.

While the birds sing, I hunt through Gospel pages to find samples of miraculous cures. In one, Christ enters another bedroom and announces that the 12-year-old child lying there is not dead, only sleeping. Amid the scorn and mocking laughs, he takes the child by the hand and says, "Stand up." And she does, giving the scoffers something better to laugh about. He tells them, "Give her something to eat," as if traveling through the valley of death had made her hungry.

Here I plead with Christ. "Once you raised a little girl from the dead. Now I beg you to raise my brother Joseph from near death. After all, he bears your father's name."

Here I keep begging, birds keep singing, my brother keeps sinking. Back to his bed with the five pillows. *Keep, keep* my brother alive, I pray.

Here is June 22, the longest day of the year. Friend Janet and I visit Joe midmorning. This day we have brought family pictures, and show them slowly. He recognizes only one and says, clearly, "Ma."

We each kiss Joe fondly and tell him we love him.

Four hours later, my youngest brother calls to say our oldest brother has died.

We are stunned. Dumb. Inert. For two weeks, very little happens. The undertaker comes. My brother's body leaves. Outside the window, the birds sing. But nobody listens.

Back home, I look at $200 I will never spend. My brother's last birthday gift. Janet looks at a photo of the two of them with a cigar hanging out of their mouths. We laugh and cry.

My brother was a gambling man all his life. Atlantic City, Vegas, life. As we all know, in the end, the house always wins. And this is true. In more ways than one.

Just before Christ died, he said, "I go to my Father's house to prepare a room for you."

And that is where Joseph Anthony Sauro lives now. He is eternally home. As is every single person in *your* life who has left.

And we miss them, more than words can say, here on earth.

August 22, 2023

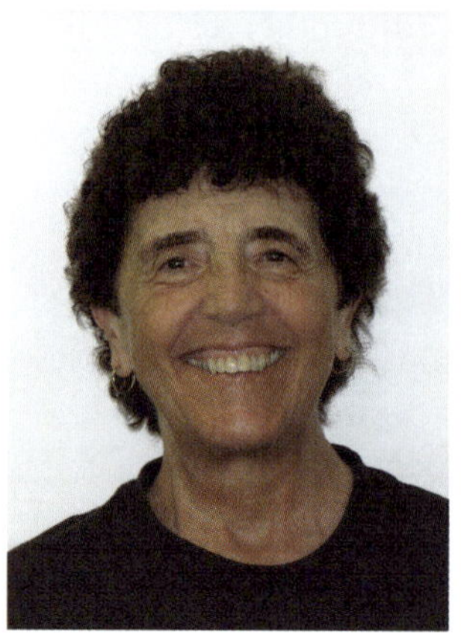

Joan Sauro, a Sister of St. Joseph of Carondelet, publishes widely in the Catholic press. "We were called Sister" (U.S. Catholic) was awarded first place for Best Essay 2014 by the CPA.

Reflection

When we come face to face with death or loss what matters most to us?

Is there someone who you "miss more than words" can say? How do you remember or honor the love and the loss?

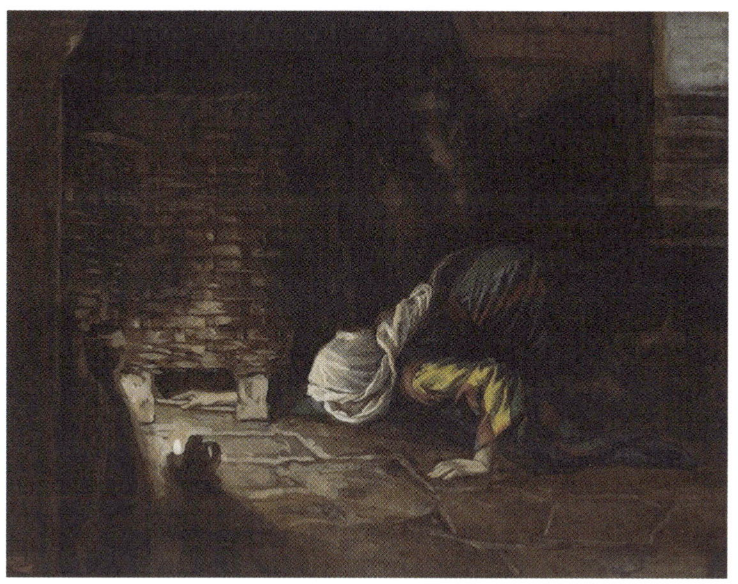

"The Lost Drachma (La drachme perdue)" by James Tissot (Brooklyn Museum)

The Lost Coin: A lesson in compassion

By Laura Hammel

Do you remember how frustrated you were the last time you misplaced something? I often misplace my keys. I know where they belong, but they are not always there when I want them. Starting a frantic search in my house, I call out to everyone, "Have you seen my keys?" Usually I'm certain that someone else has moved them; surely I am not guilty of misplacing them. I insist that all join in the hunt and there is no peace in our house until those keys are found.

In the Gospel story of the Lost Coin (Luke 15:8-10), a woman who had 10 silver coins loses one of them. Some scholars point out that this lost coin meant important money for the woman. The coin was one of 10 drachmas, a Greek silver coin that was equal to a day's wages for workers at the time. However, the respected authors of *The Collegeville Bible Commentary* suggest that this coin might well have been part of her dowry, and therefore represented her future security as a married woman.

An even more intriguing suggestion was made in *The Jerome Biblical Commentary* that this coin might well have been part of her jewelry, a part of a head band that women wore signifying their upcoming nuptials. If this were the case, then this coin was no ordinary coin, rather it is very precious to her. She lights the lamp, gets the broom and begins to sweep and search. She turns her house upside down searching for this precious coin. And when she finds it, she is so happy she calls the neighbors to celebrate.

You and I have experienced losses much more important to us than misplacing our car keys or searching for a lost coin. One of my most painful losses was the death of my parents. I was forced to face the finality of death, and I did not like the experience. I was mad at everyone and everything. My world radically changed, and yet everyone around me was going on as if nothing had happened. I felt as though I had a big hole right in the center of my heart and could not return to life as usual. I felt like the lost coin of this Gospel; lost under the couch, hurting and alone.

However, people searched me out and comforted me. They called and stopped over with food to give me time to talk and cry. Slowly, I began to heal. Soon, I began to recognize the face of God in my friends who reached out to me.

This experience following my parents' death awakened something new in me. For the first time, I knew intimately the pain of grieving and the comfort and peace it brought to have friends support me. Their care taught me what it means to be compassionate. God has shaped me in new ways through this loss. Now I approach life with more compassion and tenderness to others. Life became more precious than before.

Why is Jesus telling the parable of the lost coin, this intimate and tender story of a woman's loss? He is responding to the Pharisees who have accused him of welcoming sinners and eating with them. The Pharisees saw themselves as closer to God than others because they knew and practiced the law. Jesus makes it clear in this parable that God searches out and loves all people, even those too poor or too disadvantaged ever to have learned the formal laws and rituals.

In today's world, I believe Pope Francis is an example of what Jesus talks about in the parable of the Lost Coin. Pope Francis searches out those who are often the lost ones in the world: those who are disabled, economically poor, in prison and any who suffer prejudice and pain.

In the parable of the lost coin, Jesus welcomes and eats with those who have been excluded because he recognizes their feelings of pain and loss, their need to be found and loved.

Jesus likens God to the woman searching for a precious coin. The woman finds the lost coin and rejoices. Like this woman, God longs for us and searches for us when we are lost and in pain. When we are found by God, we gain new insight into the meaning of God's love. We find new peace and joy in our hearts and we can become more compassionate to others.

September 12, 2016

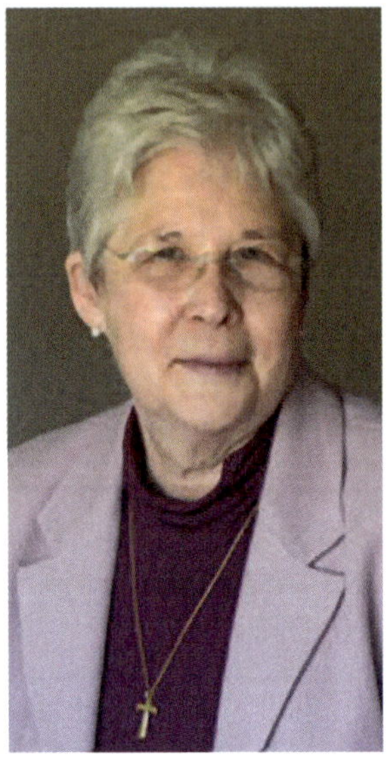

Laura Hammel is a member of the Sisters of St. Clare, a Poor Clare community in Saginaw, Michigan. In addition to the prayer ministry in her diocese, she has developed and maintained a website introducing different prayer forms useful at certain times of the year. These include an Advent calendar, contemplation using Stations of the Cross, a Pentecost Novena and Mysteries of the Rosary.

Reflection

When have you felt lost or a loss, like a big hole right in the center of your heart? Did you experience God's presence or absence in that time of loss? How has that loss made you more supportive or compassionate?

How does your experience help you seek out the lost ones in the world, those who have been excluded, or those who need to be found and loved, with the same precious love God has offered you?

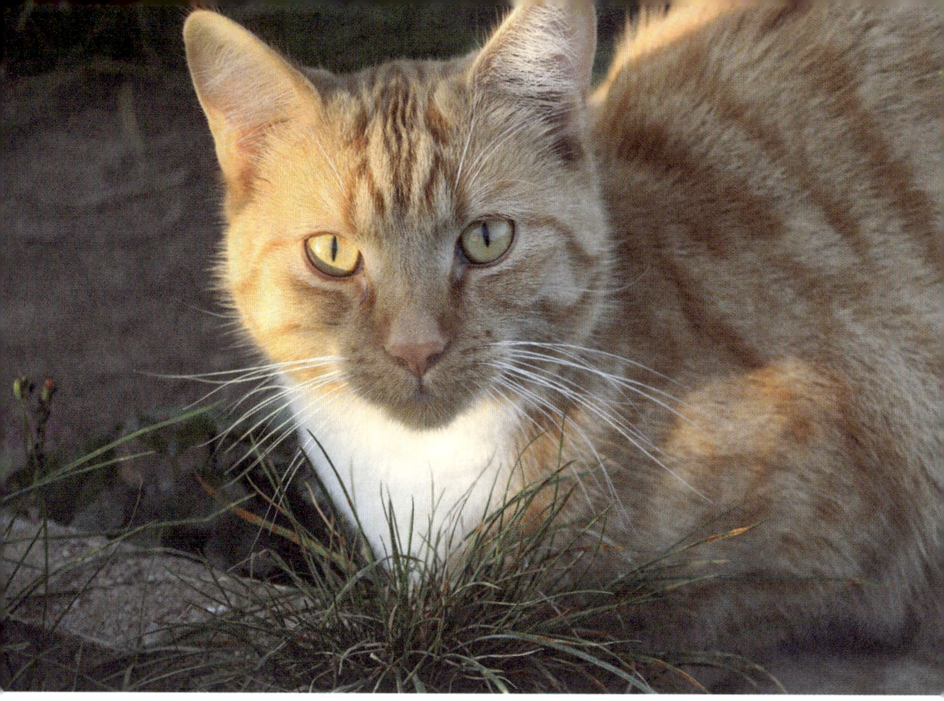

(Pixabay/Manfred Richter)

Brother Mango and eternal life

By Ilia Delio

It is now almost a week since our beloved cat, Mango, was put to sleep. His illness seemed to erupt suddenly. One day, shortly after Christmas, he refused to eat and the next day the same. It was so unlike him since he was an orange Tabby who loved a good dish of tuna. I took him to the vet and was stunned by the news: Mango had abdominal cancer and would last only another week or two. As we watched our beautiful four-legged companion become progressively weaker from lack of nutrition, struggling to get up and down the stairs, a radical life and death decision was becoming imminent. On a cold winter late Tuesday afternoon, when the sun was setting amidst a cloudy sky, we placed Mango in his carrier and tearfully drove to the City

Paws Veterinary Clinic on 14th Street. The young woman doctor who assisted us was extremely sympathetic to our impending loss and gave us time to say our "good-byes" to this white and orange ball of fur who stole our hearts.

We rescued Mango a little more than eight years ago after we began to notice a small white head with two funny ears bobbing up amidst the ivy ground cover in the backyard. One day, we put a small bowl of milk on the back stoop, and the rest, as they say, is history. Once inside the house, Mango had found himself a real home. He was not a lap cat but a very faithful one, almost dog-like. He answered the door, welcomed people inside by rolling over, and otherwise showed up, like clockwork, for his two square meals and midday snack. He liked to sleep in the chapel and often joined us for prayer in the evening. Mango was a real presence. And it is his presence that is sorely missed.

Recent trends in ecology and theology have prompted questions about non-human life such as, do animals have souls? Do animals go to heaven? Theologically, we can address these questions as intellectual ones, drawing upon various concepts to sustain our ideas. Without becoming entangled in theological discourse, I want to say quite clearly, Mango was ensouled. His soul was a core constitutive beingness, a particularity of life that was completely unique, with his own personality and mannerisms. To use the language of Duns Scotus, Mango revealed *haecceitas*, his own "thisness." Scotus placed a great emphasis on the inherent dignity of each and every thing that exists. We often perceive individual things through their accidental individual characteristics (ex. size, shape, color) but Scotus calls our attention to the very "thisness" of each thing, the very being of the object which makes it itself ("this") and not something else (*not-that*). *Haecceitas* refers to that positive dimension of every concrete and contingent being which identifies it and makes it worthy of attention; that which can be known only by direct acquaintance and not from consideration of some common nature.

If *haecceitas* is that which is known by direct contact, then *haecceitas* best describes "soul." Thomas Merton wrote, "God utters each living being as a partial thought of himself" – each living being gives glory to God by its unique, core constitutive being. Soul is what God first utters in every incarnation of the divine Word. Divine love pours itself out in otherness and comes into space-time existence through the life-giving Spirit. To be a creature of God is to be brought into relationship in such a way that the divine mystery is expressed in each concrete existence. Soul is the mirror of creaturely relatedness that reflects the vitality of divine Love.

I did not have to wonder whether or not Mango had a soul; I knew it implicitly by the way he listened to me talk to him (or think aloud sometimes), the way he sat on my office chair waiting for me to finish writing so he could eat, or simply the way he looked at me – eye to eye – in the early morning, at the start of a new day. Soul existence is expressed in the language of love. I don't think Mango loved me in the same way that I loved him, but his very presence touched my soul in a way that sharing life with Mango enriched all of life. In the spirit of St. Francis, who called all creatures "brother" and "sister," we called Mango "brother Mango" and included him as part of our community.

Teilhard de Chardin realized that the prime energy of the universe is love, unitive energy that unites center to center, generating more being and life. Love is not a thought or an idea, it is the transcendent dimension of life itself, that which reaches out to another, touches the other and is touched by the other. When we do not share in the fields of love; when we do not feel the concrete existence of another, we can easily abstract the other into a number, a data point, or even a joke.

When we recounted Mango's rapid decline to a neighbor, the flippant response was, "Hah! Your first community death!" Without direct contact of core being, without love, a living soul can disappear into the vapors of intellectualism, and we wind up constructing a world of hierarchical ontology, of lesser beings over greater beings, a ladder of existence in which the human alone stands before God. An intellectualizing of love can lead to hardness of heart, a hardness that can be harder than any rock, as Bonaventure wrote.

The death of Mango has impelled me to reflect on what matters most in life, what breaks the human heart, and what nurtures the deep, relational dimension of all life.

"If I have prophetic powers, and understand all mysteries and all knowledge, and if I have all faith, so as to remove mountains, but have not love, I am nothing," St. Paul wrote (1 Cor 13:3).

Love makes us something; it makes us alive and draws us into the dynamism of life, sustaining life's flow despite many layers of sufferings and disappointments. The person who cannot love cannot suffer, for she or he is without grief, without feeling, and indifferent.

Dorothee Sölle claimed: "When a being who is free from suffering is worshiped as God, then it is possible to train oneself in patience, endurance, imperturbability and aloofness from suffering."

If God is love then the vitality of love, even the love of a furry creature, *is* the dynamic presence of God.

Hans Urs von Balthasar spoke of the vulnerability of God's love: "It is God's going forth into the danger and the nothingness of the creation that reveals [God's] heart to be at its origin vulnerable." Out of the fullness of God's self-giving love, God shares in the pain and suffering of the world. God bends low to share our tears out of a heart full of mercy and love – and we are caught up in his embrace.

Divine love bending low is what gives the *haecceitas* of every creature a mark of eternal endurance. Every creature is born out of the love of God, sustained in love, and transformed in love. Every sparrow that falls to the ground is known and loved by God (cf. Mt 10:29); the Spirit of God is present in love to each creature here and now so that all creaturely life shares in cosmic communion. Bonaventure said that Christ has something in common with all creatures and all things are transformed in Christ. Heaven is where all tears and sufferings are wiped away, where each life is opened to the unlimited, divine creative love, and a cosmic communion of all created life is realized in the fullness of Christ.

As I reflect on Mango's death, his *haecceitas*, and the mystery of love, I have no doubt that his core love-energy will endure. His life has been inscribed on mine; the memory of his life is entangled with my own. My heart grieves for my little brother, my faithful companion, but I believe we are intertwined forever and shall be reunited in God's eternal embrace.

February 9, 2015

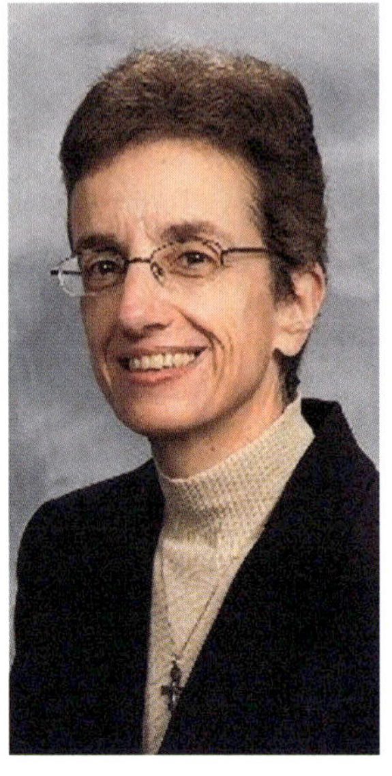

Ilia Delio, OSF, holds the Josephine C. Connelly Endowed Chair in Theology at Villanova University. Her area of research is systematic-constructive theology. She holds a doctorate in pharmacology from Rutgers University, Graduate School of Biomedical Sciences and a doctorate in historical theology from Fordham University. She is the author of twenty-four books including *The Hours of the Universe: Reflections on God, Science and the Human Journey*, which won the 2022 Gold Nautilus Book Award, *Making All Things New: Catholicity, Cosmology and Consciousness*, a finalist for the 2019 Michael Ramsey Prize, and *The Unbearable Wholeness of Being: God, Evolution and the Power of Love*, which won a 2014 Silver Nautilus Book Award and a 2014 Catholic Press Association Book Award. She is founder and director of the Center for Christogenesis, an online spiritual and educational resource for the integration of science, religion and culture.

Reflection

The author points to the expression of divine mystery in the concrete existence of every creature of God: Every sparrow is known and loved by God. Have you felt the reverence for life in creatures because of your own experience of a life or a death?

What if we embodied the spirit of St. Francis of Assisi and called each living creature "brother" or "sister"? How would being in that kind of relationship change how we acted to all living things?

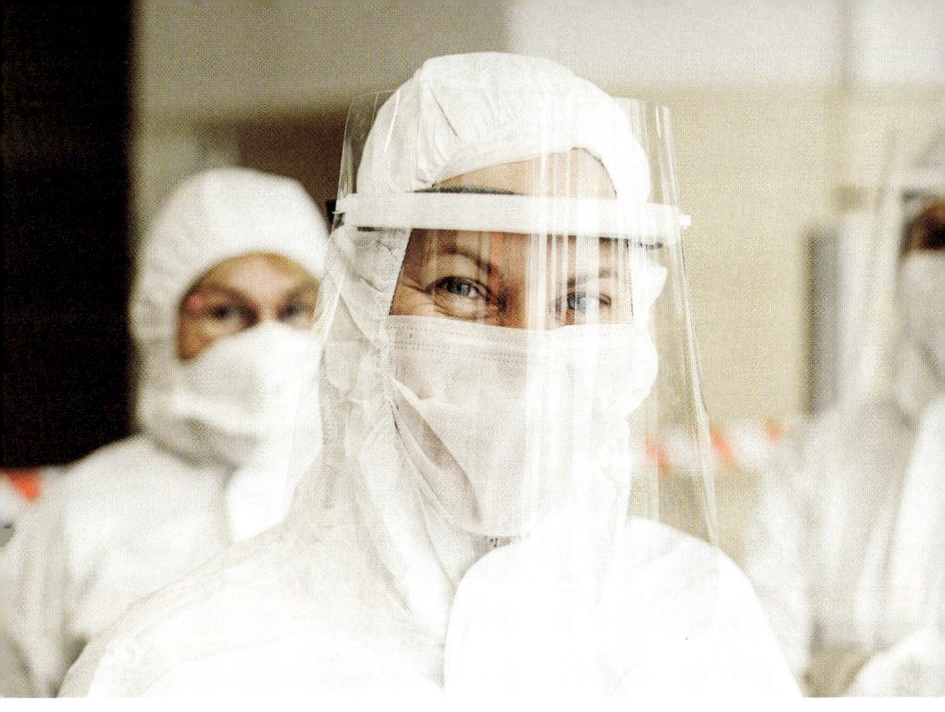

(Pixabay/Helena Jankovičová Kováčová)

Despite the pain and brokenness of COVID, Pentecost offers hope

By Mary Catherine Redmond

After I left full-time ministry as chief physician assistant in emergency medicine at North Central Bronx Hospital in New York City to assume the role of president in our congregation, I was asked by a reporter if I had it in me for a third wave of COVID.

I reflected and sadly responded, “No.” I, like all health care providers, poured myself into my ministry in March 2020 and faithfully answered the call of COVID and then the delta variant a year later. I still marvel and am humbled by the fact that I am alive. I, along with my colleagues, was bathed in

COVID in the early days. Lack of personal protective equipment, lack of knowledge about the illness, and lack of resources left us in a life-threatening position. As Brené Brown said in a CBS 60 Minutes report, "You will not find courage in a person without vulnerability." And vulnerable we were! And vulnerable we continue to be!

Although I am now in congregational leadership, my heart and support are still with my co-workers. I have provided sessions of Helping Healers Heal, a program set up even before COVID to give medical providers a space to share experiences with others who could empathize. This program was invaluable during COVID and continues to be today. I even went back to do a 12-hour shift when the staff was stressed by the deaths of family members, emergency surgery, and yes, even the birth of a baby who came early. When I facilitated the Helping Healers Heal session, I was struck by the many feelings of the staff. Those feelings ranged from fear, dismay, anger and disbelief that they were in the midst of another wave of COVID.

COVID, whatever the variant, even if its symptoms seem like the common cold, is COVID. My body has a visceral reaction when I hear the word "COVID." I see people about to die from this horrible virus. I see families ravaged with grief. I see body bag after body bag.

COVID caused me to close my circle tightly, and this past Lent, I made it my intention to widen my circle and open myself up to things I hadn't done for the past two years. There was great anxiety as I traveled (by car) to North Carolina to attend the wedding of a friend's son, fear as I went places where there were crowds, and I experienced anxiety like I have never known before. Widening my circle meant being in crowds of people—some of whom didn't even believe COVID was real, some who didn't believe in getting the vaccine and some who thought getting COVID now was better than getting it earlier.

It is difficult to be with people who don't believe what I saw and lived so vividly. It is difficult to reconcile how a pandemic so tragically divided so many—when my experience with my circle of co-workers, family, community and small circle of friends meant pulling together to protect, save and support one another. My story echoes the story of many health care workers who are still in the midst of wave after wave of this virus.

I did widen my circle, but it was not easy. Part of widening my circle was leaving the small group of co-workers, close family, community members and friends who surrounded me during my darkest time. The hardest was leaving my co-workers who knew the fear and anxiety I was talking about without me having to explain too much. I fervently tell people that health care workers are burnt out. When the new chief physician assistant (PA) came to me for advice about what to do to help the staff, I told her to encourage each person to do what they need to do for their own physical, psychological and spiritual health. Then I suggested she go to the PA on staff who is a military veteran and ask her what they do in the service when people are fighting for long periods without a break. Essentially, that is what is happening in medicine.

Right after Easter, after a six-month absence, I went back to the emergency department for a shift. Many of those I had worked with had retired, and some left for other departments. Those I worked with on that shift are broken healers who are still desiring to do their jobs and trying to figure out how to best do what they are called to do while taking care of themselves and their families. As I continue to talk with people and hear their stories—the sisters in my community and others in religious life, people of all different occupations and those in college and school, I know that COVID has had lasting effects on so many. The isolation, fear, lack of support, as so many were in survival mode dealing with the unknown, has left all broken, vulnerable, searching; not one person has escaped the effects of COVID.

COVID is only one part of a world where division continues. There is so much that fractures our families, local communities, our states, country and world. We have become a world where people stay in their own camps of belief and fail to reach out to the "other." We have lost the ability to be curious about others, to say, "Help me understand" and to be willing to listen. We all have been in our own survival mode for so long that it is hard to see others and respond.

I hope as we experienced Pentecost, we were invited by the Holy Spirit to call on the gifts of the Holy Spirit: wisdom, understanding, counsel, fortitude, knowledge, treating God with respect, and discerning the will of God in all we do. May we widen our circles, little by little, and continue the work of building the kingdom of God on Earth. May each person in her/his own way cross boundaries to understand, welcome and share life with another. This is needed now more than ever.

In a recent episode of the TV show "New Amsterdam" a doctor —dismayed by how she was treated by some after COVID— asked, "Where is the hope?" The reply: "You are hope." My prayer is that we recognize the hope that each person carries, and we all believe that we *are* the hope at this point in our history.

May the Holy Spirit bless us all with whatever gift we need this Pentecost season. As we talk in our own language in our upper rooms may the blessing of the Holy Spirit inspire us to go out and spread the gift we receive.

June 6, 2022

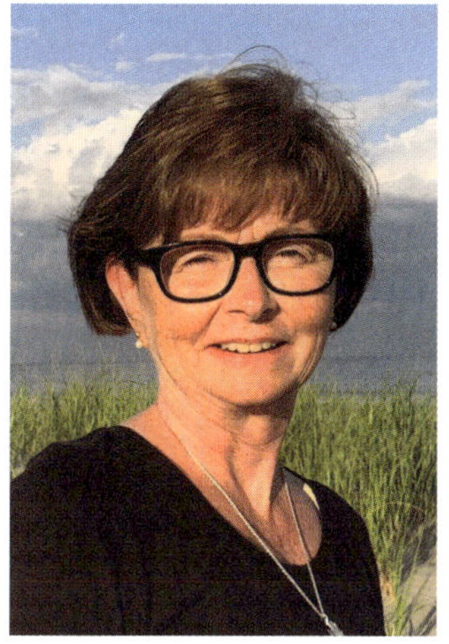

Mary Catherine Redmond is a Sister of the Presentation of the Blessed Virgin Mary. She has ministered in various aspects of healthcare and served as chief physician assistant in hospital emergency medicine, serving the underserved of New York City. She has also worked in her congregation in vocation and formation ministry. Her formal training in counseling and facilitation has also led her to do spiritual direction, retreats, and small group faith communities and to facilitate groups around new membership, leadership, and "new member" gatherings. In August of 2021, Mary Catherine was elected sister president of her congregation and she will serve in leadership until 2027.

Reflection

Most of us have times of anxiety and stress, no matter the cause. The COVID pandemic was certainly one but there can be others even more personal that cause us to close inwardly. How could you widen your circle? What gifts of the Holy Spirit might give you strength or courage?

Where in your relationships or life situations might you express curiosity and use the statement "Help me understand" to open the way for deeper listening and talking?

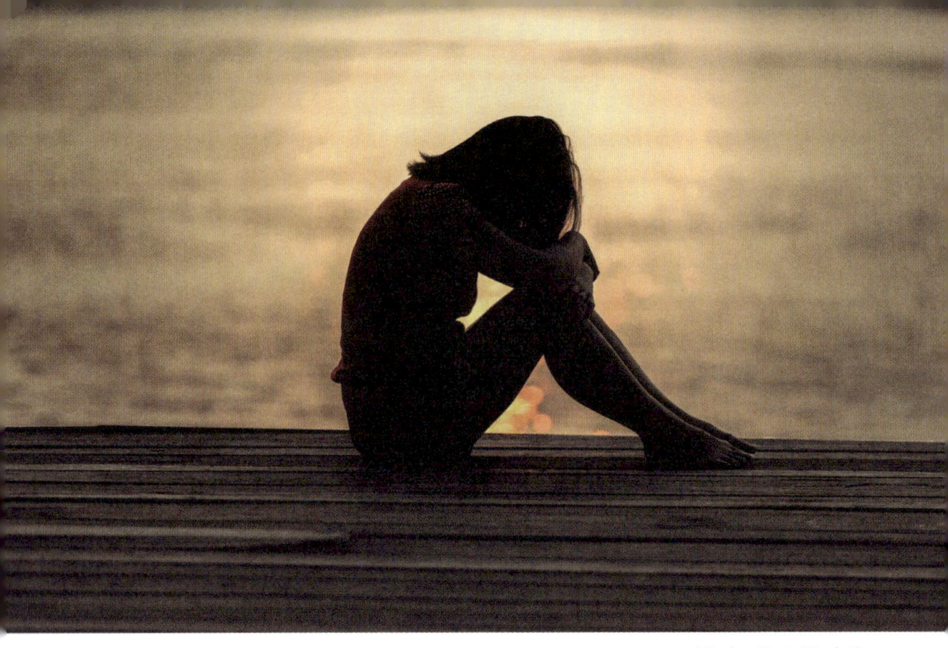

(Pixabay/Sasin Tipchai)

America's pandemic of grief

By Cecilia A. Ranger

The song is ended, but the melody lingers on. – Irving Berlin

I have been observing and mulling over her presence for a long time, especially during this last decade. Her name is grief.

Women and men religious have experienced personal and congregational losses and endings throughout their lives, including numerous forfeitures during this post-Vatican II period. They have said goodbye to women and men they have loved for decades, sisters and brothers who have left them for their eternal home and who have not been replaced by incoming postulants and novices. They have been meeting together and in inter congregational settings to speak of transformation, mergers and even endings as they watch numbers decline.

Generous, competent laity are replacing religious women and men in parishes, educational institutions, hospitals, social agencies and in the wide variety of venues where they have served God's people since the 1800s. Additionally, they are leaving behind the energies of 50 years and learning to embrace the gradual loss of physical and mental strengths and abilities that empowered them to serve in those missions and ministries: memory, hearing, sight, mobility, ability to organize complex systems and adeptness with technology.

Each change of health, ministry, move, and every letting go of what was means a new loss, and with it, an experience of grieving. These add up, and she or he often raises questions about self-worth or identity, as well as deeper questions about the meaning of one's vocational commitment, faith or life itself. We grieve. Many happenings in our current lives take us back to our losses. Colette, the French author wrote:

It's so curious; One can resist tears and 'behave' very well in the hardest hours of grief. But then someone makes you a friendly sign behind a window, or one notices that a flower that was in bud only yesterday has suddenly blossomed, or a letter slips from a drawer . . . and everything collapses.

There is, however, a larger picture. American citizens in general "move on" from one site or job to another, often in quick succession, before they have time to grieve elements of the complex world they had just left. Moreover, watching the traumas in the world around us leaves us in a heap of grief: earthquakes, floods, fires, political discord, sexual identity confusion, church divisions, school shootings, domestic violence.

All of us need "grief time," "breathing time" or "retreat time" after this bucketful of losses because each loss affects us physically, emotionally, spiritually and intellectually.

Emotionally, people are affected differently; some have difficulty concentrating, some withdraw, some turn to drinking, smoking or using drugs. Some people have thoughts of hurting themselves or others, or of destroying property—one possible explanation for the destructive violence in our society, such as mass shootings and hate speech.

Physically, some people feel exhausted or suffer from insomnia or find that their immune systems have been weakened, making them prone to colds or illnesses. Others lose their appetites or gain weight, and some experience stomach aches or headaches.

Spiritually, people have reported that they dream of loved ones, feel their presence or hear their voices. Others find that losses lead them to search for meaning, examine their faith, question the existence of God, consider the relevance of their vocations or explore their spiritual beliefs in general.

As time goes on, many people do find a positive value in grief, saying that the losses helped them grow. They gained a new sense of wisdom, became more mature, and grasped a deeper meaning of life itself. Many individuals find it healing to talk about their grief with friends or to form and attend grief groups. Shakespeare, in "Macbeth," put it this way:

Give the sorrow words; the grief that does not speak knits up the o-er wrought heart and bids it break.

Many learn to cherish not only what was, but also what will be. Helen Keller, whose losses and deprivations were so beyond anything most of us can imagine, assured us:

What we once enjoyed and deeply loved we can never lose. . . . For all that we love deeply becomes part of us.

While most of us ignore or resent the "she or he's in a better place" talk, or, "Something good comes out of what was bad" assurances, it has been the case for most, or at least many people, that they find consolation in the reality that there is a creative force in the universe, a God or Absolute Being, who can assist people of any age in growing as they process and live with their losses, and in finding light where darkness had clouded their everyday lives.

When our days become dreary with low-hovering clouds of despair, and when our nights become darker than a thousand midnights, let us remember that there is a creative force in this universe, working to pull down the gigantic mountains of evil, a power that is able to make a way out of no way and transform dark yesterdays into bright tomorrows. – Martin Luther King Jr.

September 18, 2023

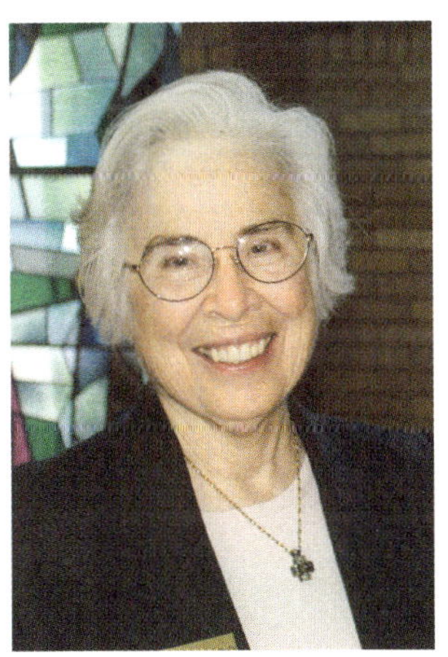

Cecilia A. Ranger is a Sister of the Holy Names of Jesus and Mary. With a lifelong commitment to education, philosophy, theology and spiritual direction, she taught and did spiritual direction at several colleges, universities and seminaries, and served in university administration and on boards. Other ministries included pastoral ministry, facilitation, and consultancies for leadership groups; she also served as president of the Oregon Sisters of the Holy Names. One of her primary interests was dialogue among religious traditions; she was spiritual and retreat director for persons of many faith traditions. She is now retired at Mary's Woods in Lake Oswego, Oregon, where she does some teaching, parish or personal retreats, and writing.

Reflection

When have you experienced the hardest hours of grief? Was it for a loss from death? A change of geography? A lost relationship? A diminishment of health? Where did you find the space to grieve? Where did you feel God's presence (or absence) at that time?

Is there a place you are able to find "breathing space"—where you can take care of yourself—when you must grapple with personal or world trauma?

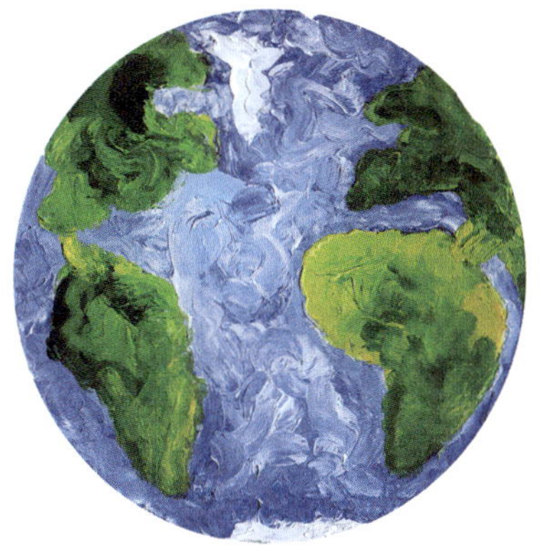

Advent and Christmas

So Christmas is giving, self-emptying, empowerment, self-surrender, obedience, simplicity and humility: In short, it is the feast of vulnerability. God is compassionate. Compassion inspires justice, equality and fraternity. So let us learn to be one with the people who are helpless, downtrodden, rejected, neglected and poor. Let us take this message and celebrate this Christmas with its true meaning.

Sujata Jena

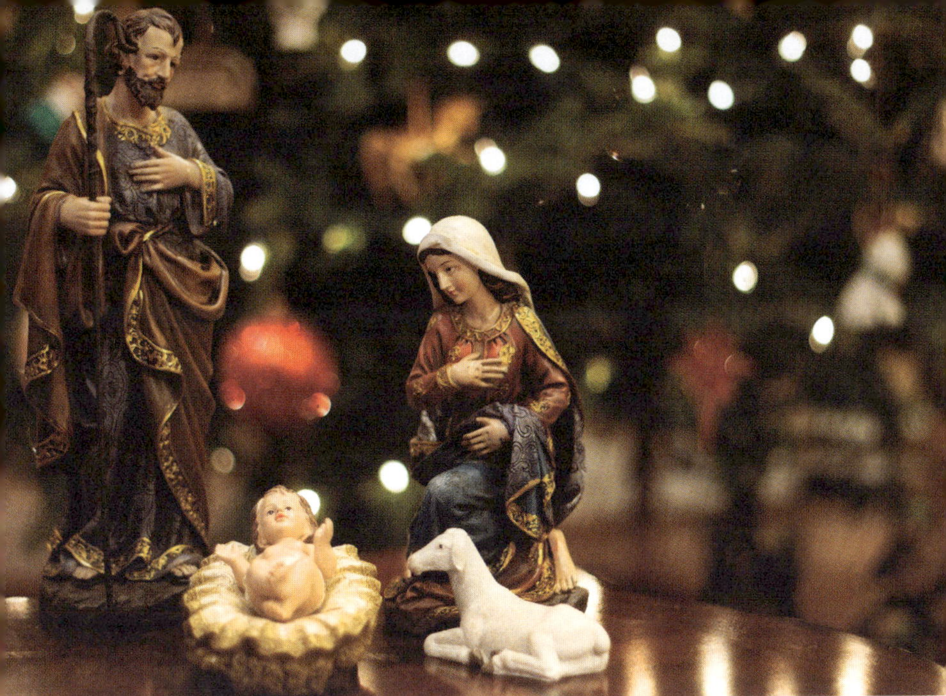

(Pixabay/articgoneape)

Pick up the phone. It may be a call from the helpless babe of Bethlehem.

By Tessy Jacob

I was on a telephone conversation with one of my cousins. While speaking about random issues, she mentioned that one of her neighbors was thought to have cancer, and described her pathetic circumstances. Money was her biggest concern. After a while we changed topics, spoke about a few other things, and ended the call.

A little while later something occurred to me: I had heard about the pathetic situation of a person who is unknown to me. I had two choices before me: Either ignore the entire story or seek a way to find a solution. I chose the latter. I have a mobile phone with internet with me at all times. I do have people among my contacts who are rich, generous and charitable. It took only a shameless attitude and a few messages to get a sum of rupees credited to that woman's account. Although it didn't mean everything, it would definitely mean something to her.

Christmas is the story of unconditional giving and loving. Mary, Joseph, shepherds, magi—all had something to offer. They were called to give without delay, almost in an instant. Their selfless giving brought the word incarnate into our midst. And ultimately, Jesus was the offering for all humankind. Their Advent, which marks the beginning of the Christian liturgical calendar, calls us to be ready to receive a message to be at the service of others.

Reading through the story of Christmas, we also encounter selfish and cruel characters: the innkeepers who denied a room for the couple and Herod—a symbol of jealousy. Advent is the season to check our hearts, to see: Do I feel the pain of those who come to my doorstep?

The chaos created by the pandemic has thrown everyone's life out of gear. Poverty, unemployment, psychological traumas, layoffs, grievances—even death—seemingly have defeated some people's hope. It may seem impossible to recall all the dreary moments each individual had to live through. Though the pandemic closed many doors, that is not the end. Many new doors opened. One of those new doors was the diffusion of technology, which helps everyone stay connected. The connectedness comes with a responsibility: to know the other and be part of their world—virtual and real.

Jesus came to a world in misery, where the social conditions manipulated the lives of simple people. The poor, sick, needy, the despised, women—everyone needed someone to hear their unvoiced cries. They could express themselves only in limited ways, as society passed judgments about them. Most of their cries were lost in the cacophony of the crowd that was hurrying around them, making a living even at the cost of someone else's life.

Think of the paralytic at Bethsaida. Had any onlooker in all those years lent him a hand? How many women might have been caught in adultery and been stoned to death because there was no one to defend them? Take any of those instances: When did they receive salvation? It was only when Jesus sensed, paused and listened to them.

Technology is useless unless it is used well. We spend many hours in conversations but are hardly affected by the issues that need attention. Technology can turn us into beings with shorter emotions—be it happiness or sadness—lasting only till the next click.

The pandemic and our survival activities have proved that we can still make this world a better place. There were innumerable good Samaritans, starting with the front-line warriors, who went out of their way to reach out to the needy. The Nobel Prize-winning mystic poet Rabindranath Tagore said, "Every child comes with the message that God is yet to be discouraged with [humankind]."

Indeed, the pandemic has shown us that the good side of us has not yet died off. Perhaps it has become a little rusty or has slowed due to irregular usage. Or maybe it has not even been installed yet, because we have not thought of using it.

Using our God-given gifts for the greater goodness of his own creation is the best way to thank the almighty. God never lets this world go completely down. Had not our brains developed enough to make alternatives and antidotes for this pandemic, where might the world have ended up? Thank you, Lord, for making us co-creators of the universe!

Connectedness to each other is the need of the hour. The God who dwells in heaven transcended to earth to be with his people—to walk their streets, to feel their pain, to help in their need and to give life through his own life. Meditating on these manifestations of the humanness of God, can I imbibe his attitude during this Advent? Can I become a sign of hope for someone else's life? Can I use all my resources—time, talent, technologies—to alleviate someone's pain? Can I create Christmas every day by doing my bit to be the Christ, bringing good news every day, to the people around me?

"He comes, comes, ever comes!" Be vigilant. The next phone call may be the cry of the helpless babe of Bethlehem. Let us behold him the best way that we can.

December 20, 2021

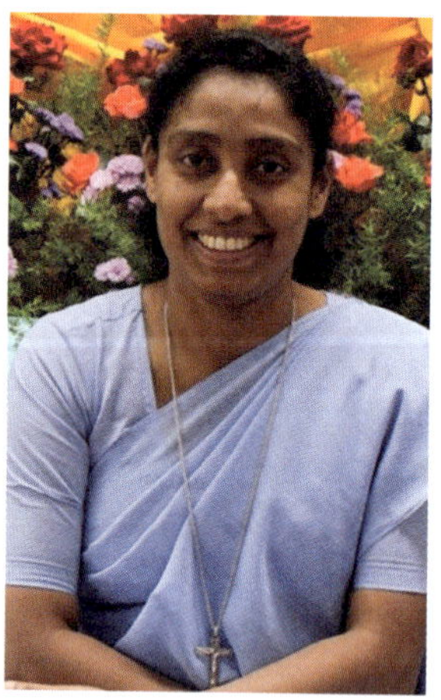

Tessy Jacob is a member of the Missionary Sisters Servants of the Holy Spirit. She is Indian in nationality and has an interest in evangelization through mass media. She is the vice president of the Indian Catholic Press Association and serves as the communication coordinator of her home province. Currently she is pursuing her doctoral research studies in media and communication from Xavier Institute of Management, Bhubaneswar.

Reflection

Meditating on all the places (and faces) where God is being manifested every day offers us a way to be aware of every encounter as a moment of grace to experience God. How might you create an Advent practice of reflecting upon those daily encounters (journalling, prayer, meditation, art, etc.)?

The author offers examples of the good and bad of technology. What might be one way during Advent you could allow technology to transform either your own or someone else's life/situation?

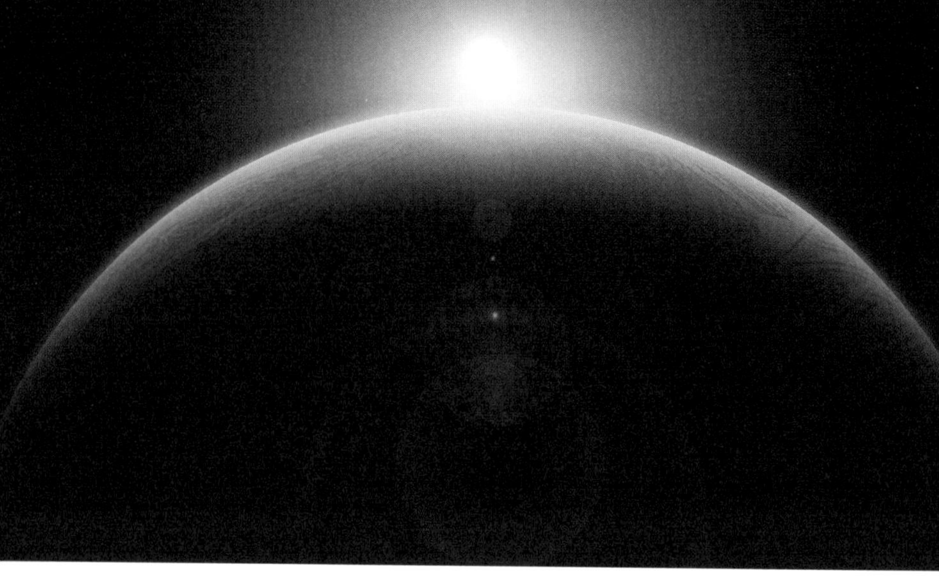

(Pixabay/LoganArt)

We are called to a new incarnation

By Cheryl Rose

I have always loved this word: *Incarnation*! It captures the glorious mystery of God becoming human in the person of Jesus! Incarnation was a sacred word, bringing a sense of awe to a grade school child who waited in joyful anticipation for the greatest moment of the year—the wonder of Christmas! Of course, it also meant the lights and decorations in our homes and towns that turned dark winter days into glittering, glowing wonderlands.

Yet even as a child, something way more than Santa Claus stirred in the air for me as our purple-shrouded church joined the centuries of faithful people longing for the coming of a savior. Each Advent candle that we lit reminded us to be patient, for he *would* come! Despite the natural excitement of toys and gifts, and cookies and trees, the plaintive, haunting notes of "O Come, O Come Emmanuel" stirred a longing that every soul sensed at some deep level.

The silence of winter nights drew us into our longing for something to ease the darkness and sadness that lurked in the shadows of life on this earth. Young and old alike yearned for the Messiah to bring light to the weary world. Disillusioned hearts searched for something real that no amount of tinsel could promise: *incarnation*—the unimagined gift, the outrageously hopeful miracle that God would enter our human experience and take on the full gamut of this journey of ours, and for one reason—to help us know how to be human!

How many years have I welcomed that Advent season, ready to enter deeply into pondering the darkness around me—in my own little life, and in the midst of seemingly unsolvable, desperate problems encircling the world? From every corner came cries for justice, mercy, compassion and peace. Advent waiting became Advent longing and yearning and aching for a peace we could not construct ourselves. And as we grew older, the sobering realization dawned on us that only "*You* satisfy the hungry heart."

But finally, there came a time when things shifted a bit for me, and I began to realize that I, too, was *incarnated*! My soul took human form so that I could learn many great lessons on this human journey. My "incarnation" meant experiencing hunger and physical pain—and accidents and disappointments, and heartache and failure—all *great* teachers of incalculable lessons. So, too, my incarnation has meant delicious feasts and the warmth of human touch, and the boundless freedom of dance and running and swimming! It has meant tender love, rich relationships, listening with compassion and touching the pain of others. It has meant a million human joys and delights . . . great books, breathtaking music, and ecstasies over the beauty and wonder of Earth's skies and rivers, oceans, mountains and forests!

Incarnation opened my human mind and heart to experience the holiness of an infant's face, a child's innocent play, a bird's effortless flight, a beloved elder's familiar, worn hand, so sacred in mine. And God walks among us in all of this, showing us how to bear ecstasy as well as sorrow.

My incarnation baptized me into discipleship, set my feet on his path, and began an apprenticeship of "putting on the mind and heart of Christ Jesus" (Philippians 2:5). Meditating on his life dispelled many false assumptions about who God is, what being a good person involves, and what really matters in this human journey. The incarnated Christ modeled living without ego, without duality. He embodied the amazing truth that all are one! We are *one* with God, we are one with every person of every culture and religion, and with every blade of grass, every drop of water, every plant and animal cohabitating with us. His example was so clear, his words so unequivocal it's hard to understand how anyone could miss or skew the message. If we celebrated not just his *coming* to Earth, but his *living* on Earth—how he saw things—"*You have heard that it was said . . . but I say to you*" (Matthew 5:21-22); how he treated people without judgment, without excluding, without anything but mercy and acceptance—the world would look vastly different. How can anyone fail to see who he was and the example he set for our human living?

This year, I am longing once again for the Messiah's coming, all too aware of the weight of darkness: of the shocking gun violence in our country, of the wrenching suffering of Ukraine and other places of staggering injustice, of lies and truth-spinning that have ignited hatred and division. And as I pray for the coming of the light, I'll also be thanking Jesus for entering our human experience and coaxing us to a new consciousness. Early on, he called us to come and follow him, telling us we could do all he did and more, inviting us to leave all the nonsense and walk on water with him. Let's pick up *our* incarnation.

Let's expand our incarnated selves to Jesus proportions! Advent is about incarnation—his and ours!

December 27, 2022

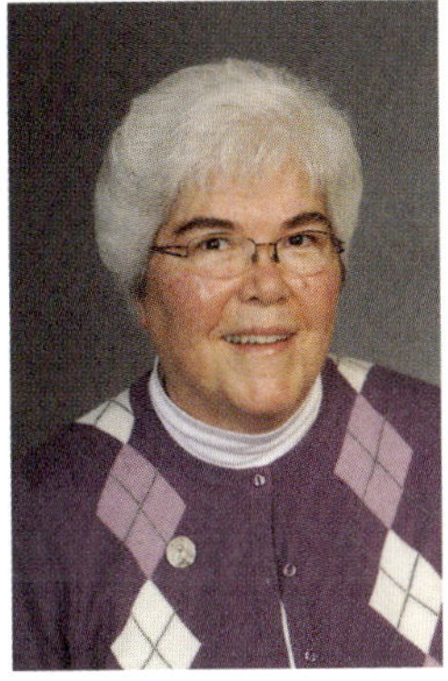

Cheryl Rose is a member of the Sisters of the Humility of Mary. With an academic background in science and math and a Master's in Religious Studies, she taught high school chemistry, physics and theology for 26 years. She also did vocation ministry for 20 years for her community. Presently she works full-time as a spiritual director and retreat director, offering many kinds of contemplative retreats, programs and Enneagram workshops.

Reflection

Perhaps you have a childhood memory or practice during Advent that you remember from anticipating Jesus' coming. As an adult, what remains important to you about the coming of God into the midst of humanity? Have you found a way to make that a part of your reflection or practice during this annual Advent season?

How does Advent give you hope in the midst of places of darkness or injustice that the author suggests? Is there a Scripture passage that reminds you of this reason to hope?

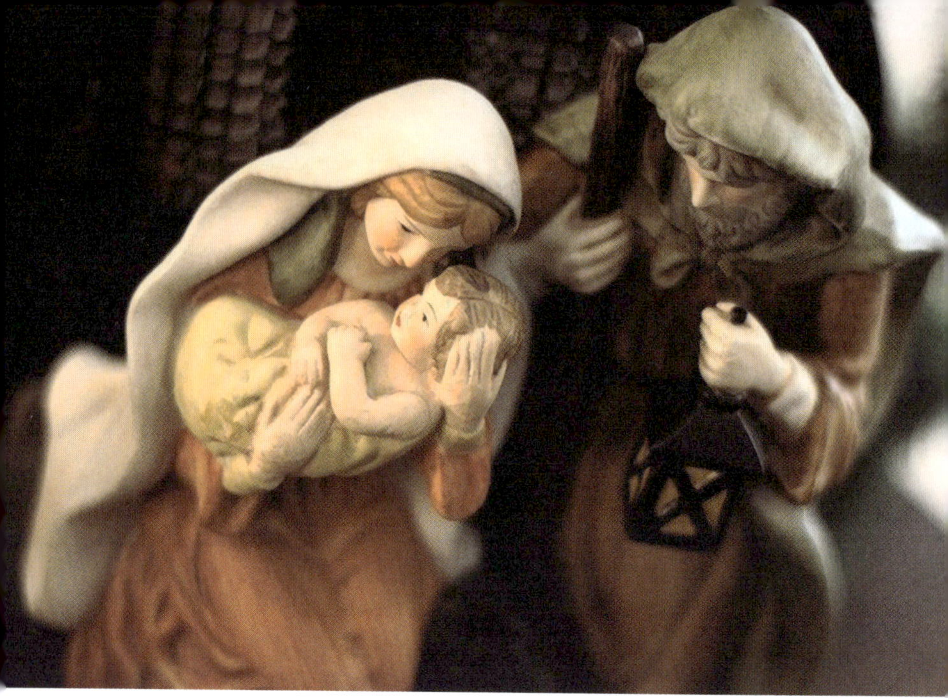

(Pixabay/Vickie McCarty)

The meaning and challenge posed by the first Christmas

By Sujata Jena

Since the first day of Advent, I have been reading, listening and reflecting on the mystery of God becoming human, the Immanuel "God with us"—the first Christmas!

I understand that Christmas is not about jingle bells, plum cakes, glittering costumes, sumptuous parties, or seven-star palaces. It is about the refugees and migrants; the internally displaced; the struggle of Elizabeth to have a child; night watch shepherds; the martyrdom of innocent children; homeless wanderers; and daily wage laborers. For me, this is the true meaning of the Nativity of Christ, the first Christmas Day.

Christmas is a great feast not only for Christians but for the whole world, for humanity at large. Almost everyone celebrates Christmas, regardless of any differences: caste, creed or language. Unfortunately, today this great feast is commercialized, and the importance of the feast of God becoming human—and one among us to unite us in his love—is lost. It has become a mere social celebration.

I would like to reflect more on the deeper meaning of Christmas so that I may realize and be able to celebrate the coming Christmas in a meaningful way.

Today, it seems like the world is governed by a few powerful corporations, and a few crony capitalists control the world order and geopolitics. We find power struggles everywhere. Even in some families, there is a power struggle between husband and wife, parents and children, or brothers and sisters. In society, there are struggles between the rich and the poor, the powerful and the powerless, and the elite and the bourgeois. Even in some religious communities, there are power struggles among members.

Every nation wants to be powerful, which is one reason why we witness prolonged wars in some parts of the world. When power meets power, the outcome is a power struggle. When a powerful nation helps a poor nation, the outcome is alienation: the powerful nation looks upon the vulnerable as one who depends on them and subjugates them by meeting their needs and never allowing that nation to come into equal relationship. As a result, when power meets vulnerability, the outcome is alienation, separation and dependence.

However, when vulnerability meets vulnerability, the outcome is intimacy.

That's what we find in the birth of Jesus. God—so powerful, almighty and omniscient—meets the vulnerable human beings enslaved by the powerful. God comes down and becomes one among us to save and set us free—from every form of slavery and sin.

That is why Christmas becomes a feast of vulnerability to experience freedom, dignity and the grace of God in and through Jesus. This feast invites us to become vulnerable, to join with the vulnerable. This is the entire message of Jesus.

Jesus is born in Bethlehem as a vulnerable, helpless baby. Mary and Joseph came to the stable when there was no place for them; Mary and Joseph gave birth to the child Jesus, wrapped him in swaddling clothes, and placed him in the manger. God becomes vulnerable in meeting us who are weak.

Today, when we ask about the meaning of Christmas, many equate it with cakes, new dresses, toys and Santa Claus. This is how we destroy the real meaning of Christmas.

To understand the real meaning of Christmas, we need to reflect from the perspectives of those who were related to the first Christmas in history.

For God the Father, Christmas is *giving* as we find in the Scripture, "For God so loved the world that he gave his only Son" (John 3:16). Hence, giving is Christmas. Today, the giving culture is slowly getting lost. We need to learn to give.

For Jesus, Christmas is *self-emptying*: "Who, though he was in the form of God, He did not count equality with God. . . . Rather, he emptied himself, taking the form of a servant being born in the likeness of man" (Philippians 2:6-7).

Christmas for the Holy Spirit is *empowerment*, as in, " 'The holy Spirit will come on you, and the power of the Most High will overshadow you. Therefore the Holy One to be born will be called the Son of God' " (Luke 1:35). We are to empower ourselves with God to empower others.

Self-surrender is Christmas for Mary: "And Mary said, 'I am the handmaid of the Lord. May it be done to me according to your word' " (Luke 1:38). If she had not surrendered, Christmas would not have been a reality.

For Joseph, Christmas is *obedience*. Joseph did not understand what was happening and what God was telling him through the angel but obeyed God's will (Matthew 1:19-24). When we live a life of obedience God becomes a reality in our life.

For shepherds, Christmas is living out of a life of *simplicity*. The shepherds were ordinary people living in hilly regions. They listened to the angel (Luke 2:8-16) and went ahead to meet Jesus.

Christmas is *humility* for the wise men, the Magi. They were humble enough to accept the little child in the manger as their king (Matthew 2:11).

So Christmas is giving, self-emptying, empowerment, self-surrender, obedience, simplicity, and humility: In short, it is the feast of vulnerability. God is compassionate. Compassion inspires justice, equality and fraternity. So let us learn to be one with the people who are helpless, downtrodden, rejected, neglected and poor. Let us take this message and celebrate this Christmas with its true meaning.

Today in the context of war, corruption, exploitation, discrimination, rape, drug abuse, and broken families, the invitation is to listen intently to the heartbeat of God. We need to think like God and dream like God. Listening intently to the heartbeat of God and effectively living it in our daily lives will make Christmas a reality.

I pray that the virtues of the first Christmas guide my life as I accompany the vulnerable in an attempt to build his kingdom here on Earth.

December 23, 2022

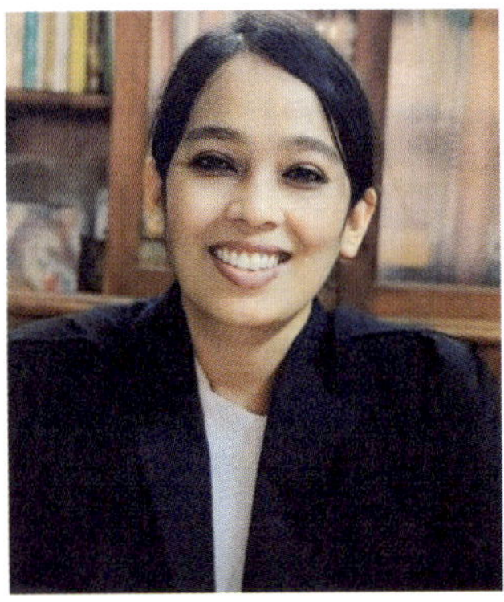

Sujata Jena is a religious sister of the Congregation of the Sacred Hearts of Jesus and Mary based in the eastern Indian state of Odisha. She is a grassroots activist, a freelance journalist, and an advocate with a specific cause of the poor, Dalits, Tribals, women, children, minorities, migrants and homeless. Sister Sujata is the recipient of the Best Journalist Award 2021 by the Indian Catholic Press Association for authentically and consistently being the voice of people's rights, especially of the poor, Dalits, and Tribals. She was conferred with the Salvador Memorial Award 2022 by Bombay Catholic Sobha in the category of individual who has contributed significantly to the field of social work.

Reflection

Christmas does celebrate the birth of a vulnerable baby in a stable. The author says, "When vulnerability meets vulnerability, the outcome is intimacy." *When we see people who are vulnerable (refugees, beggars, those suffering injustices, the homeless) it can touch a vulnerable side of ourselves if we let it. What then would intimacy with these "others" look like? What kind of compassion would you have to find within to recognize that vulnerability?*

The author offers several Scripture passages that reference the coming of the Messiah. How could you incorporate taking time for reflection on those passages into an Advent practice this year?

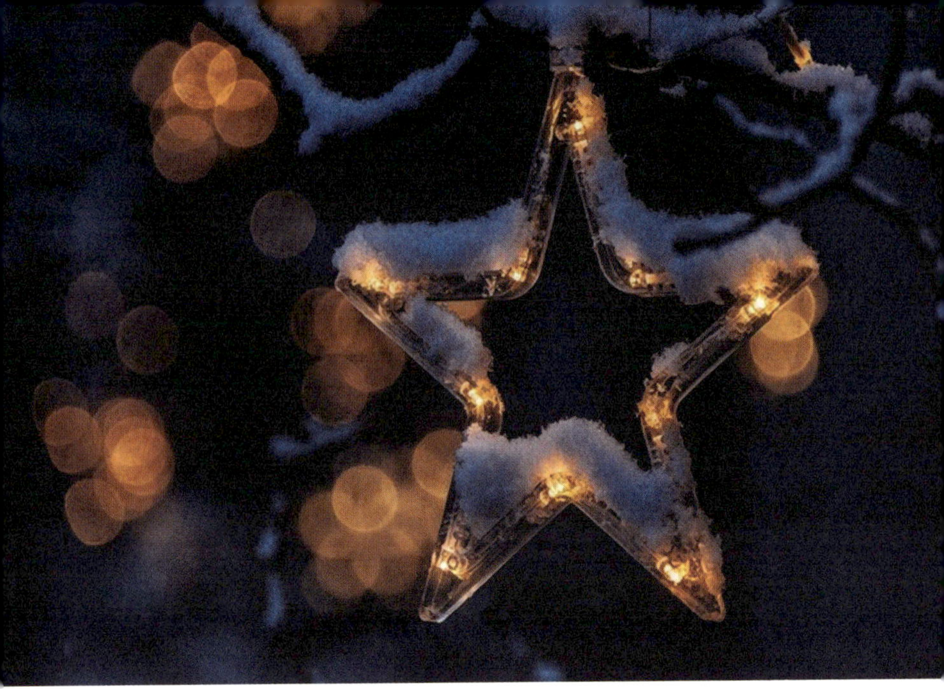

(Pixabay/121385620)

Living the spirit of Advent means making the rough ways smooth

By Mary Nguyen Thi Phuong Lan (Nguyen)

When the weather turns cold, it signals Advent; the new liturgical year is coming. In Vietnam, the social and religious (especially Christian) activities become joyful as we move eagerly toward the Christmas festival. Everywhere we listen to hymns about Advent and Christmas. It seems very sacred, holy and profound. Different styles of caves (manger scenes) decorated with colorful lights and pretty stars, all kinds of evergreen trees, Santa Claus, decorations—all are displayed around the parish, in shops, restaurants, parks and village roads.

Vietnamese sisters prepare prayer songs or prayer shows for Christmas vigil performances. People also start sending each other beautiful Christmas cards with meaningful wishes. The atmosphere of the Christmas festival becomes more and more bustling and joyful. However, looking on the surface is not enough; the faithful need to go inside the depths of the Christmas mystery to experience the meaning of waiting for the Savior.

Indeed, Advent is a good opportunity for us to recall God's love for humanity through the history of salvation. Through reliving this mystery, we experience human weakness as well as God's great love, and then we will live more worthy of God's gracious salvation for humankind today. For Advent to be fruitful, every member of the faithful needs to hear and respond to the call of God and St. John the Baptist.

In the liturgical season of Advent, God calls us to be awake and to pray because there are many people who live as if they will never die. They are lulled by worldly pleasures, drunkenness, worries about life, injustice, corruption, deceit, heartlessness and cruelty. They are fascinated by their passion for fame and power, but they forget that there are surprises that will come in death. For this, Jesus invites us to watch and pray always: "Beware that your hearts do not become drowsy from carousing and drunkenness and the anxieties of daily life, and that day catch you by surprise like a trap. For that day will assault everyone who lives on the face of the earth" (Luke 21:34-35).

We are called to wake up to realize the truth, to recognize the things in life that we should stay away from lest they lead us to death. To realize the truth, to recognize the wrong, we must pray constantly with God, who shows us how to know the dangers of the enemy. In that quote from Luke, Jesus listed two of the most dangerous enemies to avoid—drunkenness and worries about life—which make the body heavy and the mind tired. When we are tired and heavy, we no longer have enough wisdom and energy to do what God wants. Worrying about life includes things like fame, power, money and carnal desires. All of these can make us no longer desire the Kingdom; "for where your treasure is, there your heart will be also" (Matthew 6:21).

And St. John the Baptist proclaimed: "Prepare the way of the Lord, make straight his paths. Every valley shall be filled and every mountain and hill shall be made low. The winding roads shall be made straight, and the rough ways made smooth" (Luke 3:4-6).

The high, rough road could refer to arrogance, deception, cunning, hatred, lack of morality or lack of faith. If the winding, rough road can make us feel uncomfortable, our vices will also disrespect God and make God unhappy. Obeying St. John, we should correct the lifestyle of our hearts and get rid of bad habits to welcome the Lord for the Christmas festival, while looking forward to the day of the Lord's return—especially welcoming the Lord at the hour of our death.

To welcome the Lord at Christmas means that we need to think of others, and bring love and charity to them. God will not be happy if we make a retreat, confess and receive Holy Communion very fervently during Advent—with hearts filled with pride, jealousy and hatred. And welcoming the Lord during the Christmas season will become meaningful when we care about the plight of the poor . . . by helping them share the warm joy of the day God's child was born.

Our Dominican community is trying to live the spirit of Advent, preparing our hearts to welcome the coming of Christ to the world by going to meet the poor workers in the neighborhood where they live. Because of the COVID pandemic, the lives of workers in Vietnam have become more difficult because workers' wages and incomes have been reduced. Although the epidemic has been safely controlled and life has returned to normal, the workers have to rent rooms in hostels. They have to spend frugally, not daring to think about eating and drinking enough nutrients, because, with their small salary, they have to pay for rent, electricity and water, and school fees for their children.

Understanding the plight of the workers in the hostels, we visit, share, and give lovely gifts to their children on Christmas day. We hope our visits will help them and their children feel the joy of Christmas despite their life's difficulties and challenges. We especially wish them and their families a Merry Christmas season filled with the joy of the Child Jesus. Our benefactors join the sisters in becoming ambassadors of God's love for everyone, and we wish them—who supported us with Christmas gifts for the poor children—abundant grace and the joy of Baby Christ.

As we wait for the Lord's coming this Advent, may each of us Christians change our lives with concrete actions: living the faith, practicing charity and love, living justice, and respecting one another because when the Lord comes, He will judge us by the standard of love and charity. At the last judgment we will hear: "Whatever you did for one of these least brothers of mine, you did for me" (Matthew 25:35-40).

December 16, 2022

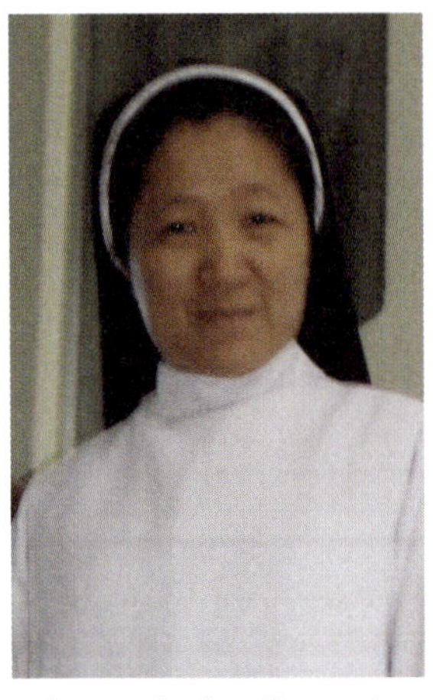

Mary Nguyen Thi Phuong Lan (Nguyen) is a Dominican Sister of the St. Rosa Lima congregation of the Sai Gon Archdiocese in Vietnam. After studying at universities in Vietnam and in Manila, Philippines, she worked in formation programs in Vietnam. Now, she is an English teacher for the Catholic college of the Xuan Loc Diocese in Vietnam, and a regular contributor to Global Sisters Report.

Reflection

The author speaks about being aware of our surroundings so that we might be responsive during this season. John the Baptist told us to prepare the way and Jesus reminded us to stay awake. By noticing those in need or in difficulty around us and responding, we are bringing God's presence into the world. Where do you see the possibility of bringing God to birth in your surroundings?

It is important that we do a periodic examination of our own lives so that we may see what keeps us from becoming closer to God. Advent is an exceptionally good time to do this kind of reflection. What concrete steps would you take this season to make time for such an examination so that you might be confident you are on the path to giving witness to the coming of God?

In Immokalee's immigrant community, the Christmas story unfolds among us

By Judy Dohner

It was Dec. 23 and I was making a last-minute run to Family Dollar store. To my surprise, Christmas was being put away and Valentine's Day cards and candy were being stocked on the shelves.

Before Christmas becomes a memory, let me share how the Christmas story is being lived out today in a poor little town in Florida. Immokalee (home of the Coalition of Immokalee Workers) is an unincorporated farming community made up of Mexicans, Guatemalans and Haitian immigrants. Jesus is there. The Gospel is alive. One just has to look.

In early fall there was a tsunami of Haitian refugees arriving in Immokalee from the Texas border. It has slowed to a small, steady stream. Most of these refugees are young couples with very young children. Many of the women are pregnant. And this is where Luke's Gospel comes alive, where Jesus is revealed: "And this will be a sign for you."

Mary and Joseph's journey from Nazareth to Bethlehem most likely took about five long days. The young Haitian couples coming from Chile and Brazil travel more than 7,000 miles, mostly on foot, for two or three months. Mary was in the last weeks of her pregnancy. These young mothers-to-be are also in the last months of their pregnancies and probably have received no prenatal care. Upon arrival in Immokalee, the young families "come to the church" seeking help and are either "with child" or have recently given birth.

"In those days a decree went out that the whole world should be enrolled" (Luke 2:1).

When the Haitians arrive at the Texas border, they are registered and placed in detention. Then, they are sent to addresses of family or friends who have agreed to accept them. The reality in this very poor community is that, upon arrival, they are told there is "no room for them" because the host families are also very poor.

The Thursday after Thanksgiving, a Holy Family visited our center. A young man and his nine-month pregnant wife said they had left detention in Texas and went to stay with relatives in Miami, but these relatives in Miami told them they had no room. They brought them to Immokalee "because there was work."

But the law says undocumented people are not permitted to work. No family, no friends, no home. So they slept in the woods. Then they were told, "Go to the church. The church will help you." Our center does not provide housing. I phoned three local hotels hoping to offer temporary shelter to the couple. Each one said, "We have no room." We found a Haitian woman with two children in a two-bedroom apartment who offered this couple one of the bedrooms until they could find more permanent housing.

"While they were there, the time came for her to have her child" (Luke 2:6).

Two other women—one from Brazil and one from Chile—arrived in Immokalee with their spouses in the days before Christmas. Both had been nine months pregnant when they arrived in Texas in late November. Marie Ange delivered her premature baby girl the day she crossed the border. Nadia gave birth in detention two days after her arrival at the border. Both had come seeking help to get their babies' birth certificates, which they were not able to obtain while in Texas.

The Haitian asylum seekers continue to find their way to Immokalee. God continues to speak to them through "angels" who offer good news of help and acceptance. These courageous young men and women are not afraid. They simply trust that God is with them.

"Do not be afraid for I proclaim to you good news of great joy for all the people" (Luke 2:10).

So, look around! Emmanuel is "God-with-us." God is revealing the Good News everywhere we look. We just have to have eyes to see and ears to hear.

After the shepherds visited the child, "they made known the message that had been told and all who heard it were amazed." May we, like the shepherds "glorify and praise God for all we have heard and seen."

January 10, 2022

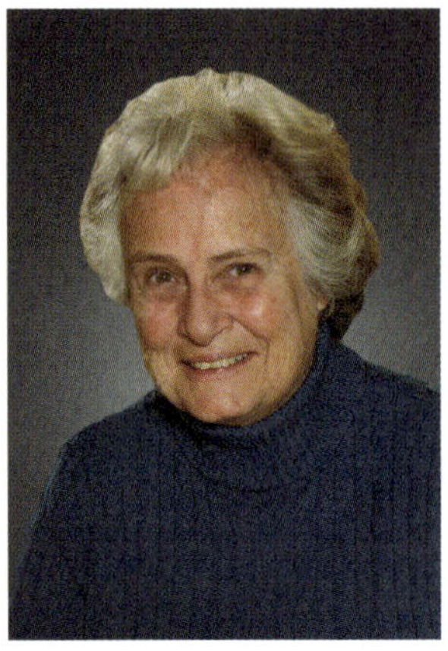

Judy Dohner is a Sister of the Humility of Mary from Villa Maria, Pennsylvania. She has worked with migrants and immigrants for the past 30 years. She returned to the United States in 2018 after ministering in Haiti for 16 years and currently works with Haitian immigrants and refugees in Immokalee, Florida. She has written for Global Sisters Report and the National Catholic Reporter.

Reflection

Luke's Gospel story about Mary and Joseph tells the story of them seeking a place of refuge and being turned away. World news outlets tell the stories of the painful plight of refugees across the world's borders who seek safety from many threats including famine, war or natural disasters. And they are often turned away. Hold our sacred story and the world news in each hand. Pray and reflect. What response are you called to make?

The author writes of the courage of those she encountered; they trust in a God who hears their cries. Where are you called to have that kind of radical trust in God?

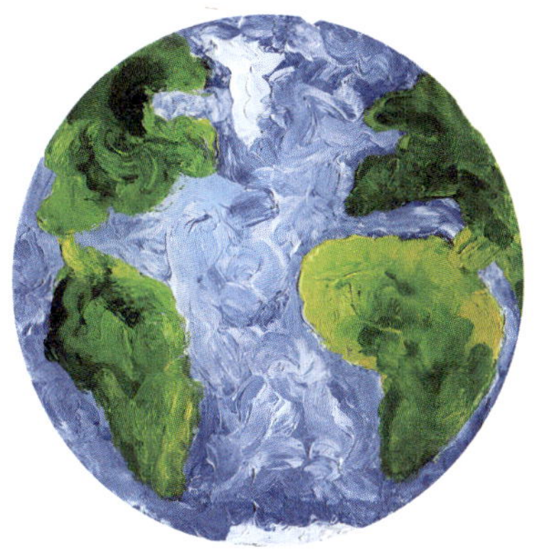

Lent, Holy Week and Easter

It's messy, it takes time, and it's not an easy fix. But I imagine, if we give God's grace the space to stretch our hearts, the Holy One will replace our own shouts of "Crucify him!" with cries of "What hurts?" and "I see you," and "I'm sorry." Maybe even "I love you."

Tracey Horan

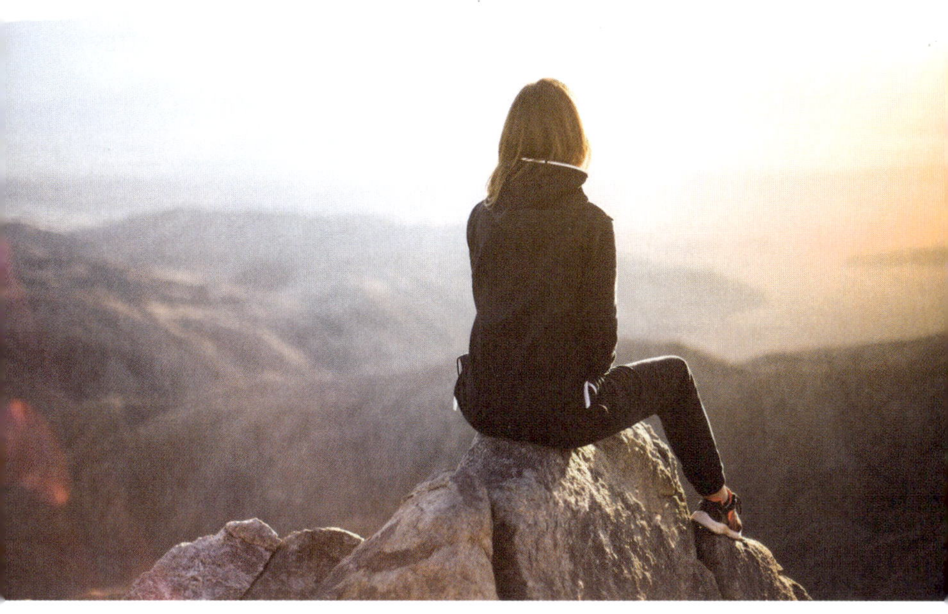

(Pixabay/StockSnap)

What I'm getting for Lent

By Christin Tomy

Lent is about to start, and I'm thinking about what I'll be getting this year.

Yes, I know I sound more like a child on Christmas Eve than an adult preparing for a season of repentance and conversion. And while conventional wisdom tells me I should be choosing what I'll give up, I'm not. This Lent, here is what I'm getting and how I hope it'll help me encounter God.

This Lent, I'm getting quiet

The Lenten call I'm feeling most deeply this year is the invitation to enter the quiet. While the gifts I receive from the quiet are manifold, two in particular are on my heart this year: rest and listening.

In a world full of needs to be met, rest can seem superfluous, lazy or even selfish. However, when we let ourselves get quiet—deep soul-quiet—we're invited into a holy rest. This kind of rest is, paradoxically, an antidote to the selfishness and laziness that threaten to numb our hearts to the cries of the other. After all, it is Jesus himself who offers us this rest, just as he invited his disciples: "Come away by yourselves to a deserted place and rest a while" (Mark 6:32). In this rest, I'm invited to surrender my need to be successful, useful, and busy.

I remember reading once that busyness is really a form of existential laziness. When I'm honest with myself, I recognize that this is true. Sometimes being busy allows me to feel important and engaged, while ignoring the small inner voice of the Spirit. Busyness tempts me to react rather than respond. It allows me to do *something*, but not necessarily to do the right thing, or courageous thing, or the well-discerned thing. It's only when I drop the defense of busyness (even the kind of busyness that purports to be about helping others) that I can truly rest in God and begin to listen. "Our hearts are restless," writes St. Augustine, "until they rest in God."

I have no illusions that I will be any less occupied this Lent. I won't give up my commitments and move into the desert, but I will try to take small steps to shift my attitude, to move from self-centered busyness to other-centered purposefulness. Getting quiet is the first of those steps.

This Lent, I'm getting outside

Of course, getting quiet won't do me any good if I am living in a cocoon. In his 2017 Lenten message, Pope Francis urges us to "favor the culture of encounter in our one human family." If my

Lent is going to be about more than a few cozy me-and-God moments, if it's going to invite me further into this culture of encounter, then I have to get outside: outside my own head, outside my biases, outside my comfort zone.

This requires me to move. I'm part of a community that names itinerancy as a part of our charism; St. Dominic was an itinerant preacher who traveled wherever he was called in order to bring the Good News. In our times and in my own life, I believe the call of itinerancy is more nuanced. We are called not just to move, but to *be moved*—to let ourselves encounter God in others and in unexpected places, and to let it change us.

As Sirach 1:9-10 reminds us, God has "poured forth [wisdom] upon all his works / upon every living thing." If I am going to encounter God's wisdom in other living beings, I first have to put myself in a position to encounter them. For me, this includes: truly seeking to know my neighbors, spending time in the natural world, and getting off Facebook and into real conversations.

This Lent, I'm getting lost

If I'm *really* getting outside my comfort zone, I'm bound to get a little disoriented. It's only when I push the boundaries of familiarity that I can begin to let go of my prejudices, biases and maybe even some of my beliefs. It can make me feel lost for a little while, and I think that's okay . . . perhaps it's even good.

Now, I'm no stranger to being lost. I have a notoriously poor sense of direction, and as a proud owner of a flip phone, I didn't have access to navigation technology until I got a GPS this year. Getting lost is simply a routine part of my existence, and while it would be a stretch to say that I *enjoy* the experience (especially when I'm running late), I must admit that it has taught me a few things.

Getting lost makes me vulnerable, because unless I want to continue aimlessly exploring my surroundings, at some point I have to stop and ask a stranger for directions. I must admit that I don't know the way, and I have to trust that the other person has something to offer me. The gift of getting lost is to release my grip on self-reliant certainty and leave some room for faith.

Opening myself to the wisdom of the other—*especially* the other with whom I vehemently disagree—doesn't mean I become ungrounded or lose all my convictions. My "no" can still mean "no," but my response is more likely to be rooted in authenticity rather than fear.

Perhaps by focusing on this kind of "getting" I'll learn how to give more selflessly. I pray that through these 40 days, I'll let God lead me deeper into encounter and closer to the joy of Easter.

February 24, 2017

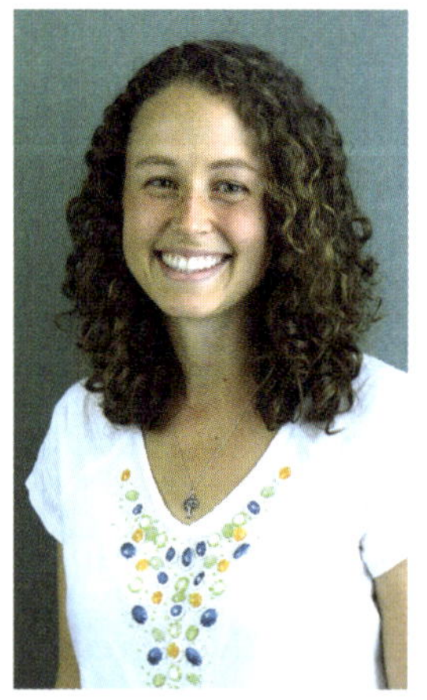

Christin Tomy, OP, is a Dominican Sister of Sinsinawa. For several years her work and interests have focused on the intersections of land, food, faith, and justice. She is currently finishing a degree at Catholic Theological Union in Chicago and ministers as a hospital chaplain. One of her favorite ways to pray in Chicago is to watch the sun rise over Lake Michigan on a morning swim or run.

Reflection

The author offers three ways she is inviting Lent to change her life: entering the quiet of holy rest, encountering God in the unexpected and allowing herself to become vulnerable. Do any of these approaches resonate as a possible theme for your Lenten practice or intention? What would you like to invite to happen?

If you approached Lent as "getting" something rather than giving something up, what would be on your list? How can you invite the Spirit of God to give you the clarity and courage to proceed?

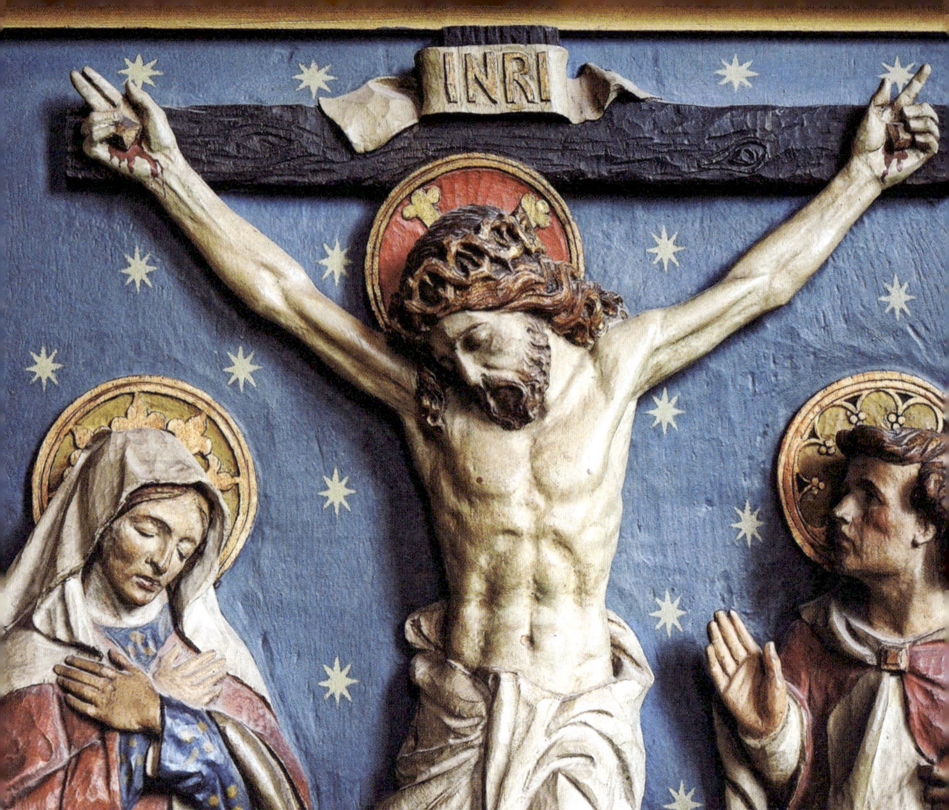

Cutline (Pixabay/Andrew Martin)

With Mary at the foot of the cross

By Nicole Trahan

Good Friday—the day we commemorate the execution of Jesus. This year, our commemoration reminds me of a quote from Meister Eckert about Christmas. In essence, Eckert asked what good it is for us that Jesus was born 2,000 years ago if he is not also born in us each day—for the Son of God always needs to be born.

In a similar way, I am reminded that although Jesus was executed in history 2,000 years ago, every day Jesus is persecuted and crucified anew in the victims of violence in Syria and Egypt, in the immigrant and the refugee, in our Muslim and Jewish brothers and sisters, in those who are executed by the state, in all those considered to be "other." Jesus dies a thousand deaths each day.

In this Passiontide, I feel a call to walk this journey through the Passion in union with Mary, who walks with her son as he carries his cross and stands with him in his final hours. As Marianists, we seek to walk each day in union with Mary as we dedicate each day to continuing her mission of bearing Christ in our world. So, this perspective makes sense for me. This approach to the Passion, though, seems even more fitting this year.

I see in Mary a companion in this journey through our modern-day circumstances. I imagine that Mary must have felt a full range of emotions as she accompanied her son—deep sadness, compassion, anger, powerlessness, and even trust in the midst of maddening confusion. And while my range of emotions may not be as deeply felt as Mary's, if I am honest, I see the same emotions in myself when faced with the current reality of our world. Deep sadness as I learn of the sufferings of those physically far from me—as I read about chemical weapons attacks, church bombings, shootings in schools and on city streets, racist and xenophobic actions against groups or individuals. Compassion as I meet people who live in fear because of their ethnicity, legal status or faith tradition. Anger as I see some in civil leadership positions with their apparent blindness, greed, fear and hardness of heart. Powerlessness because I feel so small relative to the issues I see. And yet, I also feel trust in a loving God through it all. What, then, can we learn from Mary, with whom we share these feelings?

In the face of our current reality, I think of Mary, standing at the foot of the cross of her only son. Mary *stands*. Some may see this as a passive posture. However, I see it as anything but passive. Mary's stance at the foot of the cross is one of courage, non-violent resistance, of defiance . . . and it is an act of love. She stands for justice in the face of unjust systems. It is a steadfast stance of trust in the One who overshadowed her and was with her at each step of her life. In standing there, she most likely put her own life at risk, but that was not her concern. Her concern was for the one who suffers and to stand in non-violent opposition. This, I believe, is our call as well—to stand in resistance to the systems that oppress, violate or murder and to stand with the one who suffers, who is our primary concern.

Mary stands to be present and to support. There are times when others are in such pain that our only possible response is simply to be present to them. There will be times in our current national and global reality in which we can do no more than be present to those who suffer. Perhaps we cannot be present in person, but in many situations we can. We just need clearer sight to see those in our midst who are in need of a compassionate presence.

She stands with the beloved disciple. She stands, not alone, but in community. There is a sculpture that is in our Marianist Brothers' Generalate in Rome depicting Mary and John at the foot of the cross. In this sculpture, both Mary and John gaze at Jesus—their concern is with the one who suffers. However, they are also embracing one another, supporting each other in their pain and in their support of Jesus. We cannot stand at the foot of another's cross without the support of a loving, faithful community. We cannot do it alone. The pain is overwhelming, and the work for justice too large.

In light of the reality that surrounds us, we may find ourselves asking, "How am I called to respond?" "How can I use the gifts God has given me to respond to the suffering Christ in our midst?" As we ponder these questions, let us take Mary as our model. Not the Mary of our youth—meek and mild—but Mary who stands courageous, bold and steadfast.

April 14, 2017

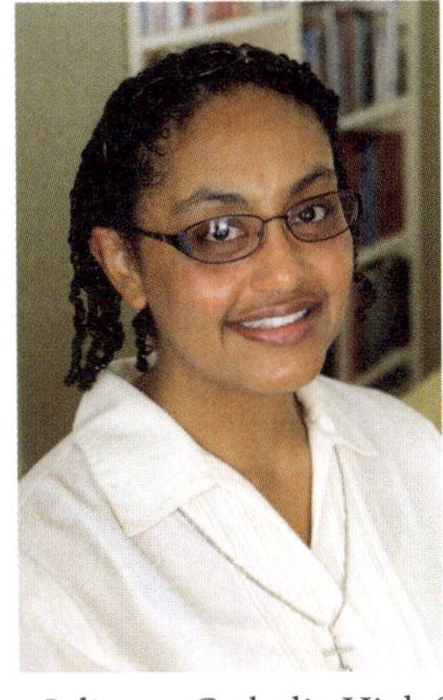

Nicole Trahan is a member of the Daughters of Mary Immaculate (Marianist Sisters) who teaches sophomore religion at Chaminade Julienne Catholic High School, serves as the national director of vocations for the Marianist Sisters, and is director of the pre-novitiate program for her province.

Reflection

The author develops the belief that Jesus is born in us each day and that we, like Mary, carry God into the world. The Son of God also dies each day when any victim of violence is persecuted or dies. In the face of this mystery, what is your work? Where are you needed to carry God?

Who is standing at a cross who might need your embrace and support? What would it be like for you to stand with them, knowing that God is beside you?

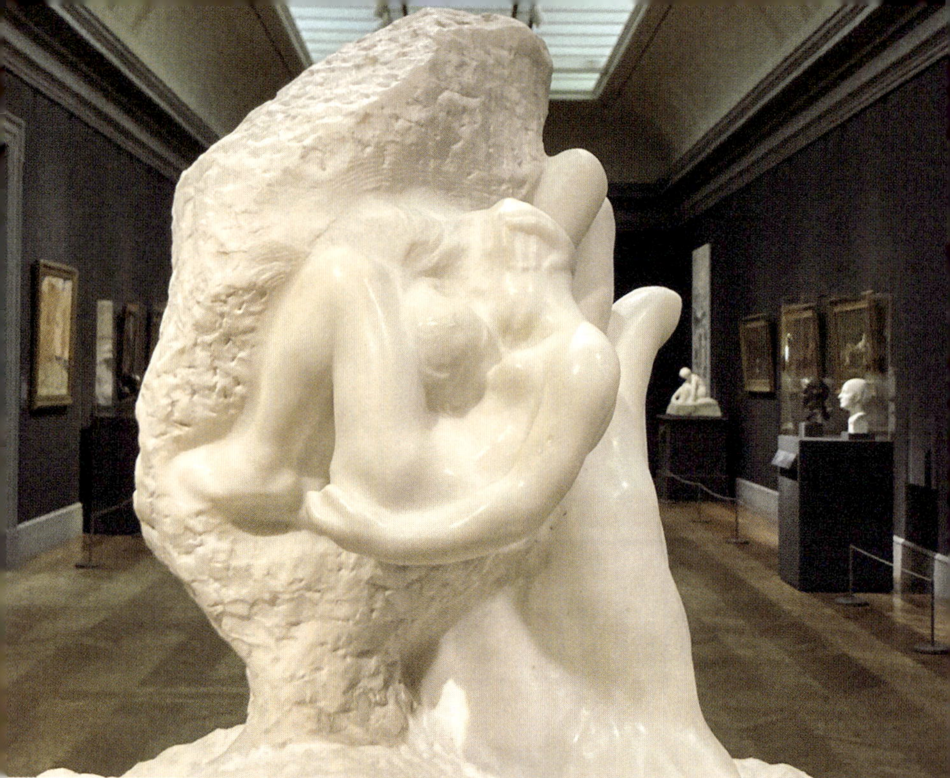

The Hand of God by the French artist Auguste Rodin, carved circa 1907, is on display at the Metropolitan Museum of Art in New York City.

(Courtesy of Nancy Sylvester)

The Hand of God comforts and encourages us with love

By Nancy Sylvester

The Hand of God is a sculpture by the artist Auguste Rodin. A few years ago, I was given a picture of the marble sculpture during my annual retreat and was quite taken by it. It became an icon for me during those days of prayer. Earlier this year, when I was visiting a friend in New York City, we went to the Metropolitan Museum of Art. On our way to the exhibit we had come to see, there it was: The Hand of God right in front of me.

Startled, I just stood and took it in once again. The beauty of the work, the curves, the entanglement of the figures, the gentle strength conveyed in the hand and the rough marble awaiting emergence.

The Hand of God comforted me the first time I encountered it, as it still does. I feel Divine Loving Energy encompassing me, holding me within the tangle of relationships. Letting me know I am not alone, ever. The Loving is steadfast and encouraging me to be who I am. The Loving Hand holds and caresses and will never let go as the yet to be carved "I" emerges out of that Divine Loving.

Rodin revered Michelangelo, who often spoke about how when he looked at a block of marble, he saw the image—the David or the angel—and simply carved to set it free, revealing what is there already so that other eyes might see as well.

That is what I learned from praying with that sculpture. I am, we all are, like a block of marble held in the energy of Divine Loving as we set free who we are as we see beyond all the rough spots, the selfishness, the negativity restraining us, keeping us locked into who we are not.

Setting free who we are becoming is a good Lenten practice. Begin by reflecting on Jesus' life through this lens of emergence. Jesus began his ministry with 40 days in the wilderness. He created the space to see himself in new ways. Jesus confronted the lure of power, prestige and wealth. He resisted and emerged committed to preaching what was in his heart.

His Sermon on the Mount put forth a vision of how to be in this world. It is paradoxical and challenging. Yet it took shape in him as he embodied the Beatitudes. The Last Supper Discourse in the Gospel of John brings a fulfillment to how he saw himself.

> I am the Way, the Truth and the Life (John 14:6). . . . Believe me that I am in God and God is in me, or else believe because of the works I do. The truth of the matter is anyone who has faith in me will do the works I do and greater works besides. . . . On that day you'll know that I am in God, and you are in me, and I am in you. . . . As my Abba has loved me, so have I loved you. Live on in my love. . . . This is my commandment: love one another as I have loved you. There is no greater love than to lay down one's life for one's friends.

Yet there was still a bit more to be chipped away. Jesus' final moment on the cross set him free. Jesus completed his sculpture by surrendering to Love and in Love emerging forever in the Hand of God.

Look now to your own emerging sculpture. Try to see what is keeping you from becoming your true self. Chip away at the temptations in your life; the addictions that make you less than you are. Polish and make smooth the values and beliefs that hold you and give you meaning. Embody them until they shine so that others can see "you" becoming whole. Carve the marble deeply to touch into the life deep within: the life you share with Jesus and our Abba God. Stand, feel yourself emerging, then fall back and know you are held in the Hand of God.

Rodin is inviting us to learn how to see—see within and without. See what sometimes looks impossible. He invites us to see with a contemplative heart. We have begun the carving, and we must continue throughout our lives—becoming our best selves regardless of the cost.

April 6, 2023

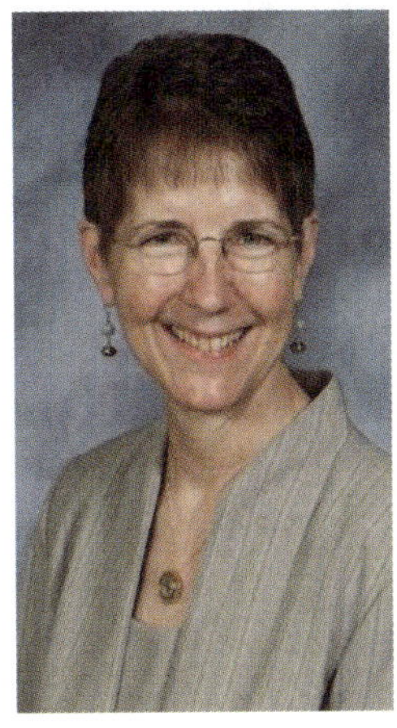

Nancy Sylvester is founder and director of the Institute for Communal Contemplation and Dialogue. She served in leadership of her own religious community, the Sister Servants of the Immaculate Heart of Mary, Monroe, Michigan, as well as in the presidency of the Leadership Conference of Women Religious. She also served as the National Coordinator of Network, the national Catholic social justice lobby.

Reflection

Can you recall being led deeper into the mystery of God and God's unceasing love by a piece of art, sculpture, music, etc.? What did you encounter in that moment of grace?

During Lent, we can practice letting go of how we see ourselves in order to see how God truly sees us. In doing so, we can confront the things that block us from fully expressing love of God, neighbor and one's self. How can you engage in that practice during this season or a particular moment in your life?

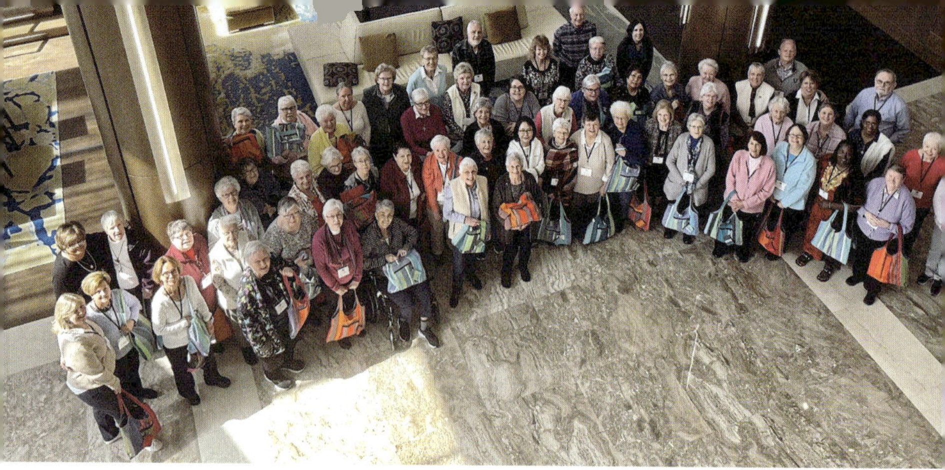

The Sisters of Saint Joseph of Peace at their 2022 chapter.

(Courtesy of Susan Francois)

We all need a “reset” button

By Susan Rose Francois

What if life came with a “reset” button that you could push when you got knocked down, and everything would be made right? Think of the reset button at the bowling alley that rights the pins that have been knocked down and thrown against each other, blocking the lane and stopping play. One push of the button and the rack comes down from the sky, wipes the errant pins out of the way, and replaces them with new ones ready to stand straight and face whatever comes their way.

In life, of course, there’s no magic reset button. We are responsible for righting our own figurative bowling pins in this thing called life, even as we might try not to knock down our neighbor’s pins by accident. “I get knocked down,” sang the lead singer of Chumbawamba in their 1997 pop hit song, “Tubthumping,” “but I get up again, you are never gonna keep me down.” (Yes, this song has been stuck in my head as I have been pondering this reflection. If it is now in your head, you are welcome.)

No matter our worries, the sun will rise in the morning, and if we are blessed to live another day, so will we. Life goes on. Yet there is also an undeniable weariness that comes from hearing the news of death and destruction raining on innocent families in distant villages, or the stark reality of systemic racism, or the anxiety of the climate emergency. Hearts are broken each day through interpersonal conflicts that seem, in the moment, to be beyond repair. In a reading from Jeremiah (20:10), someone somewhere just now has been knocked down by rumor and gossip:

> I hear the whisperings of many:
> "Terror on every side!
> Denounce! let us denounce him!"
> All those who were my friends
> are on the watch for any misstep of mine.

Who has not felt this way at some time in their life, whether on the playground or in the board room or even the parish hall? If we are honest, we've probably been on the whispering side too.

No doubt despairing, Jeremiah looks to God for his reset button . . . *But the Lord is with me* (Jeremiah 20:11).

The usefulness of my analogy ends here, however, because while Jeremiah finds his reset in God, he also is counting on God's vengeance against those who denounce him. Vengeance and violence, in my experience, are not particularly helpful responses; they are also not representative of a God of peace and love.

More and more, I am convinced that we need a collective reset in God's love. We need to know, believe, and rest in God's love and then act accordingly. This is our spiritual crisis point, and the reset is the antidote. Maybe it is just that simple.

I recently had an opportunity to rewatch an interview on racial justice with Fr. Bryan Massingale. "People are not willing to make significant sacrifices," he said, "unless they can see their life as part of a broader religious and spiritual narrative. I think part of our problem is that we have not preached the fact that God loves us immensely. And when I stand in awe of the immensity of God's love, something else takes over, and that is I want to make sure that all human beings are treated as beloved children of God."

We are knocked down, we knock others down, when we don't know in our core that God loves us and everyone else immensely.

The reset is to know who we are and whose we are.

Last month, I joined with other members of my religious community, the Sisters of St. Joseph of Peace, for our Congregation Chapter. As our constitution says, the chapter "is the highest decision-making body in the congregation. In this event we celebrate our unity, renew our life and spirit, reflect together on the call of the Gospel, and make decisions in fidelity to our charism." I find it significant that, when discerning our collective response to the signs of today's times, our focus was not so much on *what* we were called to do or *how* to do it, but rather on *who* we are called to be as people of peace.

"These new times demand a change of heart: to be, think, and act differently," we wrote in our Chapter Act, "To Be Who We Say We Are": "Our spiritual lives require deep re-examination and transformation; our outward actions must confront privilege and power in ourselves and society." Our Chapter Act commits us, in collaboration with others, to:

- Intentional living of interculturality, anti-racism, and inclusion;

- Addressing, healing, and being present to the wounds and broken relationships among ourselves and all of God's creation;
- Resisting every form of war and violence;
- Making a place at the table where all are welcome and gifts are honored.

We embrace these promptings of the Spirit, to be who we say we are, with courage, humility, hope and trust. We have only begun to unpack these words that we call ourselves to live.

During these days of Lent, I pray for the courage, humility, hope and trust to believe this impossible truth of God's immense love in my innermost being. I pray that you believe this too. I pray that we live into this reality in ways that only God can imagine.

Ready. Set. Reset.

April 8, 2022

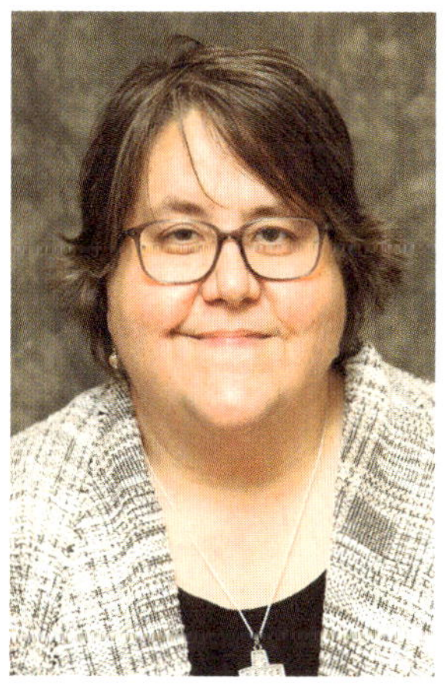

Susan Rose Francois is the assistant congregation leader for the Sisters of St. Joseph of Peace and the author of *My Friend Joe: Reflections on St. Joseph.*

Reflection

Lent is a time when we are invited to reflect on our lives with an eye on transformation. The Christian church calls this time of examination by the Greek word metanoia, *which means changing one's mind. It's an invitation to change one's heart. The author invites us to consider a "collective reset in God's love" so we can know, believe, and rest in God's love and then act accordingly. What do you need to reset this Lent?*

What issues weigh on your heart or perhaps make you wonder how you can make an impact or change? How can you use the season to examine and imagine what witness God might be inviting or calling you to offer to an often broken world?

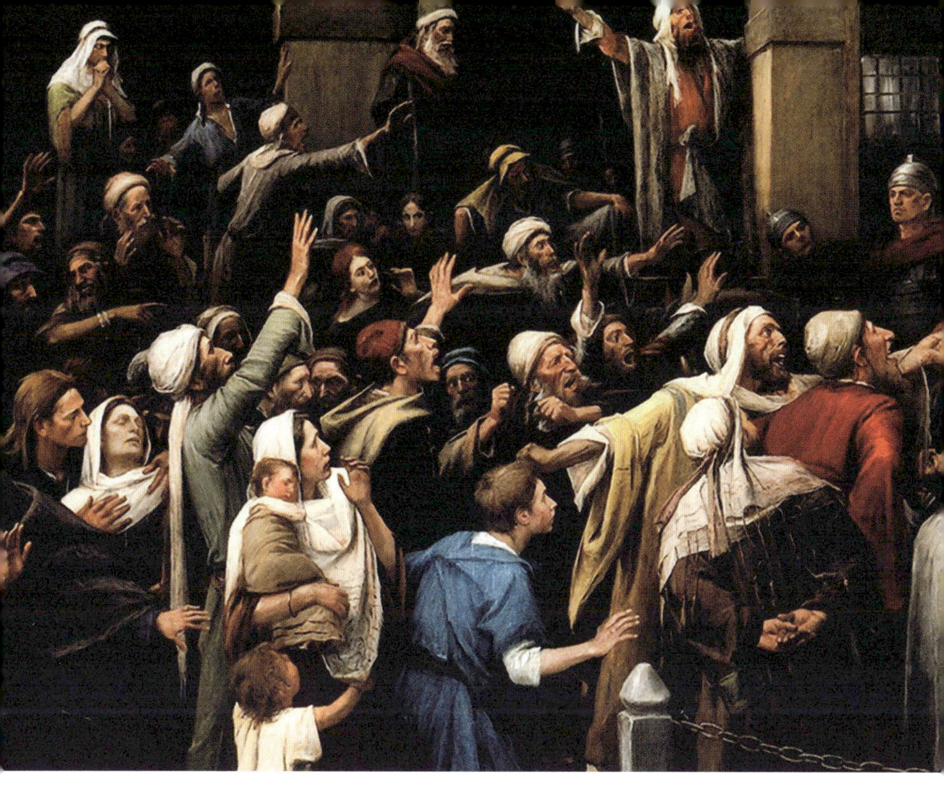

Detail from "Ecce Homo" (1896) by Hungarian artist Mihaly Munkacsy.
(Wikimedia Commons)

Crucify him: Stepping aside from the angry mob on Good Friday

By Tracey Horan

Every year during Holy Week services, as we read the story of Jesus' passion and death, I find it hard to say the words, "Crucify him!" out loud. Perhaps part of it is my own theology. I do believe that Jesus died for the sake of our collective liberation. I don't, however, resonate with the idea that my own sins are the thorns or the nails that pierced Jesus.

This year, as I was reflecting on the Passion narrative on Palm Sunday, my attention was drawn to one detail included in Matthew's version of the story: "The chief priests and the elders persuaded the crowds to ask for Barabbas but to destroy Jesus." Shortly thereafter, those same people in the crowd are yelling that they want Jesus to be violently killed.

In the 30-some years I have been listening to the Passion narrative read aloud during Holy Week, I don't think I've ever thought much about the people in the crowd. Who were they? Why were they there? Were they drawn in by curiosity?

Maybe they had witnessed Jesus speak in public or heard rumors about him. Maybe a family member or friend had been healed by Jesus. Maybe they just happened to be out shopping in the market or running errands. Maybe they were moms or dads who themselves had been feeling the weight of the oppressive Roman regime and were looking for an outlet. Did they desire desperately to fit in, to be enough, to be able to put food on the table for their own families?

Perhaps some of them came already in disagreement with Jesus, whom they saw as an agitator threatening the status quo. Others may have come into the crowd unsure of where they stood and then convinced by the authority figures who whispered fear into their ears.

Whatever the case, within a few hours, they were all swept up in a political spectacle to place blame on a man who had been preaching, teaching and healing among them for days and weeks. Something moved these people enough that they were inspired to shout, "Crucify him!"

As a "One" on the Enneagram, I can resonate with the temptation to judge and want to find blame outside myself. I have a constant inner critic just itching to point out imperfections and look for ways I or others around me need to change. This inner critic says things like, “Ugh, how inconsiderate!” when the man next to me on the plane takes his shoes off.

Critic says, “Get to work, Tracey. Now is not the time to take a break,” when I’m staring down at a long to-do list. And when I notice the person in front of me at the grocery piled a bunch of sodas and sugary snacks onto the conveyor belt, critic certainly has something judge-y to say about the health impacts of such irresponsible decisions.

Not quite, “Crucify them!” but this voice of judgment does seem to fit well among the voices in the crowd ready to place blame alongside the chief priests and elders.

My own conversion is a work in progress. Even as I walk my journey toward acceptance and empathy, I spend a lot of time at my ministry engaging others to do the same. In my work in education and advocacy at the Kino Border Initiative, I accompany people as they learn about the reality at the U.S.-Mexico border, with a hope to transform hearts, minds and policies toward more dignified migration.

It turns out that conversations about people on the move can sometimes resemble the finger-pointing mob the evangelists describe in the Passion narrative. As I accompany students, parishioners, seminarians and teachers from all over the U.S., I sometimes hear comments like, “Well, why don’t these people fix their own country instead of coming to ours?” or “How do you know someone is telling the truth when they say they are fleeing violence?” or “We need to keep migrants out because they’re bringing drugs into the U.S.”

Something softens in me when I hear these comments because I can relate. Earlier in my life, when I felt far away from people in migration, I had some similar sentiments.

I've learned that hurling back my own judgments just creates more fear and distance. So instead, I try to get curious and tell stories. After all, that's what Jesus did: ask lots of questions and tell stories.

Last month, I traveled to one of our partner institutions to give a presentation. I invited those present for the event to turn to the people at their table and share what words, phrases or images came to mind for them when they heard the word "migrant."

I then sat down at the closest table just in time to hear the woman next to me say, "Well, I think of the words 'legal' and 'illegal.' I just think people should come the legal way. I have a family member trying to migrate now, and he's going through the whole process: filling out the paperwork, paying the fees, and other people are just coming in without doing that."

I took a deep breath and nodded as I processed what she was saying and discerned how I would respond. My heart was pounding, but I wanted to get curious and learn more about this woman.

"That must be really hard to have someone you love who wants to access a process and reunite with his family and can't," I said. "What has that been like for your family?"

I listened as the woman described the frustration of having to wait, the ways that family separation has affected her loved ones, and how living with such uncertainty meant their future was on hold.

Then I said, "You know, what you're sharing reminds me a lot of the families who are waiting in Mexico to access safety. They arrive with the intention to follow an orderly, legal process to seek asylum but feel frustrated by the barriers that the U.S. government has put in place. Many people have been waiting weeks or months, like your relative, and simply don't know what to do."

There was something freeing about putting aside my inner judge, looking this woman in the eye, and listening to her pain. As I remember the encounter, I can imagine the two of us moving away from the angry mob in the Passion narrative so we could hear one another and take a beat before shouting, "Crucify him!"

I don't know how the woman felt after our conversation, but I walked away full of gratitude. Our encounter left me wondering how our world would be transformed if, instead of gathering in angry mobs, we could replicate over and over this space to ask questions and tell stories.

It's messy, it takes time, and it's not an easy fix. But I imagine, if we give God's grace the space to stretch our hearts, the Holy One will replace our own shouts of "Crucify him!" with cries of "What hurts?" and "I see you," and "I'm sorry." Maybe even "I love you."

April 7, 2023

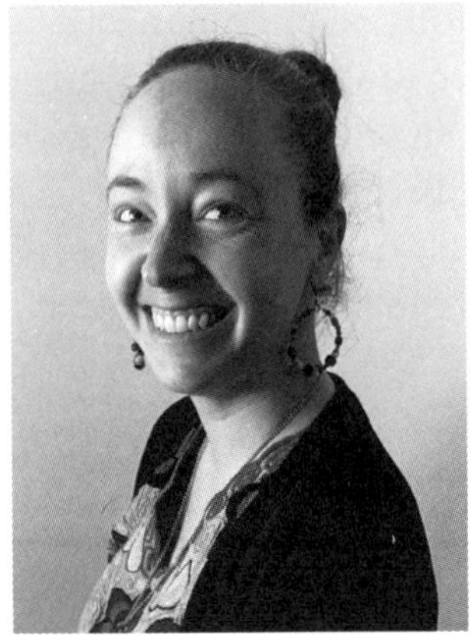

Tracey Horan is a member of the Sisters of Providence of St. Mary-of-the-Woods, Indiana. Her first deep conversation with this community occurred in a melon patch during her time as an intern at the Sisters' White Violet Center for Eco-Justice. She has ministered with Latinx communities for over a decade as a teacher and community organizer and currently serves as Associate Director of Education and Advocacy for the Kino Border Initiative in Nogales, Arizona and Nogales, Sonora, Mexico.

Reflection

The author likens our own quiet voices that judge and criticize others to the loud angry mob that yells, "Crucify him!" During this season, where might you recognize your instinct to judge and instead invite someone to find a safe way to tell their story? Or at least imagine another possibility from the one your instinct jumped to first?

What might be one topic or issue that seems black and white now where you might seek the gray areas in between and invite the Spirit of God into that exploration to give you guidance and wisdom?

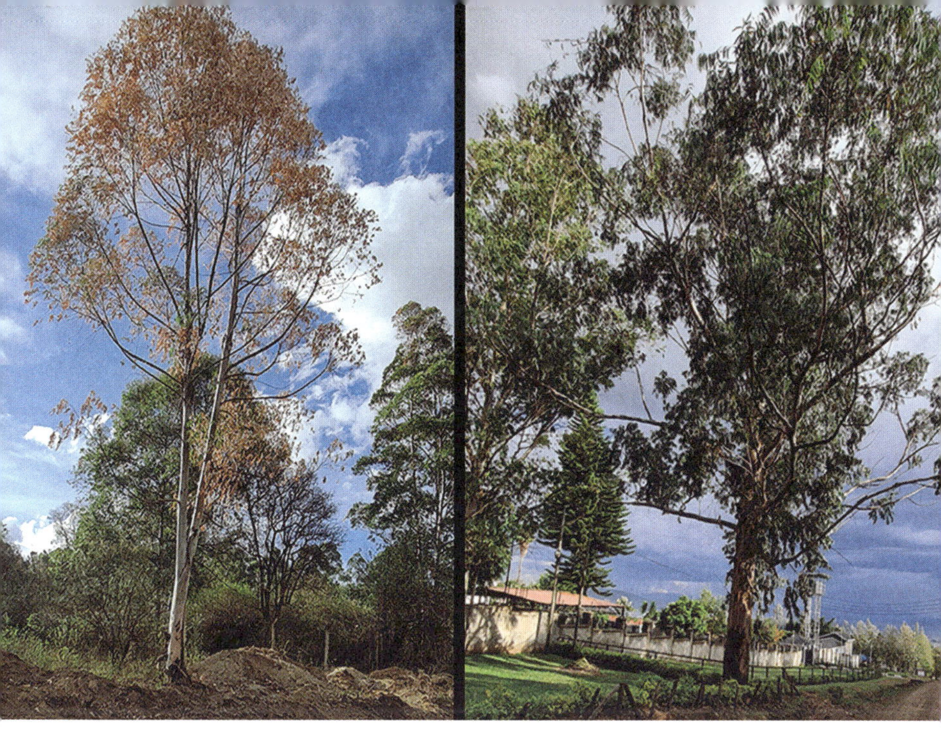

Pictures of a dry eucalyptus tree, left, and a green eucalyptus tree; during a walk through the forest Rosemary Wanyoike noticed dried up eucalyptus trees, which she says is very unusual.

(Courtesy of Rosemary Wanyoike)

Easter, "the rain of our lives," comes as we're about to give up

By Rosemary Wanyoike

Recently, I took a walk through the forest. I had not gone through there in a long time. In Kenya, it has been very dry since the beginning of the year, with the grass all burned up by the scorching sun. Now something very unusual caught my attention. I saw some eucalyptus trees that had dried up, and others showed signs of drying up soon. I have never seen this before!

In my home area, this is the most feared tree, known for its long taproot that anchors it and its deep root systems that enable it to absorb water and nutrients fast. This tree is said to be a heavy feeder needing a lot of water—it is nicknamed "the water taker." If it grows among crops, it takes away most of the water from the crops. And it is evergreen. So this sight worried me and I could hear a voice in me saying, "*If the eucalyptus can dry up, what else will remain*?"

This experience made me think about the days following the crucifixion of Jesus, before his appearance to his disciples after resurrection; the days preceding Easter. We read in the Scriptures that the disciples were behind closed doors for fear of the Jews (John 20:19). Like the eucalyptus that I saw, people around them probably looked up to them to draw hope, but their sadness would not have allowed them to be there for anyone.

Continuing my walk, I realized there had been some signs of rain and in some parts of the country—in particular where I live—we had received about three rain showers. At this, I concluded that with this kind of tree drying, the drought cannot go much beyond this; now it is time for the rains to fall; surely this is the beginning of the rainy season.

This experience spoke to me deeply about Easter and I realized that Easter is "the rain of our lives." It comes when we are almost giving up, and brings water to our drooping spirits. When the disciples were at their lowest point, the resurrected Jesus appeared to them, gifting them with joy and breathing the Holy Spirit upon them. After that, all the sorrow was forgotten. They got new energy! Think of Mary Magdalene running to tell the brothers about the Resurrection.

This inspiration made me think about life differently. As a staunch Christian and religious, like the first disciples, Christ has been reminding me that—besides the hundredfold reward—

persecution or at least challenges in life will be part of the package of discipleship. With every challenge, our inner hope increases and we gain trust that the current situation will pass and joy shall return. This helps us to accept reality as it comes.

People around me may watch how I approach life, hoping to gain some encouragement and confidence in facing their own share of sorrows. But if I am thrown into despair by situations in my life, they might be surprised—as I was by the perceived "resilient" tree drying—and begin to say, "If she is this broken, who can stand?"

The eucalyptus experience consoles me. Instead of being sad when I see her drying up from the drought, I can say confidently, "It is time to bring out the containers to collect water because the rainy season is just about to begin."

Easter comes to help us rise to another level of existence with the risen Lord. I can only imagine what the death of Jesus could have meant for his disciples; it was a loss beyond description, as any of us can attest after losing a loved one. But then, in a little while, he appears again!

While we cannot change our past experiences of hardship, Easter comes as a reminder that there is life after all these struggles. The season encourages us to carry our crosses patiently and ungrudgingly since this is not the end but the beginning of a new life—characterized by a deep awareness of the power of God which conquers even death.

We realize that the peak of his suffering was the beginning of his victory over sin and death for our sake.

Jesus died for us, and his rising marks our rising, too. This "aliveness" has to be sustained. Easter is a time to thank God for what has been. In times of crisis, people come together, brought by the need to support one another through hard times. In the resurrection narrative, we see the disciples gathering in the upper room; they needed the companionship that gave them the courage to face another day without Jesus in their midst.

Our life situations put us on the cross now and then, so we are familiar with "crucifixion" in our lives. Equally, we have experienced coming out of an illness or financial constraints. It is a time that brings a lot of joy and a sense of achievement.

We live Easter pondering on the graces obtained through our pains and struggles, with joy and celebration. I want to sustain this joy, but after a short while I tend to forget that there is a season for everything—and whatever happens is for my good—and I begin complaining again. I am invited to the realization of the end to which the suffering points. It brings me closer to God and my fellow human beings, and a time to appreciate people I sometimes take for granted.

Easter reminds me of the times when people have been there for me: during the long illness of a loved one, the loss of a loved one, or even the wedding of a loved one, when I could not have managed on my own.

The disciples remained united after Jesus was crucified, and from that moment on, a community was formed. They had something in common; they had undergone the loss of a loved one and the accompanying humiliation and misunderstanding.

Humanity is the same, the world over, and Easter is a reminder of how much we need one another. The end of one problem should mark another Easter, earning us more favor with God and with fellow human beings. This becomes a cause for sustained joy since with every "Good Friday" challenge is an Easter: The problems will pass, and we will have a reason to celebrate.

Let the realization of the love of God, who gave his *only begotten son so that those who believe in him might not perish but might have eternal life* (John 3:16), mark our renewed relationship with God that has its peak at Easter.

Then every day becomes Easter, and our spiritual drought becomes a thing of the past since the joy of Easter continues to water our hearts sustaining our inner lives. Arise with the risen Lord and cheer up! Be happy, not because there are no challenges, but because this is the path to our true happiness.

April 9, 2023

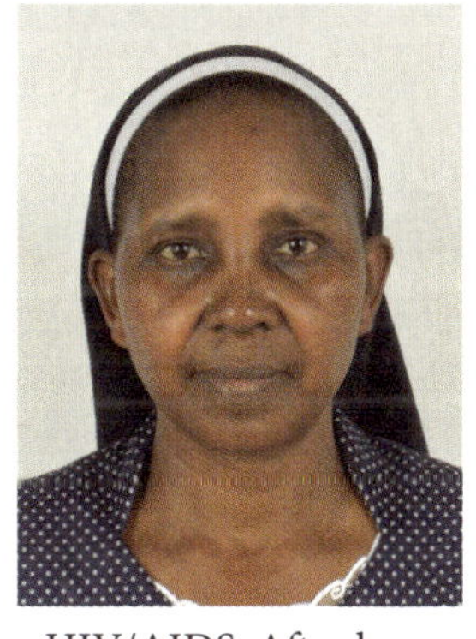

Rosemary Wanyoike was trained as a nurse before joining the Sisters of Mercy in Kenya. She has worked in Turkana, Kenya, and in Zambia, where she served people with HIV/AIDS. After her perpetual profession in 2008, she attended a formation program in Ireland and now directs her community's formation program in Kenya.

Reflection

When has "the rain of our lives" come for you, perhaps at your lowest moment or when you were ready to give up? What did the rain bring for you?

The news of Jesus' resurrection gave the disciples new life and energy. (Consider Mary Magdalene running to tell the news to her brothers.) But the energy must be sustained especially during times of difficulty. How do you sustain your witness? Who helps you continue?

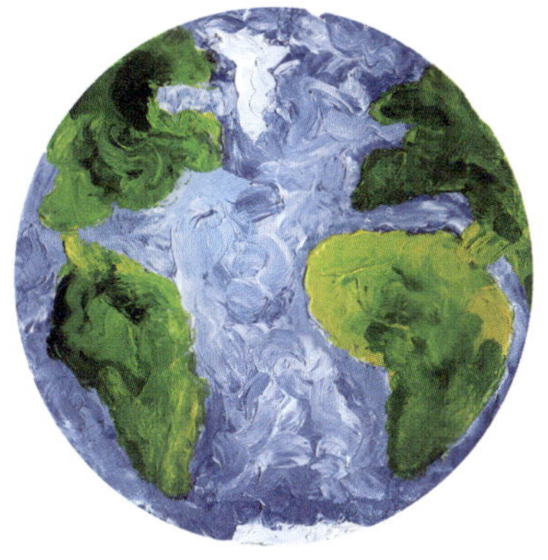

Ministries: Anti-Trafficking

In the women's stories, I heard strength of soul and a deep connection with life beyond suffering. They are women of hope and have much to teach us about suffering and the human spirit.

Kathleen Bryant

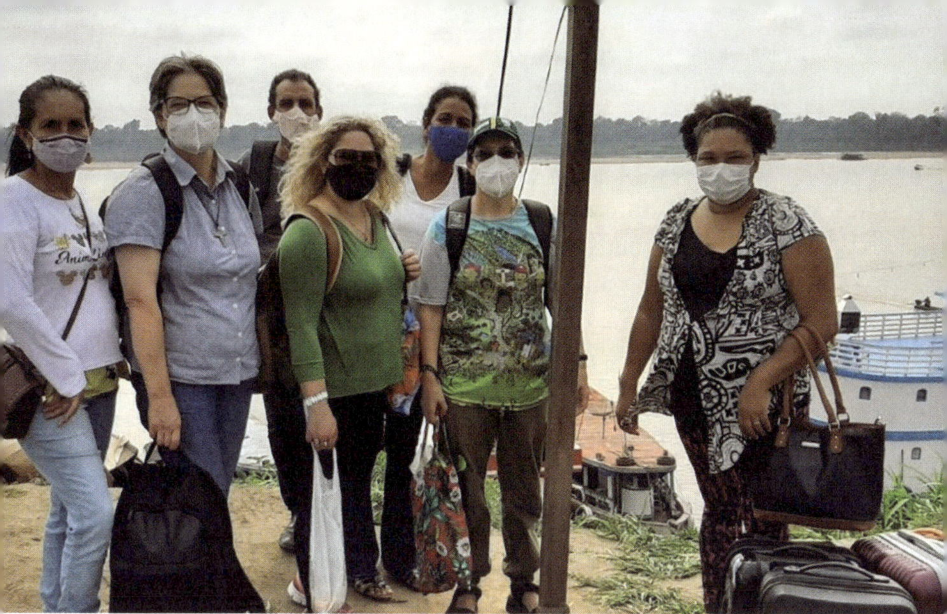

A group from the anti-trafficking network A Cry for Life prepares to leave for a trip down the Amazon River to work with women.

(Courtesy of Caterina Ingelido)

A Cry for Life: Sisters combat human trafficking in Brazil

By Caterina Ingelido

For the last three years—out of 21 working in Brazil—I have been working in the Amazon Basin, in the state of Rondônia, coordinating the network A Cry for Life and facilitating workshops for people who live along the river. This network is an integral part of the Conference of Religious of Brazil, which emphasizes "evangelizing action in the face of the dehumanizing reality of human trafficking."

Many people in this region fall victim to human trafficking because of the geographical position of Porto Velho, Rondônia's capital, and its international airport that effectively connects the trafficking routes. One of my tasks is to make the network known in schools and parishes and to make people aware of the significant problem of human trafficking.

Many victims work in exchange for a plate of food, and they often remain in debt to those who contract them for work because they are charged for traveling expenses and work tools. As for the women, they almost always end up being sexually exploited or working as domestic workers. A Cry for Life has followed up on many cases. Still, there are several challenges: first, to help the trafficked person recognize that he/she is being trafficked, then encourage him/her to denounce and/or run away, and, finally, to support the victim because he/she has nothing: no shelter, no money and no documents.

The following story reflects the situation of most of the victims. A young woman living here in the north of Brazil was convinced by a friend to go to Europe to work. She set off to go to Europe, leaving her two young daughters with her parents. At São Paulo's airport, a stranger was waiting for the woman. The person told the woman that her friend, who was supposed to travel with her, had been arrested because she was carrying drugs in her suitcase.

When the woman arrived at her destination, another person was waiting for her and she was forced into sexual exploitation. She was allowed to communicate with her parents, but always in the presence of her traffickers—to ensure that she would tell her parents only what the traffickers wanted her to tell. At first, she called weekly, then monthly, then every other month, and finally every three months. When her parents asked her when she would be back in Brazil, the answer perplexed them because she said she had to work long enough to cover the cost of the trip.

Fortunately, one of her aunts acquainted with A Cry for Life contacted us, telling us what was going on with her niece and her intuition that something might be happening to her. With the assistance of the network and the intervention of the federal police, the woman's whereabouts were traced through the phone calls.

When the police rescued her, the network provided a hidden place away from her parents' house and psychospiritual therapy till she was in a condition to take care of herself and her daughters. Then she and her daughters were relocated to an unknown place to keep the traffickers from finding them. As you can imagine, once a person falls into this trap, the way out is difficult; many victims die by suicide, or the traffickers kill them.

Our commitment to preventing people from being trafficked is shown through our efforts to make as many people aware of this reality as possible.

In Porto Velho, the network works to prevent the human trafficking of Venezuelan immigrants. Since 2018, Venezuelans have been passing through Porto Velho City, intending to move to bigger Brazilian cities. However, the pandemic stopped them from reaching their goal, and they had to settle here. The significant number of people and the few job opportunities made them a vulnerable population that struggled to meet their basic needs, especially food. That made them easy victims to fall into the traffickers' hands.

In Porto Velho, the network works with Venezuelan immigrant women through workshops on handicrafts, cooking and baking. The objective of the training is to ensure that the women will have a source of income for their families and won't be lured by false promises. During the pandemic shutdown, each woman persevered in doing her best to sell her products. Recently, after the reopening of activities, we held the first town fair to offer their products. In addition to selling their products, the goal was to make people aware of the women's work, expecting that local people or businesses would eventually employ them. The network will continue training women as long as people of goodwill continue supporting the project.

It is rewarding to see how happy the women feel having the leading role in providing for the needs of their families. One of them testified that her life was very difficult and told us she cried every morning, knowing that she didn't have anything to feed her three children. When the network offered the woman the catering training course in Caritas, she thought she could not learn, but the situation she and her children were experiencing motivated her to try. Today, she is grateful and proud of what she has accomplished. She is now the first one to encourage other women never to give up the opportunities God sends through the people they meet in daily life.

Unfortunately, we face many challenges, especially that of a lack of financial resources for mobilizing and printing materials to continue making other people aware of the evils of human trafficking. Because of limited resources, it is difficult to follow up on the various commitments and provide more coverage in schools and pastoral activities. On the other hand, this lack of resources motivates us even more to continue training new leaders to multiply the activities as far as possible.

Sometimes we encounter obstacles to partnering with other networks in the city. We realize that many people do not believe what is happening in their communities; they find it difficult to see and accept the reality of trafficking. The denial of this reality that is right in front of them makes them more vulnerable to becoming victims themselves.

The trauma and suffering the victims went through motivates and strengthens us as a group to continue walking and defending life! Life that is often seen by society and the globalized systems as worth only what it gives in exchange—and in the language of trafficking, that is only profit. Trafficking is a crime because it violates human rights. Our network will keep listening for the victims' "cry for life."

February 8, 2022

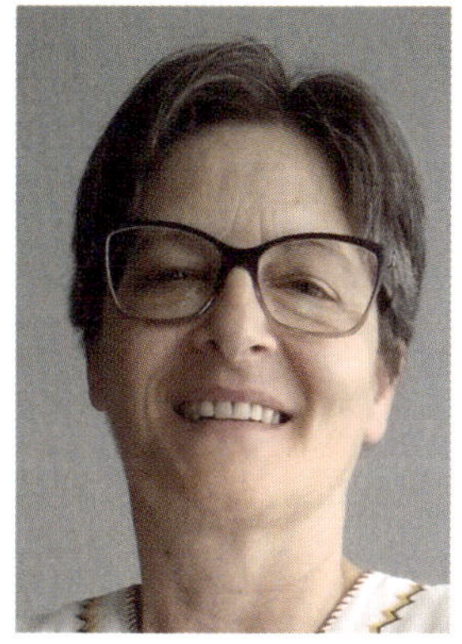

Sr. Caterina Ingelido, a Combonian missionary, is Italian and has lived in Brazil for 23 years, the last four in Porto Velho, Rondônia. She was involved in the pastoral formation of her parish, in mission outreach and coordinated "A Cry for Life," a network committed to the prevention of human trafficking. Since March of 2023, she returned to Italy for an internal congregational service, where she lives in Verona.

Reflection

Trafficking continues to grow because people find themselves in vulnerable situations. What kinds of conditions, both locally and globally, exist that allow or even assist trafficking to continue in so many places in the world?

How is making ourselves aware of trafficking situations and aiding victims a movement to support the sanctity of human life? Are there ways you can concretely assist in your local community? If you are not sure, how can you do some further research to see how to assist in the effort?

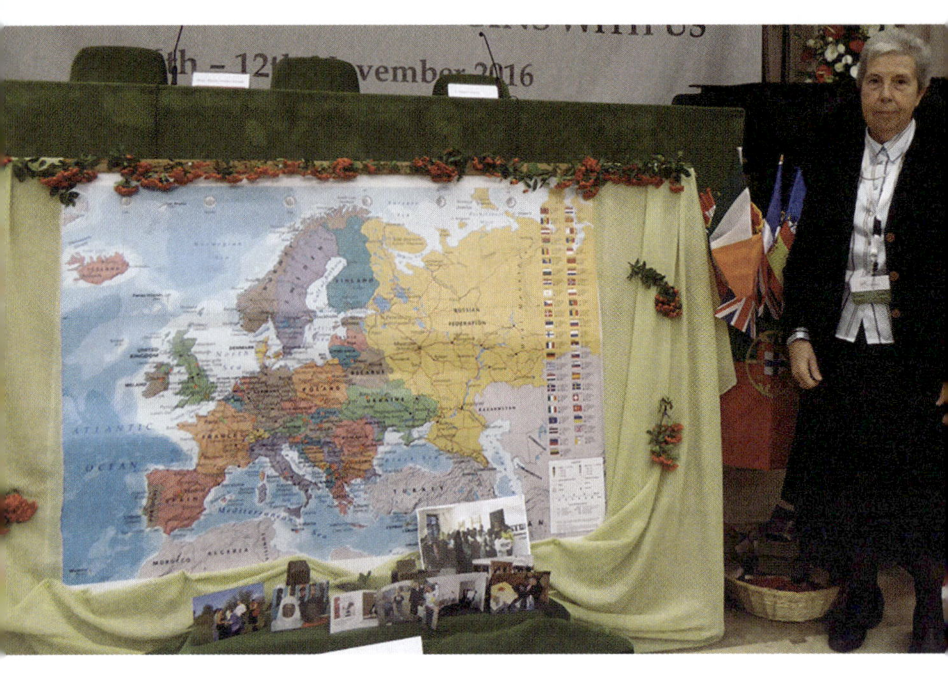

Sr. Begoña Iñarra at the 2016 RENATE assembly in Rome.

(Courtesy of Begoña Iñarra)

Walking with women on their way to freedom

By Begoña Iñarra

After years in Africa—the Democratic Republic of the Congo, Uganda, Ethiopia, Mozambique and Kenya—first teaching sciences and later on doing adult education and justice and peace ministry, I spent some years in Brussels lobbying the European Union on African economic issues. In January 2016, I was sent to Paris with the mission to get involved in the fight against human trafficking.

I discovered a part of the "hidden Paris" where women are trafficked for sex exploitation. I spent Monday mornings at the

Jorbalan Home teaching French to formerly trafficked women who were rebuilding their lives. On Thursdays at the Open Day Center Bakhita, I welcomed trafficked women working on the street. And on Tuesday afternoons and evenings, I visited Nigerian women obliged to sell their bodies along the Pyramid road at the Vincennes Wood, southeast of Paris, in the open air—in rain, snow, cold or heat.

As a volunteer with the Christian association "Liberation to Captives," I worked in the organization's truck, which had a sitting room where the women used to come to chat, do some French, and protect themselves from the cold, the rain and the police. But more often, to get help with their papers, ask for a paper to see the doctor, or share a small decision like their readiness to begin the French course.

We invited them to go on Thursdays to the Bakhita Center in Montmartre, where they could cook Nigerian food, enjoy a good meal and choose their activity: meet the social workers, take French lessons, take art therapy, computer classes, cooking, or just sit and chat. In my weekly seminars on being healthy, I used the Emotional Freedom Technique, which helped them a lot.

The time with the women was sacred to me. I saw Christ in them. Their faith, resilience, and energy of life encouraged me to continue fighting against human trafficking and accompanying them, even if at times it was hard.

The weekly meetings helped us to create bonds with some women. Then, we opened a little door toward freedom, evoking their dreams, their projects for life.

With some, we saw that coming out of prostitution was possible; for the minors, it was easier, as the police could take them to a protected place. But they all needed a lot of courage to get free from the psychological hook of the juju, the oath they had taken to keep silent, obey and pay the debt to the madame.

The decision to take the road to freedom depended on them. We just accompanied them on that hard road, as they faced loneliness, leaving the world they knew for an unknown world, in an unknown country. But quite a number overcame the difficulties!

I just got news from Joy, a Nigerian who, after three years at the Vincennes Woods, decided to come out of the life of prostitution. She overcame many difficulties. A refugee organization accepted her in its program, and she lived for some months with a French family, got her asylum status, made friends, prepared for a job, and now she has her apartment and a steady job at a supermarket. She even feels ready to start a family.

As part of the team of RENATE (Religious in Europe Networking Against Trafficking and Exploitation) in France, I raised awareness in parishes, religious congregations, Catholic high schools and Christian groups—bringing to light what was hidden, aiming at potential clients and working toward a greater church involvement on fighting human trafficking.

When my community, the Missionary Sisters of Our Lady of Africa (often called the White Sisters), closed our only community in Paris, I was sent to Madrid with the same mission, as fighting human trafficking is a priority in our congregation.

Being a member of RENATE, I knew some congregations accompanying formerly trafficked victims in Spain. I volunteered at the Security Hostel of the Hope Project run by the Adorers Sisters, to which women being exploited in Spain came from all over the world.

The hostel cares for their needs while they recover in body and spirit, learn Spanish, and prepare to rebuild their lives. After supper and washing up, we chat, play, watch TV, and have a few calm and joyful moments.

Some women express their joy at having all they need after their hard life. To see them overcoming the friction of daily life in common, with women from different cultures, countries and religions, challenges me to widen my own tent! They are not victims but survivors and resilient women! What a joy being with them, even if it is not always easy!

Since the pandemic, all volunteers over 65 cannot go to the shelter, as we are at-risk persons. The same happened with the Project La Casa of the Oblates sisters, where I gave computer lessons to a few women.

Some months ago, I was invited to participate in the new RENATE Law Enforcement Task Group relating to the survivors of human trafficking. We are 10 persons from seven nationalities involved in fighting human trafficking in eight European countries. We aim at changing legislation and policies to provide adequate support and protection for the victims/survivors.

I started by researching the hostels in Spain for victims/survivors of human trafficking. There are many small organizations helping trafficked women, while very few look after men. That led us to the realization that many victims are not protected and have no compensation because of "holes" in the legal aid system and its implementation in European countries.

We focused our research on access to legal aid providers for victims/survivors, limiting our research to six European countries: Albania, Bulgaria, Germany, Romania, Spain and England /Wales. We advocate for better protection and legal compensation for survivors in all EU member states.

A university in England is conducting a study on legal aid for victims of trafficking across these countries. After disseminating it in June, the RENATE advocacy group will use it in the EU countries. We are excited about the study as there is little research on this area. We trust it will help us advocate for stronger legislation for survivors' protection.

In the regional Madrid church anti-trafficking group of Catholic organizations, I invite other organizations working on this issue to join this group. I also approached Karibu, an association facilitating the integration of African migrants, where my congregation has worked since Karibu was established.

When Nicole Ndongala, an African woman who is Karibu's current director, came to the group, she shared the vulnerable situation of many women living in their refugee shelters. I felt a call to work with those women and offered my services to Nicole—now I go to one of their two shelters once a week to do activities with the women from both shelters. I am attentive to the potential victims of traffickers, and I show the volunteers the hidden reality of human trafficking, the signs of how to detect victims, and how to deal with them.

The more people know about the evil of human trafficking, the more will fight it, and it will become more difficult for traffickers to profit from it.

My commitment to these women is my way of living my Christian faith.

June 21, 2021

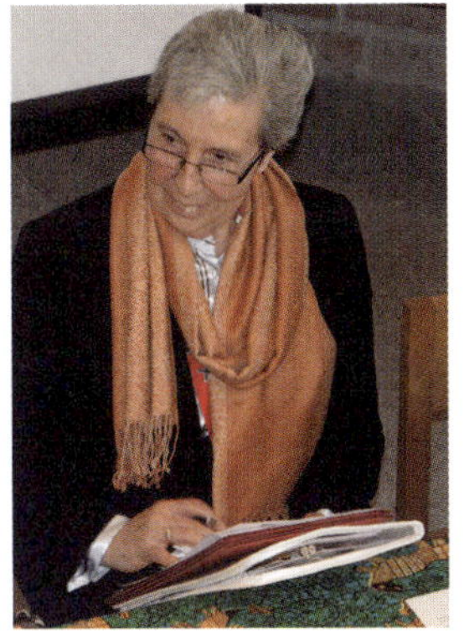

Sr. Begoña Iñarra is from Bilbao, in the Spanish Basque country. She studied music (piano) and chemistry in Spain and taught sciences in the Democratic Republic of the Congo as a lay missionary. After three years in Africa, she joined the Missionary Sisters of Our Lady of Africa. She taught in Uganda, did adult education in Ethiopia and Mozambique, and worked on justice and peace in Kenya. In Brussels, she lobbied on African issues at the European Union, and in Paris and now in Madrid, she is committed to fighting human trafficking.

Reflection

The author calls her work with trafficked women sacred saying that she saw Christ in them, and it renewed her commitment: "Their faith, resilience, and energy of life encouraged me to continue fighting against human trafficking and accompanying them, even if at times it was hard." Where do you encounter Christ or experience "a sacred moment" in those around you, especially those who are suffering? What do you recognize in them? Is there a deeper call to do more?

What could you do to explore trafficking in your local area? Do you know the signs of someone who might be a victim? Are you aware of local resources for those who might be trafficked?

Communities see anti-trafficking successes in Nigeria's Edo state

By Eucharia Madueke

No one thought it could be done. But through sustained advocacy engagement, what was thought impossible became a reality.

For many years, Edo state in Nigeria earned a badge of dishonor as the epicenter of human trafficking in Nigeria. Thousands of young women were taken out of the state with promises of job opportunities, enviable income and a better life, only to end up as trafficked victims in the hands of their prospective employers.

The agony of these victims was hushed under a cloud of fear of retaliation, punishment from the underworld, and reprisal to family members. The recruitment process involved a complex system of rituals, oath-taking, vows of secrecy, and promises of allegiance to the recruiter. The ritual was performed such that the recruited and their families believed that breaking the oath of allegiance to the recruiter had physical as well as spiritual consequences.

These predeparture rituals kept the victims in bondage, and even when they had the chance to escape, they remained trapped in their misery out of fear of the terrible things that would happen to them and their families.

From early 2017, and over a period of 30 months, the Africa Faith and Justice Network trained and mobilized a group of committed Catholic sisters to tackle this menace. The network began its activities at the grassroots, conducted town hall meetings, met with the traditional rulers, conducted advocacy activities in secondary schools and met with the association of market women.

These grassroots engagements achieved two things. First, it gradually empowered the communities to talk openly about what was happening in their communities. Second, traditional rulers who had difficulties uniting the communities to address this issue now saw the community unite behind them. This led to the closure of a famous brothel named the A-1 Hotel that served also as a transit for trafficked victims; the brothel owner and his family were ostracized from the town.

A major demand in the communities was that law enforcement agencies treat the traffickers with the seriousness they deserve. The communities noted further that when a trafficker was reported and arrested, before the community knew it, the trafficker was back in the community and emboldened even more to continue the nefarious business. Communities suspected law enforcement agencies of facilitating trafficking by not prosecuting the perpetrators.

The sisters reported these complaints to the state commissioner of police, who summoned the officers to hear the complaint lodged by the sisters on behalf of the local communities.

Following their findings, the sisters moved their advocacy to the governance structure of the state, the governor and his deputy, the minister for youth and special duties, the attorney general, the commissioner of police, advocacy letter to the paramount ruler of the state, the Oba of Benin (the traditional ruler of the

Edo people), and religious leaders, and a convention of major stakeholders in the state.

These activities at the local and state levels led to the establishment of an anti-trafficking task force by the state governor. The governor appointed one of the sisters to serve in the task force, which was chaired by the state attorney general.

The sisters conducted statewide sensitization programs for youths and local communities and produced radio and TV jingles to highlight the plight of trafficked victims. Rescued trafficked victims were brought to youth gatherings to tell their stories.

On the policy level, the state governor introduced an anti-trafficking bill to the state assembly and asked the sisters to mobilize for support. The state assembly passed the legislation, the first of its kind at the state level. The Edo state anti-trafficking legislation goes a step further than the National Agency for the Prohibition of Trafficking in Persons, empowering the state attorney general to prosecute those who contravene the state law.

Because the sisters were focused on achieving their objective rather than on highlighting their activities through press coverage, most people do not realize the role the sisters played in bringing the issue to light, in empowering community leaders to act, and in the introduction and passage of the state anti-trafficking law.

At the Africa Faith and Justice Network's convening of stakeholders in Edo state in November 2019 to strategize for statewide action on human trafficking following the passage of the law, the state attorney general personally told us that she had 20 traffickers in custody, thanks to our network's activities. We then asked the attorney general to simplify the new legislation such that it is available to and understandable by the average citizen.

While other organizations played a part in policy changes at the state level, most do not realize the leading role the sisters have played. Under the umbrella of the African Faith and Justice Network, they helped build a grassroots coalition and conduct the comprehensive advocacy activities at state levels that led to these changes. State officials, traditional rulers, and religious do recognize it!

Archbishop Augustine Obiora Akubeze of Benin City, Nigeria, was well-acquainted with the activities of the sisters and regularly supported them with the means of transportation that enabled them to reach the rural communities. He remarked that the activities of the sisters enabled the communities to openly talk about human trafficking, something that was a taboo prior to the sisters' activities.

Recent reports show a drastic drop in the number of people trafficked from and within Edo state. The Vanguard news site on Sept. 27, 2021, quoted the wife of the governor of Edo state as saying that Edo state has dropped from the No. 1 state in Nigeria in the number of its trafficking cases, to No. 5 due to advocacies, thanking her husband for responding to this issue. She noted that if Edo state has gotten it right, the rest of Nigeria should get it right.

December 7, 2022

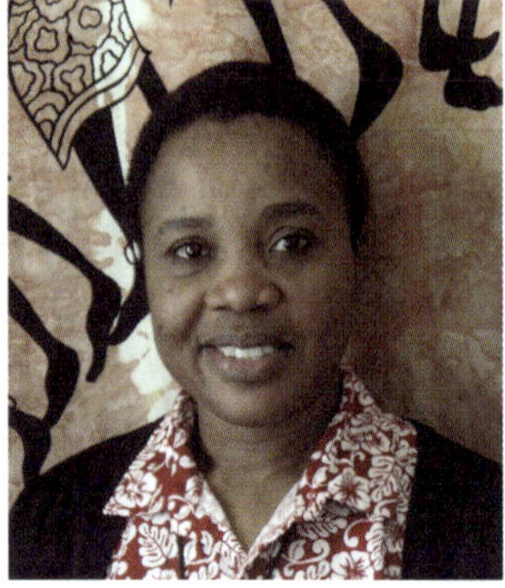

Eucharia Madueke is a Sister of Notre Dame de Namur from Nigeria. With an academic background in education, religion, development and public policy, she has taught at the secondary and university levels in Nigeria and the United States. She has led many workshops in Africa in grassroots organizing and advocacy centered around Catholic social teaching. She served as provincial of the Sisters of Notre Dame de Namur, Nigerian Province. Currently, she is the women's empowerment project coordinator for the Africa Faith and Justice Network, a religious nonprofit organization that focuses on U.S.-Africa relations.

Reflection

In many trafficking situations, the author says that victims can remain "trapped in their misery out of fear of the terrible things that would happen to them and their families." What do you know about trafficking in your own local area or country? Are you aware of any support that is available to those in need of breaking free from this entrapment?

The advocates against trafficking, including religious sisters, organized a grassroots effort that involved changing law enforcement and national policies. It took time and energy, yet made long lasting change to situations that trapped women. What situation of injustice would you be willing to give time and energy to change if you saw a grassroots effort being mounted? Could you see yourself as a potential worker or leader in this movement?

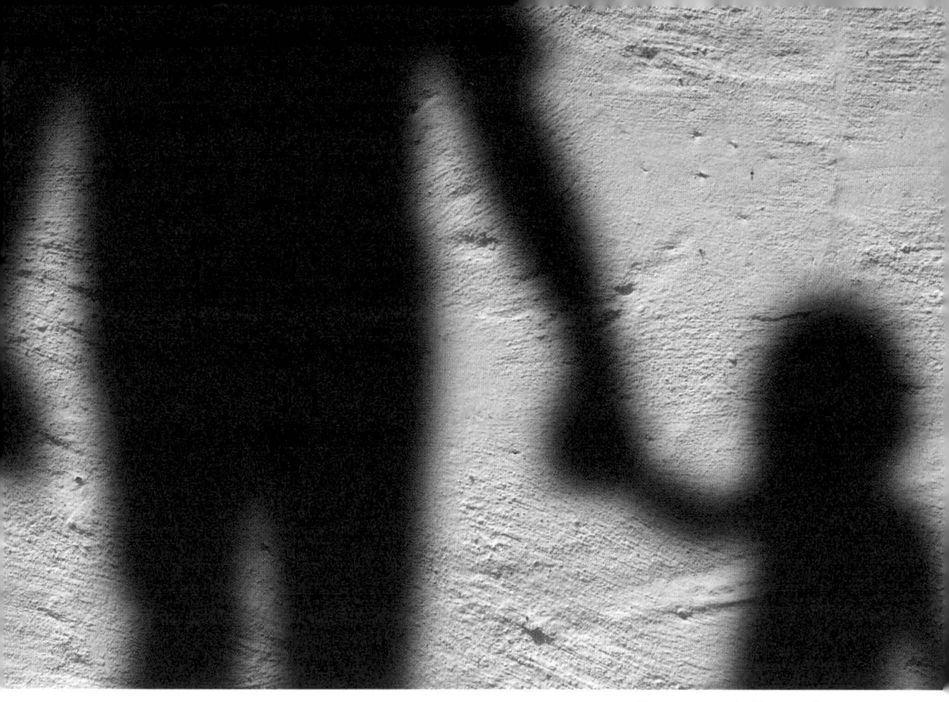

(Pixabay/Gerd Altmann)

Resilience in women survivors

By Kathleen Bryant

On February 8, we celebrate the feast of St. Josephine Bakhita, a woman who evolved from an abused child and an enslaved young adult into a strong, impressive woman religious. By popular acclaim she is known as the Patron Saint of Those Who Are Trafficked, and at the request of women religious, Pope Francis declared her feast an International Day of Prayer and Awareness Against Human Trafficking.

After being involved with anti-trafficking efforts for 10 years, I received a grant from the Louisville Institute to study the resilience of women who have been trafficked here in the United States. Through my interviews, I discovered a face of the human trafficking reality that is rarely addressed. Survivors themselves made it clear that they would like more focus on their growth, goals and strength—on who they have become in their own resilience.

What I heard astounded me. It challenged all the public discourse about Post Traumatic Stress Disorder (PTSD) and the media presentations about "victims." As the women told their stories of healing, I heard deep determination, pride in their progress and dreams for their future. Their stories reflected research by Dr. Lawrence Calhoun, head of the Psychology Department at the University of North Carolina, and Dr. Richard Tedeschi about a phenomenon they call Post Traumatic Growth, which happens more often than PTSD!

Even though these women are in some ways "success" stories, they still experience turbulent waves of recurring traumatic flashbacks that come at any moment, and they know that the healing process takes years.

As Brené Brown says, "Stories are data with a soul!" In the women's stories, I heard strength of soul and a deep connection with life beyond suffering. They are women of hope and have much to teach us about suffering and the human spirit.

Someone out there

Themes of the power of faith and spiritual practice resonated in the stories of resilience. Even when religious belief was never introduced to them, several women told me of sensing "someone out there" to whom they begged for freedom.

One said that while being abused as a young girl, she would look out the window and focus on the moon. *"I knew there was something Greater out there than what was happening to me at that moment.*" Her ability to latch on to the transcendent kept her soul alive.

Kanthi Salgadu, an advocate and activist, was trafficked into Los Angeles for labor. During her struggles, she practiced mindfulness meditation, which she learned as a young girl in Sri Lanka as part of her Buddhist classes. Going within, she found strength to continue living.

I heard a tenacious inner drive for meaning in the stories. They may not have been churchgoers, but they begged for a God to hear them. A 19-year-old girl, who had never been to church in her life, in her desperation as a victim of trafficking, said her *first prayer*: "If you are out there, help me!" Afterward, she did a YouTube search on how to pray. She prayed for a way to get out of her situation. She is now going to school and doing well. The name she called God was, "If you are out there."

The stories I heard remind me of the one about Hagar (Genesis 16), a slave woman who was used for both labor and sex according to the custom of the time. In her escape to the desert, God came to her. She gave a name, *El Roi*, meaning "The God who sees me" to this God. Hagar is the *only* one in the Old Testament who named God; yet she was the outsider, the "pagan." This is the same God whom the women experienced when they felt invisible.

Dr. Harold Koenig writes, "Belief is the most powerful survival tool in the world." These women discovered and accessed within themselves what Laurence Gonzales calls the "survival kit" inside us.

Finding her voice

One of the spiritual challenges for women's development is for a woman to find her voice and use it. On an annual march and demonstration, a survivor used her voice for the first time to shout out against trafficking in a safe context with others. She shared what a thrill that was and how she felt empowered.

After a time of healing, some of the women chose to be advocates for others and activists against human trafficking. Many of them emerged from the Coalition to Abolish Slavery and Trafficking (CAST), the first survivor-centered program in the country. The women I interviewed also told of how empowered they were when they told their stories at Congressional hearings and before state legislators. Before being trafficked, some of these women had never imagined that they could speak before an audience. Advocacy increased their self-confidence and awakened them to their own power and strength.

This phrase from Carol Orsborn in the book *Bouncing Back* about resilience in the brain resonated with them: "Mastering the art of resilience does much more than restore you to who you once thought you were. Rather, you emerge from the experience transformed into a truer expression of who you were really meant to be."

Their mission

I heard the desire to serve and to give back to the community from women who have been through years of recovery and stability. They started non-profits, opened shelters, a day care center, became licensed social workers, and joined with other survivors to advocate for legislation to protect and provide victim services. Their call to mission was life giving for them. It forged an identity beyond being a person who had endured trauma.

Our bodies

Since the body carries memories of trauma, the women mentioned how bodywork had helped them to become stronger and freer. Even though there is a resilience gene, only one third of people have it. Survivors at the early stages of healing found that they could reconnect with their bodies through acupressure and, because it is nonverbal, they were not re-traumatized by telling their story before they were ready. The women found their way to resilience through yoga, tai chi, dance, running, and gym classes.

Music, beauty and the arts

Women expressed a new-found liberation in the arts by telling their stories using drama, journaling, ceramic and oil artworks, art therapy and by creating videos. Hearing about this creative aspect over and over, I learned the arts were a vital part of their healing and resilience. Immersion in nature also was healing, as one survivor shared: "Just looking at the grass, or flowers, and sitting in the sun; the beauty of nature helped me recover."

Relational resilience

A consistent theme from the survivors of human trafficking was that they attribute their resilience to the presence of other survivors. "When I met another survivor, I realized I was not alone, that this happened to others as well."

The National Survivor Network provides both a personal presence and online support to people across the world. Mutual understanding and support help them to heal.

Relationships fed resilience, and for many of them, it was their longing to see their families once again that kept them alive while they were trafficked.

Staying in the middle place

Judith Herman, in her book *Trauma and Recovery*, notes that survivors feel like they are among the dead because they believe that their "capacity for love has been destroyed." When the victim descends into hell, "one positive memory of a caring, comforting person may be a lifeline during the descent into mourning." The most resilient gave time and space to this time of mourning and grieving. The remembrance of one person who loved them unconditionally made their healing more accessible.

The role of women religious in this work has empowered these women. Several described the unconditional love and acceptance from women religious playing a part in their rebirth and the foundation of their recovery. One described herself as extremely shy and crying most of the time but the "sisters kept saying, 'You can do it!' " She described them as her angels. Others commented that women religious were like family and truly their *sisters* as they helped them start foundations, websites and advocacy groups.

The spirituality of Holy Saturday can help us understand the process of healing for survivors. There is a middle place, a liminal space, where resilience cannot be rushed. In *Spirit and Trauma: A Theology of Remaining*, Shelly Rambo notes that as soon as Good Friday is over, we begin moving into the Resurrection celebration without waiting in the void, the silence and emptiness of the Holy Saturday. Survivors can teach us that we cannot short circuit the process of healing and that we need to learn to wait.

Josephine Bakhita's point of conversion happened when she saw the crucifix and identified with the bound and tortured Christ. Rambo explains, "There is no place that God does not go. The impact of this point is existentially powerful. We receive, in the drama of hell, assurance that there is no place that God has not been. God has traveled even to the regions of godforsakeness." For one survivor, her conversion happened in the back seat of a car when she was overwhelmed by the presence of

Jesus. It was in the very dark place of her oppression that God came to her. Resilience emerges from the darkness.

Wisdom

What can these women teach us about resilience?

From their wisdom, we can learn to rise above our own suffering. We can let their experience speak to us about healing: through waiting, using our voices, accepting support from others, engaging in the arts, enjoying beauty and reclaiming our own embodiment.

February 8, 2016

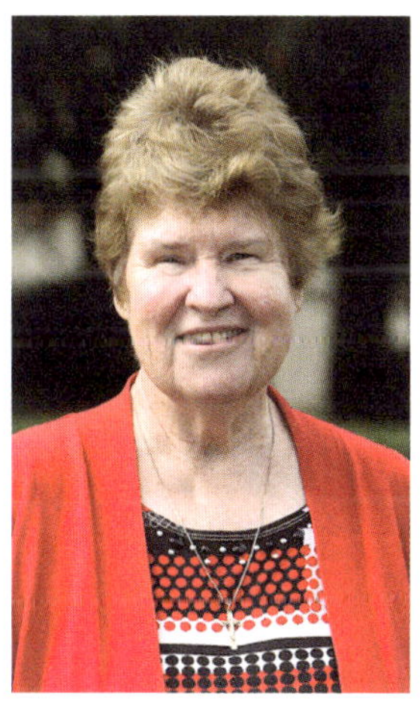

Kathleen Bryant is a Religious Sister of Charity from Los Angeles, California. She has been a member of her community since 1967 and has served as a teacher in California, Ireland and Africa, as the vocation director of the Archdiocese of Los Angeles for 21 years, and is a trained spiritual director. Currently she serves her community in a leadership capacity and gives a variety of spiritual workshops. Her work to bring awareness to the realities of human trafficking is one of her main areas of concentration.

Reflection

In recounting stories of survival, the author tells of the importance of hearing the stories; she includes one about a young woman, a victim of trafficking, who called upon a presence in her desperation. "The name she called God was, 'If you are out there.'" What names have you given to a presence/God when you were suffering, felt invisible or were afraid you were alone? (You might also read the stories of St. Josephine Bakhita, Patron Saint of Those Who Are Trafficked, or Hagar in Genesis 16 for inspiration.)

People who have been trafficked have much to teach us about suffering and the human spirit. What do we need to learn from their stories, particularly women's? If you could take one step to become more aware, understand the situation, or learn how to be of assistance, what would you like to do?

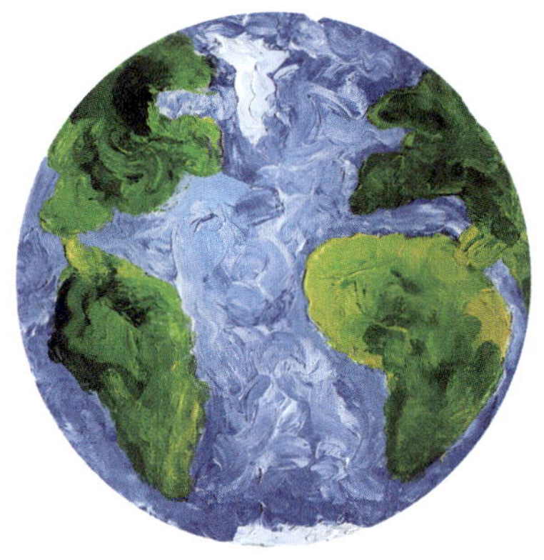

Hope Amid Turmoil

It is true that each person I accompany leaves me with new wisdom, makes me re-know myself once again, from the shared pain and from resilience that is generated in the love required for deep listening.

María de Lourdes López Munguía

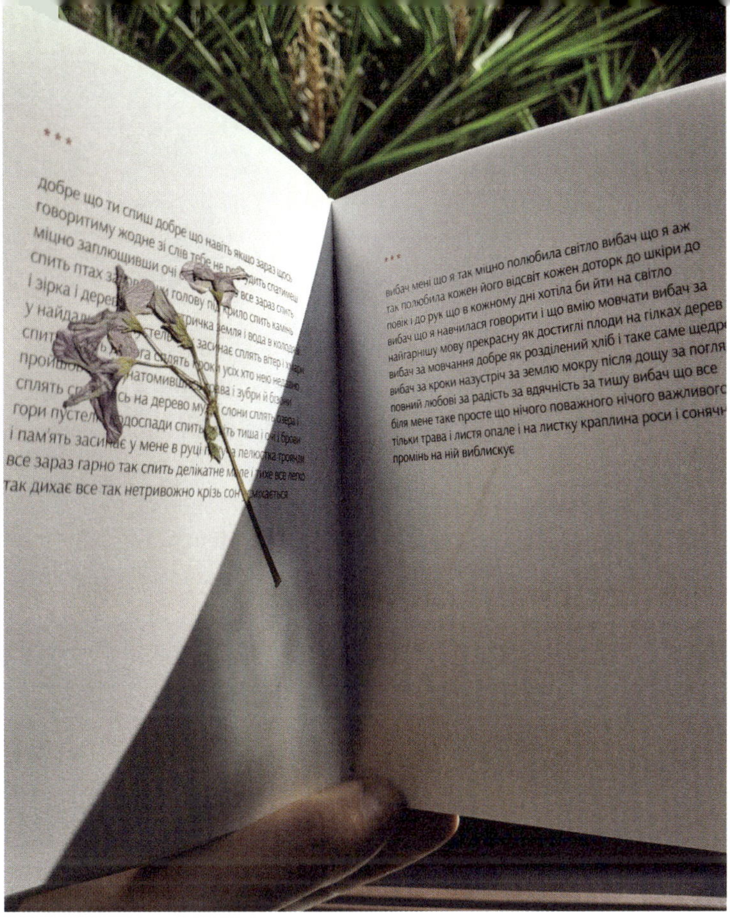

The first book that Mostepaniuk was able to read since Russia invaded Ukraine on Feb. 24, 2022 was poetry.

(Courtesy of the Sisters of the Order of St Basil the Great)

God, don't let us unlearn being human

By Teodozija Myroslava Mostepaniuk

I look at the walls of the small kitchen of our monastery (straight lines, stone flowers) and think about how deeply we humans have a longing for harmony and order. As religious sisters, we are used to the fact that from time to time we must change our place of residence or ministry. However, I am sure that the childhood memories still live in each of us: the smells and sounds of the house where we were born and grew up, the bends of the streets of our native village or town, our childhood photos on which the first features of our future adult personality can be seen through amusing faces and disheveled hairstyles.

During this year of Russia's full-scale military aggression in Ukraine, about 40 million Ukrainians were deprived of all these things. For most Ukrainians, their native home has ceased to be a place of security. On 603,700 square kilometers of the territory of Ukraine (which is twice the size of Italy and slightly smaller than the state of Texas), air raid sirens still sound and super-heavy missiles designed to destroy military targets fall on residential buildings.

The funerals of someone's sons and husbands, sisters and mothers take place daily. Those of us who have unexpectedly lost a beloved one or a parent in early childhood can testify to how much it affects our whole life. The deaths of a soldier or a civilian are not just numbers in statistical reports; each of those people was someone's closest person, someone's whole world, a guiding star that has gone out forever.

Sr. Vasylia Sivch, who was, like me, a Sister of the Order of St. Basil the Great, wrote in her memoirs about the Second World War: "Every war is terrible, and the postwar consequences are even more terrible. Whoever experienced them experienced hell on earth. Because everyone was left with deep, painful wounds on the body and in the heart and soul, irreparable losses of dear people and property, acquired by hard work and thrift."

These words sound incredibly relevant even today.

My previous column for Global Sisters Report about praying for peace in Ukraine and what it meant to be a Ukrainian religious was published on Feb. 22, 2022, two days before the start of a full-scale war. So much happened this year.

At the end of February 2022, the first refugees arrived in the city in eastern Croatia where I lived. I suddenly realized how fragile a human person is, how much he or she needs, and how we do not notice this in our daily lives.

Among the refugees, I met a woman with cancer who could not stop chemotherapy; a young girl who needed weekly dialysis; a newborn boy who made his first journey with his mother, who had no opportunity to recover after giving birth. All of them needed not just food, clothes, housing, but very specific medical care, stable conditions, on which their lives literally depended.

If you multiply this by the number of 8 million refugees and displaced persons, you can roughly imagine the scale of the vulnerability caused by Russia's attack on Ukraine.

Soon Ukrainian soldiers who needed eye surgery came to Croatia for treatment. I looked at the burned face of a man who had lost his sight; his hands, also burned, were trembling. With his fragile human body, he stood against the aggressor's weapon to protect us.

We are vulnerable, we are mortal—this is my first lesson this year.

The most difficult thing for those Ukrainians who lived abroad at the time of the start of a full-scale war was the feeling of helplessness, the feeling of guilt due to the inability to protect their relatives who remained in Ukraine. A great support for us was the helping hands of foreign friends who collected aid, accepted refugees, and were simply interested, listened, supported and assured us that they believed in the victory of Ukraine.

A young guy at a printing service who printed my document for free after seeing the Ukrainian flag on it, an old gentleman at a language course who greeted me with “Glory to Ukraine,” a library worker who asks me about Ukraine every time we meet—these simple touching gestures were a testimony of humanity and at the same time God’s touch. The cracks of fragility in our “clay jars” (2 Corinthians 4:7) made the light of kindness more visible.

The second lesson I learned from this year is that Ukraine, my motherland, is a source of strength for me. Ukrainians who, fleeing the war, found their refuge in Croatia also contributed to this.

The most memorable for me was the question that constantly sounded from the lips of children and adults: “Do you miss Ukraine? Don’t you want to return home?” Or as a 4-year-old girl said in her child manner: “Are you Ukrainian or ‘Croatinian’?”

This was a lesson for me—to allow myself this longing for home, to trust my longing. Each of us has this yearning for a true “home,” for a place where we are accepted, where we can be ourselves.

In August 2022, I had an opportunity to visit Ukraine. And I felt that my homeland, although wounded, was bringing me back to life. The first air raid siren I heard was during the liturgy when we prayed the creed (“I believe”).

And now, when hard moments come, I listen to Ukrainian music and podcasts of Ukrainian psychologists, I read poetry and essays of modern Ukrainian authors.

At the same time, whoever I choose—the brilliant poet Vasyl Stus or the composer Volodymyr Ivasiuk—it turned out that the life of each of them was violently cut short in the war of Russia against Ukraine, which has lasted not only from 2022, nor from 2014, but for several centuries of persecutions, mass deportations and famines.

The third lesson was a spiritual experience. I think that this year brought to both believers and nonbelievers the acute questions about God, about life and death, good and evil, violence and justice.

A priest—to whom I confided that since Feb. 24, 2022, I have felt some obstacles in prayer—advised me to pay attention to how God is working in people during this war. In the courage of Ukrainian soldiers, firefighters, doctors who, risking themselves, fight for human lives every day, we can see a sign of Christ's love, "lay down his life for the sake of his friends" (John 15:13).

However, at the sight of huge injustice, destroyed cities and crippled lives, the question "Why?" inevitably arises. Why is this happening?

The questions remain, they hurt, and sometimes we try to stop feeling and become petrified. The first book I was able to read after Feb. 24 was a collection of poems by the Ukrainian poet Bohdana Matiyash. I read the lines, "God of the kind and quiet, sad and wounded, don't let me unlearn crying," and I cried, for the first time in several months.

. . . While I am writing these lines, at 10:30 a.m. air raid sirens sound in the entire territory of Ukraine, because in Belarus a plane capable of carrying Kinzhal hypervelocity missiles took off. In those minutes, millions of children left their classrooms or kindergarten playrooms to go down to the basements of shelters. I can imagine how parents feel when they, while going to work in the morning, take their children to school.

My favorite Ukrainian poet and filmmaker, Iryna Tsilyk, whose husband, also a writer, has been in the war for a year, wrote in a Facebook post: "To be honest, I sometimes feel like I carry a big black hole inside me, but fortunately, under the clothes, the smile, and all these things, it is not very noticeable."

While the war is still going on, it is important to stay alive, not to succumb to the temptation of an easy and false peace, to the soothing whisper that "things are not so clear." To remain human, we need to be open to the pain of others and our own. As Oleksandra Matviichuk, head of the Nobel Peace Prize laureate Center for Civil Liberties, aptly put it, "You don't have to be Ukrainian to support Ukraine. It is enough just to be human."

"God of the kind and quiet, sad and wounded, don't let us unlearn crying." God, don't let us unlearn being human.

March 1, 2023

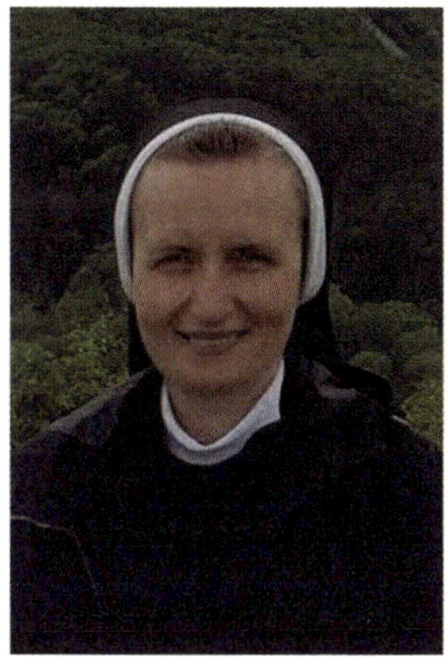

Teodozija Myroslava Mostepaniuk is a sister of the Order of St. Basil the Great (Province of St. Michael the Archangel, Croatia). She completed a master's degree in Ukrainian and English language at Kyiv National University in Ukraine and a licentiate degree in theology at Catholic Faculty of Theology at Zagreb University in Croatia. After final vows in 2018, she worked in pastoral and educational ministry in Croatia, Bosnia and Ukraine. Currently, she is doing her postgraduate studies in church history at the Pontifical Oriental Institute in Rome.

Reflection

No matter when you are reading this reflection, there will be places in the world where humanity is torn by war, violence and evil. God hears the cry of any human being in pain, and as humans, we need to also hear the pain. Where do you recognize pain in any human person, and what can you do to give comfort?

Often, in the midst of crisis or pain, it is poetry, music or art that can soothe or even heal our woundedness. Have you found a piece of beauty that has been healing for you? Is it perhaps time to look again for such a balm?

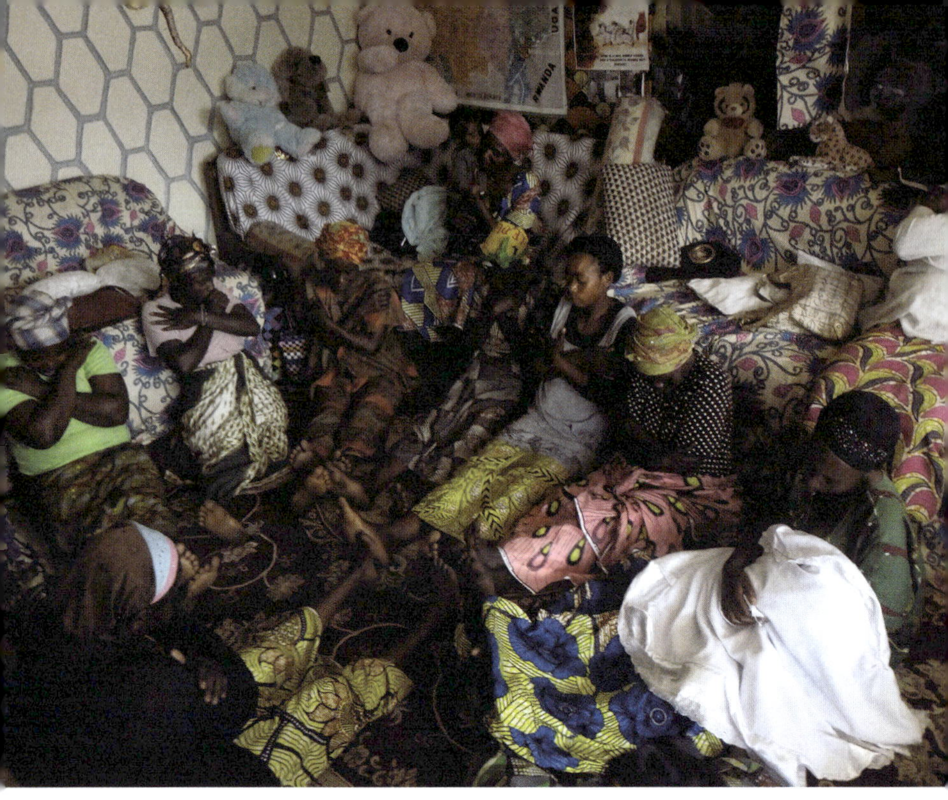

A group of women survivors in a therapy group at the Tulizeni Center in Goma, Democratic Republic of Congo.

(Courtesy of María de Lourdes López Munguía)

Your tears are my tears; your pain is my pain

By María de Lourdes López Munguía

The missionary life is a continuous process of incarnation in which a part of me remains with the people to whom I am sent and a part of the people remains in me. There are experiences that mark me deeply and fill my heart with names and stories. To quote Pedro Casaldáliga:

At the end of the road they will tell me: "You've lived? You have loved?"
And I, without saying anything, I will open the heart full of names.

In December 2019, I arrived in Goma, Democratic Republic of Congo, in the east of the country. There, people have lived in constant tension since the displacement of the Rwandan population by the genocide. Goma has been a place of welcoming refugees from conflicts that end and start over.

It is in this reality where God accompanies me, and for them I consecrate myself (John 17:19).

One of our sisters had begun to accompany women survivors of the sexual violence that comes with armed conflicts and realized the number of vulnerable boys and girls, orphaned, abandoned on the streets, sexually abused girls and ex-soldiers. That is why she founded the Tulizeni Center, which welcomes children and women who survive these realities.

Here, I have had the grace of accompanying some women who have lived terrible experiences—sexual violence linked to the situation of instability, to the fratricidal war—and women who are revictimized by their own families. We have cried together with them; we have shouted anger and impotence.

I have stayed with them on their Holy Saturday, opening my ears and my heart to allow them to tell their stories over and over again until they begin to re-know and re-create themselves. We have danced because it is in dance that these women try to express their pain, their deaths and finally begin to live again.

As a psychologist and spiritual companion, I feel deeply called to accompany people on their personal journeys—usually, for me, women who have suffered sexual violence. I do that from my formation, but much more as a call from God.

It is true that each person I accompany leaves me with new wisdom, makes me re-know myself once again, from the shared pain and from resilience that is generated in the love required for deep listening.

In another sense, the boys and girls that God has entrusted to our care at the Tulizeni Center have awakened in me a sense of motherhood that I had not experienced before, knowing that I was responsible not only for feeding and dressing them, but above all for exercising such an essential role as emotional bonding, and opening a space for listening and welcoming so that they too can retell their stories and heal. Certainly, the little ones have an incredible ability to rebuild themselves.

Last October, the war once again gained momentum in view of this year's presidential elections and political-economic interests in the region. At first, I faced fear—a different fear because it is not the fear of losing my life, but fear for the safety of the children. I have discovered in them this great trust in God that allows them to pray with all their being.

In short, in the midst of this town to which we are called, we live together with our people, with insecurity and hope.

As I write this, the rebels have not reached our city of Goma yet, but whenever they approach, the population is afraid. Nevertheless, because the people need to live, they continue struggling to survive because of their families. At the end of the day, we witness how life and hope hold them one day at a time.

A few weeks ago, as a community, we went to visit a refugee camp that is located less than a kilometer from our community.

The living conditions are shocking: There are more than 7,000 families living in small shacks made of canvas and sticks, without access to electricity and little drinking water delivered every day.

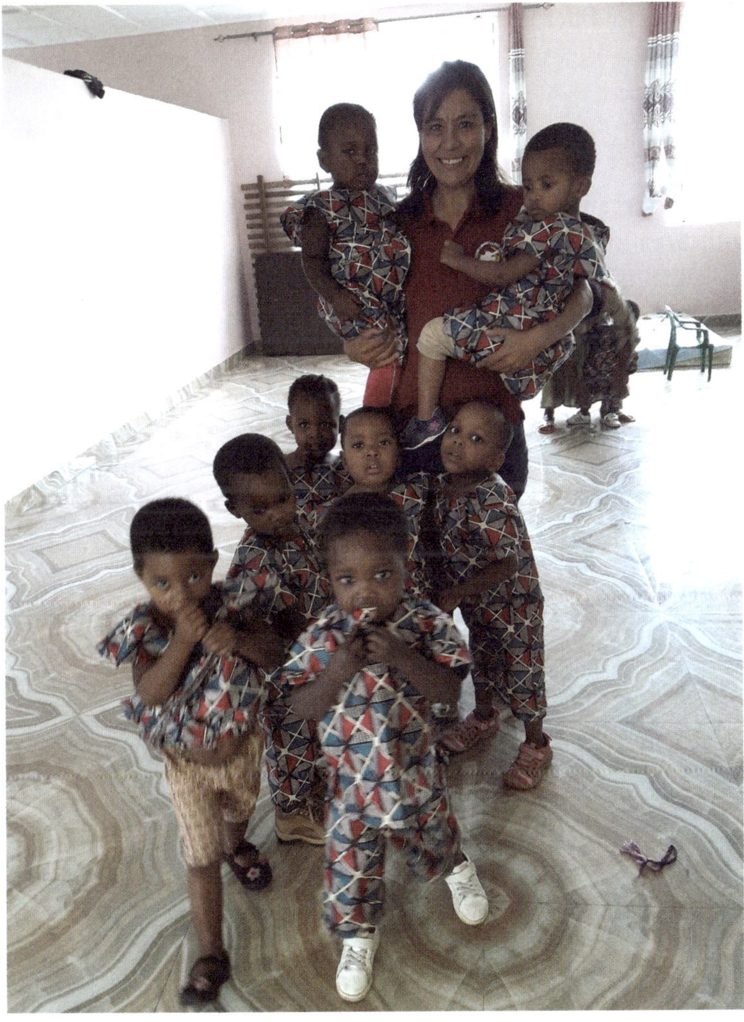

Franciscan Missionary of Mary Sr. María de Lourdes López Munguía with preschoolers at the Tulizeni Center in Goma, Democratic Republic of Congo.

(Courtesy of María de Lourdes López Munguía)

I am convinced that God contemplates through our eyes the pain of his people, the hunger of his sons and daughters. They are images that remain engraved on my retina and in my heart—and these images do not leave me indifferent. It hurts deeply to see babies and children crying for lack of food and already in different stages of malnutrition.

Here I am.

Yes, here I am, and I am not saying it as an affirmation, but rather because each day I'm becoming aware of the depth of the incarnation of God in this town and in me.

Here I am with my story, with my failures and with all the ways God is calling me.

Here I am, in a deep moment of self-reflection, allowing myself to contemplate this reality through various prisms and find that it is our wounded humanity that prevents us from finding love and reconciliation.

Here I am, in silence, because my throat has run out of voice, because it is time for the survivors to take up their voices again to seek and find justice.

Here I am, trying to listen: listen to God in the silence of each morning to discover what he is asking of us; listen to God's people, their cries, their anguish, their hopes; listen to the boys and girls who are in the center and who have already suffered enough.

Here I am, rediscovering God's invitation to "*maternar*" (mothering) in this movement to give life and to care for the life in the midst of death.

So, living in this sacred land and witnessing the visit of Pope Francis has been a *kairos* moment. Listening to his words—"Your tears are my tears; your pain is my pain"—gives a new impetus to our presence in the midst of these people, and we have felt that the world has heard what had been silenced so many times.

If today I would ask myself, how has this experience in Congo transformed me?—my first response is silence, a silence full of lives, names, stories; a silence that I find at dawn and that is a stubborn hope that does not allow death and war to win in the heart.

It is that same silence that is engendering a new way in my prayer, this letting myself be mothered by God, letting God cuddle me, allowing myself to cry in his arms so that I can later comfort and console his people.

Before, I said that there are images that are recorded on my retina. There are also images of hope, of unconditional love and gratitude that in this time I have the ability to see, welcome and embrace from my own profound experience of depending on God.

Certainly, we know that for the moment our lives are not in danger, but the lives of the people that God has given us are at risk. It is God's mercy that moves us to be signs of hope in the tissue of this humanity.

March 7, 2023

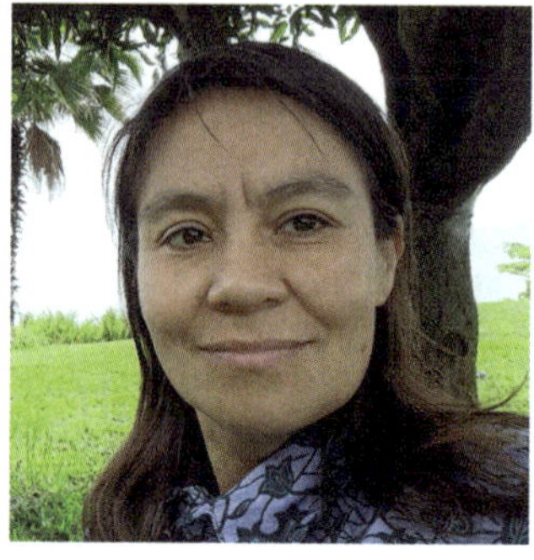

María de Lourdes López Munguía is a Franciscan Missionary of Mary from Mexico who now lives in Cameroon. She is a professional psychologist, trained in accompaniment. She received novitiate formation in Managua, Nicaragua, and ministered in Chile, the United States, Tunisia and Congo.

She has shared her life with: people recuperating from drug addiction; at-risk children; indigenous people in Mexico; inmates and women who have suffered domestic violence; immigrant children in the United States; immigrants in Tunisia; women survivors of sexual violence, and vulnerable children in Congo.

Reflection

What experiences or people have marked you deeply? What images do you carry, or whose names would you find if you opened your own "heart full of names?"

When or where have you responded "Here I am"? The author lists several of her own choices for her "Here I am" moments. How does your own litany of responding to God's presence in the world mark you as one called by God?

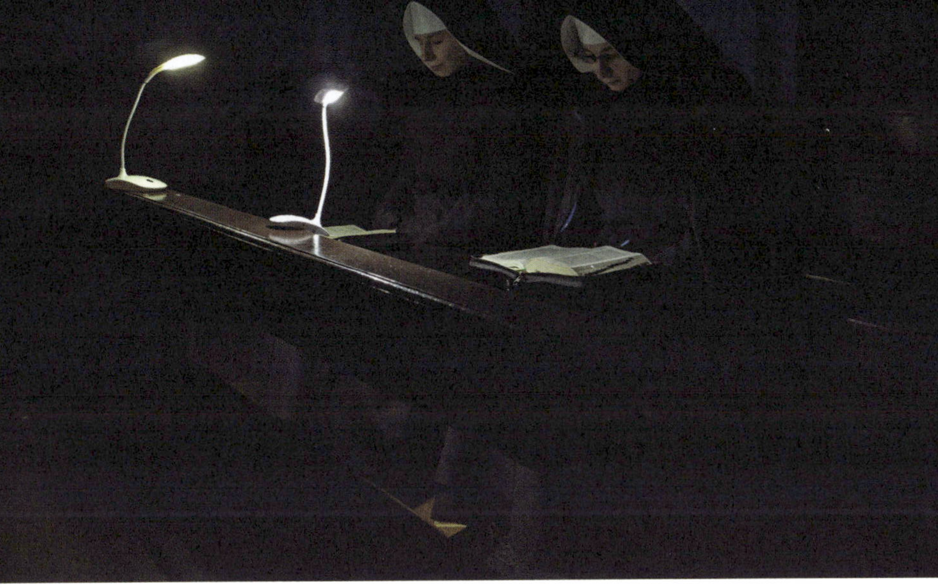

Sisters pray in the chapel of a Benedictine monastery in Ukraine when the lights are turned off.

(Courtesy of Scholastica Oleksandra Hulivata)

War has taught Ukrainians things we would not have understood in peacetime

By Scholastica Oleksandra Hulivata

I don't remember what day Feb. 23, 2022, was. I can remember almost nothing: What was the weather like that day? What was my mood? What did I do, what were my plans? I just don't know. All memories were overshadowed by the next day—Feb. 24, which was etched in memory minute by minute.

Even today, I close my eyes and hear and see again all that ominous day brought. Now, I divide my life into before and after. Sometimes, I get the impression that in just one year—since the war has been going on—I have managed to live not one but several lives.

Now, nothing would surprise me. War first stuns you with its cruelty and unpredictability, and then it takes away the ability to wonder. War takes everything away from you and leaves you with many questions—questions that will haunt you for the rest of your life—and most will remain unanswered.

War is a difficult but invaluable experience. It taught us things that we would not have understood in peacetime.

In the news or in journalists' photos, you can see bloodied bodies, destroyed quarters of the city or even entire cities. However, there are also invisible traces of war: They are inside people, and these traces are imprinted on souls. How can we live after what has happened to us? And almost immediately, the words of the Apostle Paul come to mind: *And now these three remain: faith, hope and love. But the greatest of these is love* (1 Corinthians 13:13). All we have left after Feb. 24 is faith, hope and love.

Lesson 1: Faith

Faith is something that cannot be taken away from us by Russian missile attacks, crimes against the civilian population, and terrorist acts. It is faith that tells us that suffering has meaning.

We look at the injustice of war every day and understand that anyone can become its victim - man or woman, child or elderly, rich or poor, celebrity or homeless. We are all equal before suffering and death.

However, we are not alone. When I look at the wounded or the dead, I see the suffering of Christ. He is present in every victim of war and suffers in each of us in order to lead to eternal joy.

Recently, my 8-year-old student told me that her father died in the war and would soon be buried. With tears in my eyes, I began to comfort her, and she said: "Don't cry. I know my dad was brave and not afraid of death. He wanted us to live in Ukraine and be free. And I want all people to know about my dad. Therefore, promise that you will tell everyone about him."

In the childlike faith of this girl, you can feel a strong conviction: Her father's death was not in vain and he will live forever in the hearts of the people he saved.

Lesson 2: Hope

For the first six months after the invasion, we received dozens or even hundreds of people in our monastery every day. These people had different stories, came from different cities, but they were all united by an indescribable desperation.

I will never forget their eyes full of pain and anxiety. They experienced the greatest fear when someone from the family remained under occupation or did not contact them for a long time. The pain doesn't lessen if you have to lose again and again.

Of course, people fleeing war needed shelter, food and medicine—but above all, they needed hope. They needed to hear that they were safe, that everything would be over soon, that there are people who will help them.

War erases the future. But Christ—the One who rose after suffering and death—says: *Do not let your hearts be troubled. You believe in God; believe also in me. My Father's house has many rooms. . . . And if I go and prepare a place for you, I will come back and take you to be with me that you also may be where I am* (John 14:1-3).

Every caring look or word can become a source of hope; you just need to dare to take on the pain of another person.

The slogan of one of the largest charitable foundations of Ukraine is eloquent: "Invincible when united." These words contain the whole truth about Ukraine today; our unity is a source of hope for a peaceful future.

Lesson 3: Love

My close friend, a soldier, was at the front from the first days of the war. From the beginning of March, he was in a city surrounded by Russians, to save the civilian population from murder, rape and other crimes of the Russian military. He realized that he would not get out of the encirclement alive but continued to fight until his last breath.

One day, we managed to talk for a few minutes on a cellphone, and he said: "I will do everything to ensure that my family and friends never experience what war is like."

He fulfilled his promise, did everything he could—he loved with the greatest love and gave his life for his friends. Junior Sgt. Vyacheslav Kushnir died on Good Friday, April 15, 2022, in the city of Mariupol, while performing a combat mission.

The life of the military is often far from moral ideals, but they are an example for everyone—consecrated persons as well—with what love one should love one's brothers and sisters.

We are fighting an enemy that has come into our home to destroy it and enslave us all, as it was before. The Holodomor, endless repressions and bans, the destruction of identity—this is what millions of Ukrainians went through in that prison of nations—the Soviet Union. All these crimes are still alive in the memory of our grandparents and parents.

Today, we are witnessing new crimes, which we must stop once and for all. The legendary Ukrainian military leader and statesman Roman Shukhevych said: "We fight not because we hate those in front of us, but because we love those behind us."

The war destroyed the life of every Ukrainian, without exception. The war destroyed the world in which we lived until Feb. 24, 2022.

Each of us feels the burning pain of losing family and friends at the front, fear 24 hours a day and seven days a week; discomfort from lack of light, heat, hot water; endless queues at shops, hospitals and pharmacies.

But the most important thing is that each of us feels a thirst for struggle, each of us has become a warrior of truth and goodness on our front. Another important lesson of war is: "Be where you are. Do what you do best." Not only the military, but priests, doctors, teachers, businessmen and artists are doing everything they can to bring our common victory closer.

The world can join our struggle today through prayer and moral or financial support for Ukraine.

February 24, 2023

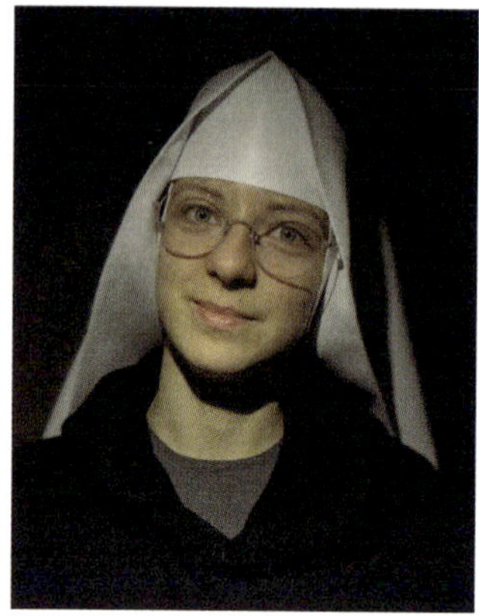

Scholastica Oleksandra Hulivata is a member of the Congregation of the Missionary Sisters of St. Benedict. Born in Ukraine to an Orthodox family, she converted to the Catholic Church at a young age. A graduate of the Theological Institute of Our Lady of Immaculate Conception in Horodok, Ukraine, she works in an orphanage in Bilohirja, Ukraine.

Reflection

Often, people do not know what to say in the face of tragedy or pain, so sometimes say nothing. The author suggests that a look or word to someone in pain brings hope. But it means we have to express compassion and "dare to take on the pain of another person." Where can you offer comfort and hope to someone even though it means looking directly at someone's pain?

Sometimes, one of the hardest things to believe is that suffering has meaning because we often cannot recognize it until time has elapsed. Is there an experience of suffering in your own life that you already have considered or could reflect upon seeking meaning?

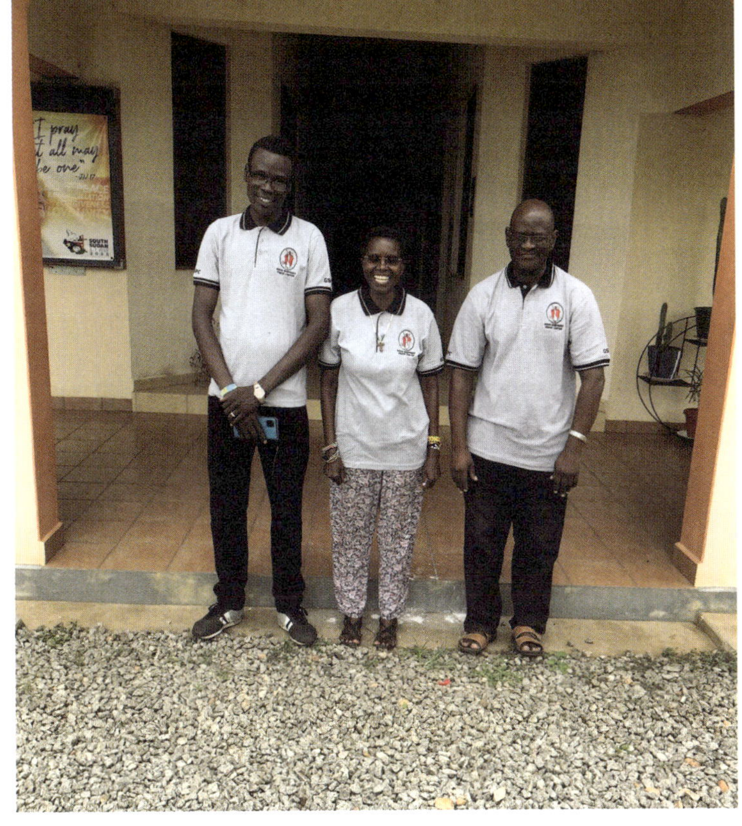

Sr. Scholasticah Nganda is pictured with two staff members of the Good Shepherd Peace Centre-Kit, a few miles south of Juba, in South Sudan. Nganda writes about how she and her colleagues try to keep hope alive in a country in turmoil and conflict.

(Courtesy of Scholasticah Nganda)

What is it like serving in conflict-torn South Sudan?

By Scholasticah Nganda

When did you last pause and reflect on your life in community and in ministry, in unfamiliar circumstances? What if you were invited to choose between your comfort zone and other zones that stress and stretch your capacities? What if you had to reimagine possibilities for thousands of people living on the periphery, marginalized by inherent systemic injustices, exploitation, violence and natural disasters?

I am ministering in South Sudan, a country in turmoil and conflict. I invite you to stretch your imagination and visualize yourself as a messenger of hope in the midst of turmoil. This reflection shares how my community and colleagues and I try to keep hope alive in circumstances of utter helplessness and vulnerability.

When I volunteered for the Solidarity with South Sudan Mission, an initiative of the Union of International Superiors General (or UISG) and Union of Superiors General (or USG), I barely knew the depth of trauma that existed in South Sudan. I was not aware that tens of thousands of South Sudanese had been killed while millions of them were living in neighboring countries as refugees. Gaining independence for South Sudan in 2011 did not usher in political stability. Shocking and paradoxical, isn't it?

Every day in South Sudan opens my eyes to the plight of women and children, who continue to pay a heavy price in the ensuing inter-tribal and ethnic conflict. While the men fight, thousands of women are left behind to carry the day-to-day yoke of fending for their families. Women are seen digging their farms and fetching water for their families while the men are fighting or away grazing huge herds of cattle. (A man who possesses many cattle is considered to be a rich man in South Sudan since cattle are used to pay bride price.)

Many families in South Sudan are headed by women since the men are absent. With absent husbands, most women live by their wits, tending small farms, minding their children and running small businesses—like selling fruits and vegetables or home-brewed alcohol—to generate income for their families.

You may find it easy to read about war, guns and bullets. You may have no difficulty visualizing troops headed for peacekeeping missions in Syria, Somalia or South Sudan. I have not found it easy to live imagining that a gun could be fired at me any time, day or night. Living in South Sudan, it is not uncommon to hear gunshots coming from all directions. In September 2022, rebel forces killed one of the seven security men who guard the Good Shepherd Peace Centre-Kit, or GSPC, where our Solidarity Pastoral Team members live. To this day, we do not know the reason for this attack! Worse still, efforts to seek justice for the family members of the murdered soldier have been met with crippling resistance.

Anytime I recall the brutal murder of our soldier Lipoy (not his real name), a cold shiver goes down my spine! Why did Lipoy have to die? What crime did he commit? On that fateful day, Lipoy stayed in the GSPC all day long. Unanswered conflict-related questions like these fill my mind as I minister in South Sudan. Likewise, some of my colleagues—both foreign and South Sudanese—struggle to find answers to similar questions. However, with fighting that often erupts with the least provocation among South Sudanese, maybe we are looking for answers to the wrong questions.

Talking to the women who participate in the Solidarity trauma healing workshops that Solidarity offers across the country, I have heard stories of women who live with the shame of gang rape or rape by a family member. Horrendous narratives, told by women and young girls forced by family to marry older men they did not know, have left me vicariously traumatized and in need of psychological support. Indeed, my lived experience since 2020 has been one of personal and professional challenge. Nevertheless, it has not all been bleak. There have been rewarding professional experiences in the moments of sadness.

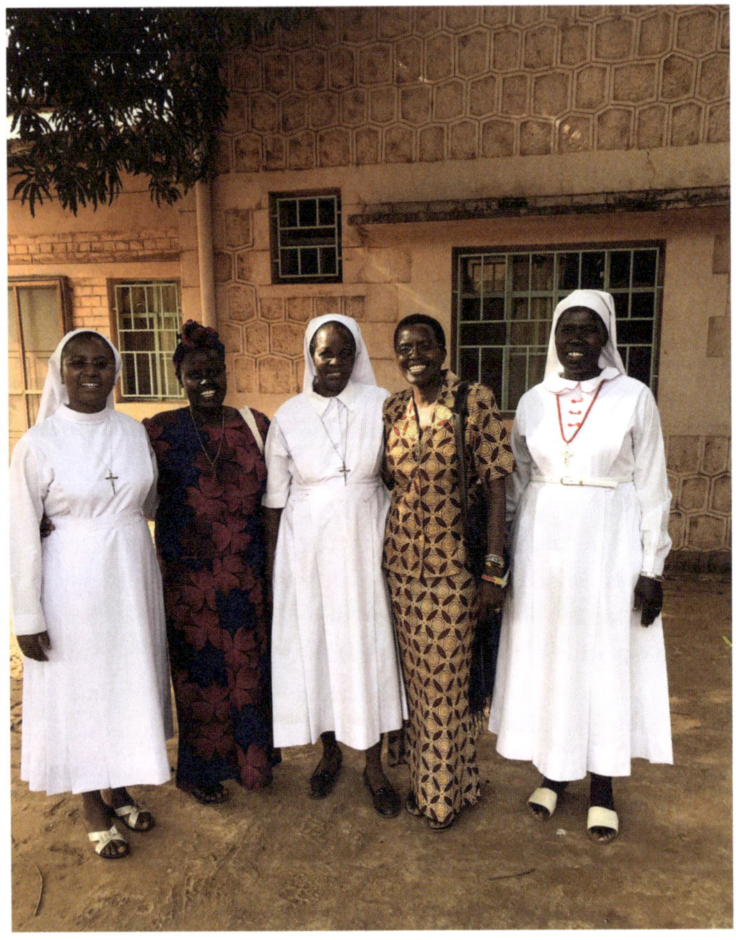

Sr. Scholasticah Nganda with religious of the Wsu Diocese in South Sudan.

(Courtesy of Scholasticah Nganda)

Sometimes, hope has been ignited in me and in those I serve. Moments of my attentive listening to people who need help have enabled the other person to become aware of their inner strengths—the power that helps in navigating challenging life situations. While it has given me fulfillment seeing others beam joyfully with revitalized hope, it saddens me to know I have no access to a formal debriefing place or a trained professional to support me in my work with traumatized people.

In vain, I have searched for a professional counselor for this support. I have found it challenging to work with traumatized people with no personal supervision of my own. I would not wish this experience for anyone! Now and then, I have accessed online supervision that proved helpful but very costly. Peer supervision is not an option as one finds oneself almost in a ministry all by him/herself. With almost no one with whom to discuss my work-related problems, I view this challenge as a dark cloud. I can only hope and wait for the sun to rise one day! In my own helplessness and vulnerability in my ministry in South Sudan, I have leaned on my faith in a loving and caring God. In God, my energy to serve has been affirmed and reinforced.

I do not expect for South Sudan to be flooded with professional psychologists working as supervisors, but I believe the psychology department in the University of Juba may train some people as professional counselors, who would then offer this needed service.

As a missionary in South Sudan, I have learned to take in the pain of my people as they narrate their horrific stories, narratives that sometimes tore my heart. I have listened and heard women who have had to travel for days, hiding in bushes and surviving on grass and wild fruit as they made their way to what they imagined to be safe haven, either with relatives in distant villages or to church grounds. Keenly listening, I have heard details of how these people navigated their way through challenging and trying circumstances, and I have been left in awe by their resilience. Their survival in an environment enveloped by violence of untold magnitude tells of a people determined to beat all odds. Evidently, the majority of ordinary South Sudanese are determined to keep alive the independence dream of 2011, to move—as the pope said on Feb. 3—"*from words to deeds.*"

Who would not want to partner with a people who aspire to self-liberation? The South Sudanese I have met and to whom I have ministered want to be actors in their own liberation. I too desire to play my role in this joined struggle for a future full of hope for South Sudan. The people of South Sudan have hope, an inspiration to work towards peace and a better future. They dream of a better tomorrow, a transformed South Sudan that will once more focus on care of its people: education for the children, improved health care, functioning infrastructure and security for all.

Visualize such a country, and you would find a reason to have physically or virtually celebrated with South Sudan as she welcomed Pope Francis, Justin Welby, the Archbishop of Canterbury and the symbolic head of the Anglican Communion, and the Rev. Iain Greenshields, the moderator of the Church of Scotland, on their recent "pilgrimage of peace" to South Sudan.

March 21, 2023

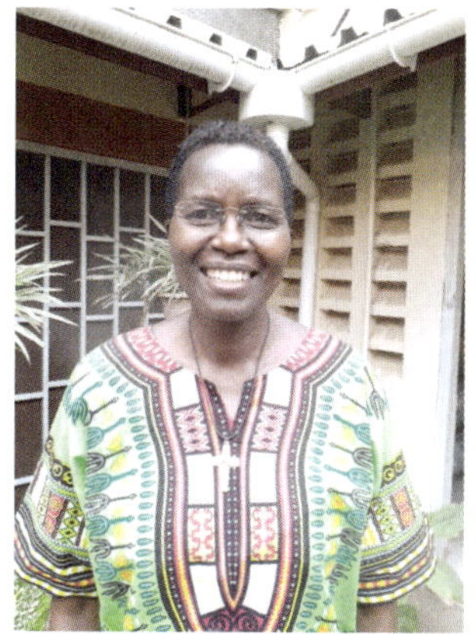

Scholasticah Nganda is Kenyan by birth and a member of the Congregation of the Sisters of Mercy. In early ministry, she taught and held leadership positions at the secondary and university levels. Her graduate work was in counseling and counseling psychology. After serving on the leadership team of her congregation, she is now serving as the director of pastoral programs for Solidarity with South Sudan, Juba, and is one of four members of the Solidarity Pastoral Team working in collaboration with the Catholic Bishops Conference of South Sudan to meet the pastoral needs of the church there.

Reflection

The author lives in a country torn by turmoil and pain, yet she is filled with hope and purpose. Even in helplessness, she says she leans into God and her faith and goes on. Where might you lean into God even in a situation you may feel is hopeless?

What would you choose—a comfort zone or a zone that stretched you? What gifts could you trust God to give you if you were willing to be stretched and, in doing so, be filled with the Spirit?

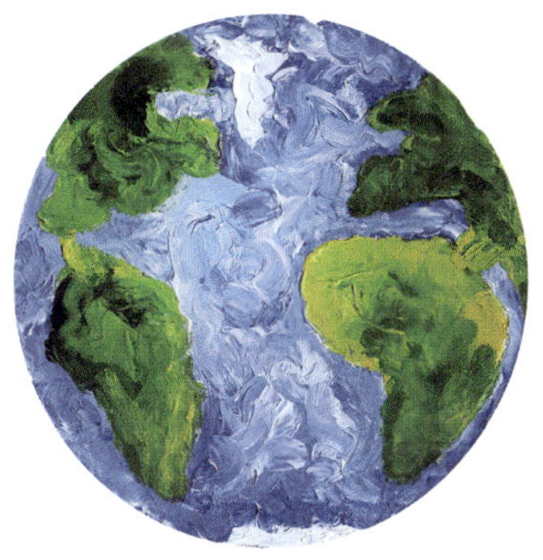

Care for Others

Be the one: it's a choice. Live for others, not yourself. Allow the gifts you carry, whether abundant or scarce or seemingly absent, to flow from you to others who are in greater need.

Marilyn Lacey

Turning a gift of $20 into loaves-and-fishes on three wheels

By Margaret Gonsalves

At Christmas, one of my friends sent me $20 as a gift. On the envelope, she wrote, “Strictly for personal use only.” The exchange of $20 in Indian currency came to 1,400 rupees.

I contemplated how best I could spend it for my personal use. I checked online the prices of shoes and clothes, but given the pandemic lockdown situation, I gave up the thought of shopping for myself.

It was Monday, and my reading and reflection were on the martyrdom of holy innocent children (Matthew 2:16-18). Suddenly, I was inspired—why not share that amount with as many people as possible, to get more personal satisfaction than using the gift for myself?

Since I am free from the old “permission culture,” on Tuesday, I hired a motorized rickshaw from 8 a.m. to 6 p.m. I agreed to give him 1,200 rupees for 10 hours driving, with 10 quick halts.

As soon as I got into the rickshaw, I told the driver, “Even in this pandemic situation, if you or I see any needy person on the street, we will offer them a free lift.” The driver agreed hesitantly.

Soon, we met an indigenous woman carrying a sack of rice on her head and holding an infant at her bosom. We stopped the rickshaw; the driver helped the woman by lifting the sack of rice from her head, placing it in the rickshaw, and then made her sit with me. Upon asking her destination, we were shocked that if we had not stopped, that lady would have had to walk for another 2 kilometers.

The driver looked at me with appreciative eyes, approving my advice to give lifts to needy travelers.

I had planned an itinerary round trip up to 50 kilometers.

After dropping off this woman, we saw another woman waving her hand for a rickshaw to carry her vegetable baskets to the market. Though the market was close by, rickshaw drivers were taking advantage of the COVID-19 situation and looting poor people with a tenfold fare. Again, the driver nodded at my request and helped this woman to load and unload her vegetable baskets for a six-minute driving distance.

We continued this pattern till lunchtime, then paid condolence visits to families with tragic COVID-19 deaths. In between, I noticed the driver getting stressed out after hearing that the house I visited had had a COVID-19 death.

I had sent prior information to the families I was going to visit. They believed that the visit of a religious person would bring blessings to their grieving family. At their request, I wore religious attire. At every house I entered, I did not disclose my prior visit to families where a COVID-19 death took place.

Every family offered me *guru dakshina* (offering to the guru) in the form of money, fresh vegetables from their gardens, full-bran rice from their fields, dry and fresh coconuts, fresh fruits like papaya, chikoos and the like. Fisherfolk families offered me fresh and dried fish.

By the time I finished my visits, the rickshaw was so full of offerings that I hardly had space to sit comfortably.

On my return journey, I made calls to orphanages and poor families and gave away those gifts—worth 3,900 rupees!

With the 200 rupees I had left, I bought a pair of flip-flops. (When shops were closed down during the pandemic, a widow had asked for my pair of flip-flops for her granddaughter.)

That night, I called my friend on WhatsApp and gave her the details of spending the $20 for my personal use.

Results and lessons I learned from that "personal use" gift of $20:

- I was a recipient of huge smiles of hope on the faces of those who had said their goodbyes to their COVID-19 patients when they left for the hospital, no more to return.
- It was heartening to hear, "Thank you, sister, for visiting us—no priest, no sisters visited us."
- When life was getting tough, I came to believe that "generosity begets generosity."
- The rickshaw driver got a lump-sum income for that day.
- One rickshaw driver from a high-caste Brahminic family was able to get rid of his ingrained bias against untouchables. He could feel the pinch of untouchables being excluded by his Brahminic culture.

My $20 was like the multiplication of two fishes and five loaves (Matthew 14:13-21). Instead of letting his disciples send away the hungry crowd, Jesus converts their attitude of exclusion into inclusion, by sharing whatever meager food that was available.

And more than just Jesus multiplying the loaves and fishes, I see a woman—the mother of that little boy—behind this miracle, who had taught her little boy to share his tiffin.

For me, the coronavirus pandemic is a providential opportunity to learn thousands of ways to minister to the *anawim*—the poor of Yahweh.

I remember the final blessing from Sr. Francisca Hardy from Carmel-by-the-Sea, California. After my spiritual direction session, she said, "Maggie, God is passionately busy beautifying the world by those who work for his poor, and the needy, and the excluded ones."

Waving goodbyes to me, she said, "Grace will lead you home, Maggie." This message has stayed with me forever.

"God is able to provide you with every blessing in abundance so that by always having enough of everything, you may share abundantly in every good work" (2 Corinthians 9:8). God's vision of shared blessings abounds for all!

When Jesus does equal distribution from just a little, why can't our leaders share a little from the wealth they have hoarded or amassed? Because of a handful of greedy people, scarcity is experienced by many. Our small decisions of sharing whatever we have and we are will bring big change—and hopefully, fuel collective actions that share compassion.

Someone has said, "You can give without loving, but you cannot love without giving."

That little boy—from whom the hungry received food and were satisfied—was given the loaves and fishes by his mother. Just as there was a mother behind the little boy of the parable, there was a sick and suffering woman behind this $20 gift. Let us mother people with compassion.

"Whatever you do, work at it with all your heart, as working for the Lord, not for men" (Colossians 3:23). Genuine freedom from within would replace the meaning of gifts designated as for "personal use only."

By sharing this small gift, I experienced the spirituality both/and! I enjoyed the gift as well as reaching out to the needy in compassion.

April 12, 2021

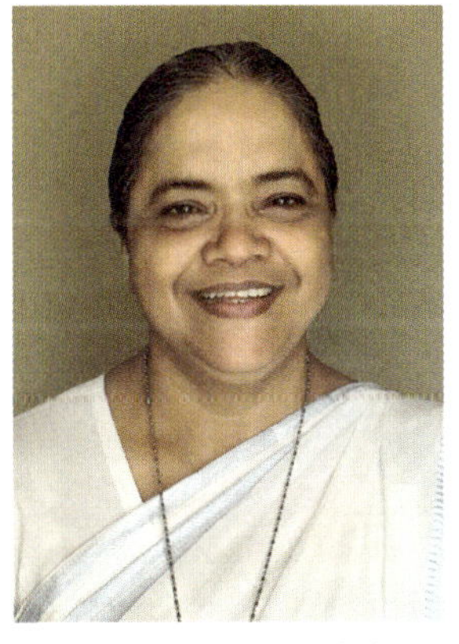

Margaret Gonsalves is a Sister for Christian Community and feminist theologian active in the Ecclesia of Women in Asia and Indian Women Theologians Forum. As founder of ANNNI Charitable Trust, she networks in solidarity with nongovernmental organizations to run free residential programs in intensive spoken English to empower Indigenous girls and women. She organizes MADness workshops to implement the United Nations' sustainable development goals as well as the spirituality of *Laudato Si'* and *Fratelli Tutti*.

Reflection

Can you imagine creating a similar story if you started with a lump sum of money and were determined to somehow give it all away where it was most needed in one day? How does contemplating that gesture make you feel? What might happen?

As you contemplated a day of giving away money where it was most needed, where did you imagine the strongest needs of God's people? Now, what will you do about it?

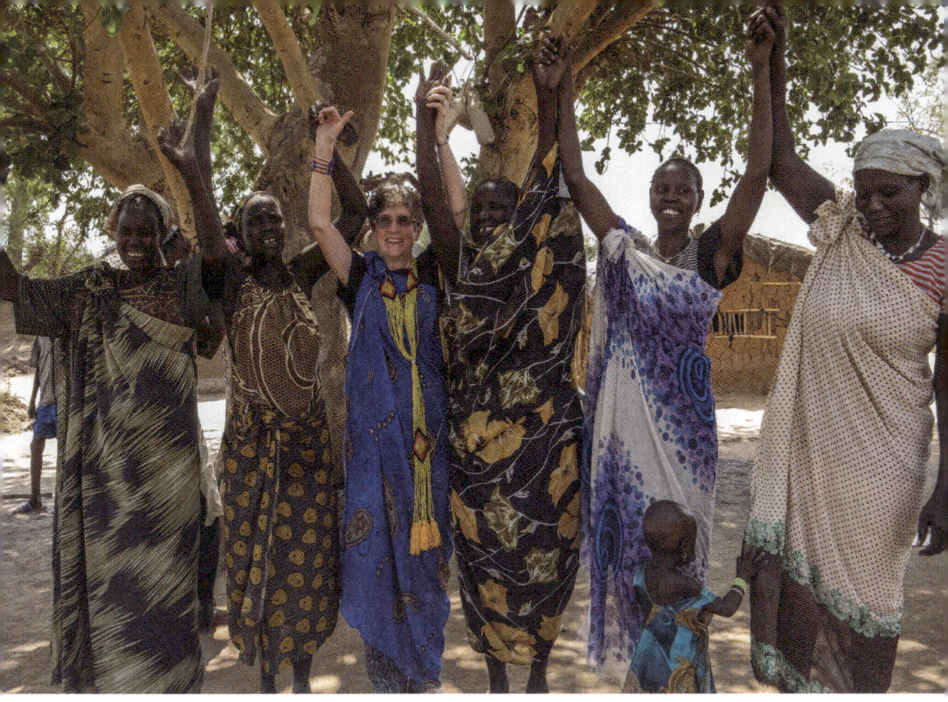

Sr. Marilyn Lacey, third from left, raises her hands with South Sudanese refugee women in celebration of the micro-loans provided by Mercy Beyond Borders. They had just draped Sr. Marilyn in blue and put a bracelet on her wrist when they spontaneously grabbed her arms and began singing.

(Courtesy of Mercy Beyond Borders/Alison Wright)

Even if you've not been fed, be bread

By Marilyn Lacey

Every Eucharist includes time for an offering of gifts. Here in the U.S., that's almost always the moment to contribute money. I've experienced other cultures where it can include contributing fresh produce from one's farm or home-baked goods to share.

In South Sudan, instead of the collection basket being passed around the pews, usually one person stands in front holding the basket; congregants walk up one by one to add their gifts. Leave aside, for the moment, the anger I often feel when I see the poorest of the poor dropping their very-hard-earned coins into the basket. Surely, the Church has this ritual entirely backward! Shouldn't the presider be stuffing the basket with cash and then passing it around the pews, inviting each parishioner to take what s/he needs for the week ahead? Isn't that how Luke describes the early Christian community in the Acts?

Backward as it may be, the weekly offering can still carry amazing grace.

In his most recent Christmas letter, Brother Paolo (an Italian Comboni medical doctor who manages a hospital in rural South Sudan) described a recent collection that moved him deeply. Tall, barefoot women—most having come to church from mud huts and many having survived violent displacement multiple times due to war—slowly walk the length of the center aisle while the choir sings above a strong drumbeat. Paolo wrote:

"I saw some stretch and open their empty hands [over the basket], evidently dropping . . . nothing."

Nothing? Paolo marvels at their humility and courage. He confesses that he, if he had no ready cash, would "remain quietly sitting in my place." Surely, we never want others to see that we have *nothing*.

There is deep learning here. In my role as director of the nonprofit Mercy Beyond Borders, I am frequently in South Sudan visiting our education projects for girls and our micro-enterprise projects with women and our leadership training of young women for advocacy. Keeping girls in school protects them from early marriages, allows them to develop their gifts, sets them on the path to pursue professional careers. The small loans we provide to women in refugee camps enable them to create sustainable futures for their families, a path upward from extreme poverty. It is easy to believe that we are the ones filling their coffers with coins.

But wait. Perhaps that, too, is backward. It is these widows, orphans, refugees and displaced persons who enrich us. They stand undefended, "the least among us," often with apparently empty hands. Yet God cherishes empty hands. Miracles happen there, precisely because God stands with those whom the world disregards.

With no material wealth to give, such women connect on a deeper level. They share their struggles, their stories, their hard work, their daily living and dying, their dreams. They know nothing of the rugged independence so cherished by Westerners. They need one another, and they know it. And when some small abundance does unexpectedly come their way, they share it.

My first experience of this emptying was in a Lao refugee camp in Nong Khai, northern Thailand, in the early 1980s. The small convent where I was living initiated a nutrition program for the refugee children in the camp's pre-schools. Long before dawn each day, the cook fried hundreds of eggs in large woks over open fires in the convent yard. Several hours later, each child received one cold, now-rubbery egg, delivered atop a leaf. Often, I witnessed children carefully folding up their precious egg in the leaf and setting it aside. When questioned, they told me they were saving it to share with their younger siblings.

One does not need a theology degree to understand that this is real *kenosis*, the self-emptying of holy ones who cling to nothing but God.

Sufis, the mystical branch of Islam that focuses on inner love rather than external religious practices, have bequeathed to the world a trove of profoundly spiritual 13th century poetry. In the experience of the Sufis, the original whirling dervishes, those who dance before God feel an ecstatic freedom that eliminates the compulsion to cling to anything.

Here is my favorite Sufi prayer, by Jelaladdin Rumi. For me, it sums up the self-offering that lies at the heart of every Eucharist:

> Be the one who, when you walk in,
> Blessing shifts to the one who needs it most.
> Even if you've not been fed,
> Be bread.

Be the one: it's a choice. Live for others, not yourself. Allow the gifts you carry, whether abundant or scarce or seemingly absent, to flow from you to others who are in greater need. Even in times of personal emptiness, when you might not feel fulfilled or acknowledged or competent or fed, let goodness flow through you to nourish others.

This is my daily prayer. Empty hands don't prevent meaningful sharing. In fact, they just might be a prerequisite!

February 24, 2020

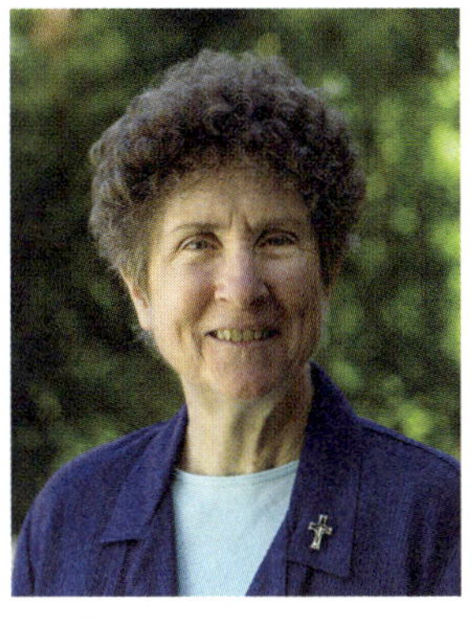

Marilyn Lacey, a member of the Sisters of Mercy of the Americas, has worked with refugees and displaced persons since 1980. In her spiritual memoir, *This Flowing Toward Me* (Ave Maria Press, 2009), she recounts stories of meeting God in strangers. She is the founder and director of MercyBeyondBorders.org, an international nonprofit forging ways for women and girls in extreme poverty to learn, connect and lead.

Reflection

Even when we are in great need we can still offer our own lives to God who accepts us as we are. In your own life, have you ever experienced "the self-emptying of holy ones who cling to nothing but God" either in your own offering or seeing an offering by another?

In the early Christian community, none of the members were ever in need because they shared everything in common. How can we do that in today's communities? How does that make us bread for one another? How might goodness flow through you to nourish others?

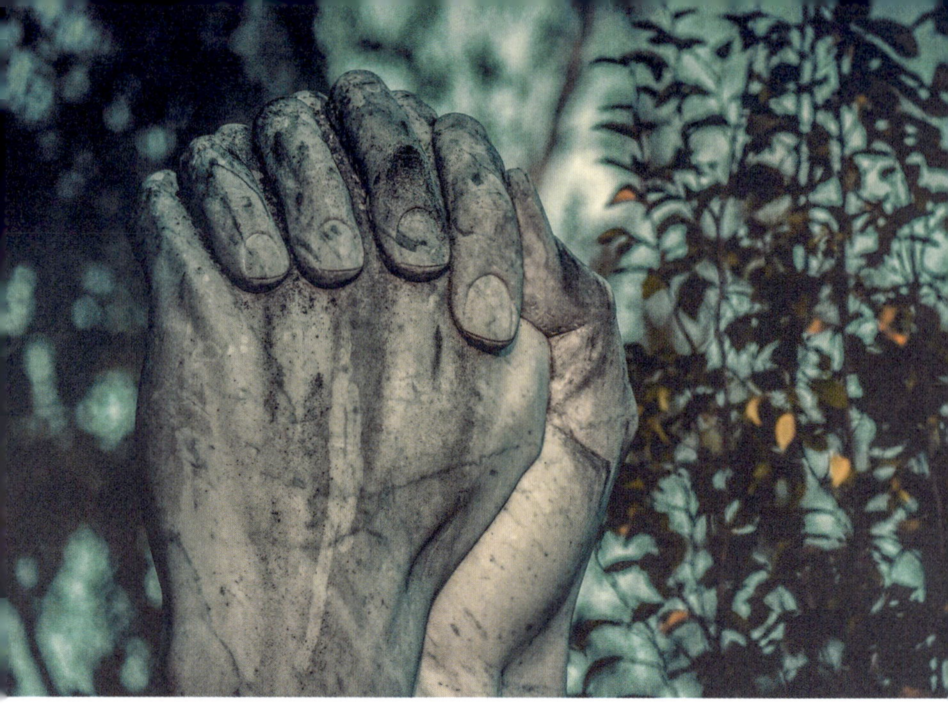

(Pixabay/Ilo)

Contra spem spero: Against all hope, I hope

By Lavina D'Souza

The feeling of hopelessness is familiar. All of us have probably been through times when we have felt hopeless. It could have been at the news of a terminal illness of a loved one, or at a relationship that's on the verge of falling apart, or during a stressful job, and so forth. In those trying moments, what kept us going?

It was probably *contra spem spero*, which translates as "against all hope, I hope." The phrase became popular after a poem with the same title was penned by one of Ukraine's most revered poets, Lesya Ukraïnka, in 1890. Lesya battled an illness that weakened and exhausted her, both physically and mentally.

In this poem, she articulated her unwillingness to be conquered by her illness. It was hope alone that sustained and carried her through life to not give up and give in to the disease.

Hope is not a simple fairy tale wish. A wish is something that someone longs to have, but hope is the expression of a possibility. It is a "looking forward to." Jürgen Moltman, a German theologian, expressed hope as "forward looking and forward moving, thus revolutionizing and transforming the present." Hope expresses confidence of a high possibility of an event occurring or not occurring, whatever the case might be.

I noticed this forward-looking attitude in one prisoner under trial in a prison in India during one of my visits there as a volunteer. She had been accused by her in-laws of murdering her husband, but she shared that her husband had committed suicide, unable to bear the stress resulting from financial debts. She couldn't afford to pay the legal fees for her release and has been incarcerated for the past eight years despite the efforts of her aging parents and siblings.

Though imprisoned and unable to help herself, there were no words of despair in her conversation. As she narrated her story, I recalled the words of Karl Barth, a famous theologian, who wrote, "All that is not hope is wooden, dead, hampering as ponderous and awkward as the word reality. There then is no freedom, but only imprisonment." How fitting this quote was to this imprisoned woman. I felt life in her. She seemed hopeful—imprisoned, yet free. *Contra spem spero*!

Her proactive attitude made me reflect on two aspects of hope: believing and progressing. Hope-filled people whose hope has its roots in faith in the divine have Believing Hope. Their faith in the divine leads them to have faith in themselves and in the process of growth itself. Hope and faith are inseparable companions, and those who believe can anticipate that truth will be revealed. Faith is the foundation on which hope rests, nourishes and sustains.

Hope affects faith, too. The unremitting, renewing and restoring hope invigorates faith again and again. Hope has the power to overstep the closed walls of suffering, guilt and pain. This Believing Hope helps one to cross and transcend the bounds of a prison to progress in hope.

For a prisoner under trial, to move beyond her past and beyond the present in order to discover her future means a lot. It requires hope that progresses and matures over time. Hope, for them, is not built upon a wish-fulfillment, but embedded in the process of continuing anticipation of being proven innocent, of being released, and being able to live the peaceful life of an ordinary person.

They are people who move around like a lamp with a flickering flame but would not let the outside forces blow it away. They make efforts to progress toward the "not-yet"—the radically new and transforming future. It is the daily progress in hope that provides them with the inexhaustible inner resources to seek justice. Justice and hope are indeed partners on life's journey despite being surrounded by overwhelming injustice. It is through hope that we know there are people who still continue to fight for justice.

Though injustices prevail, we still hope. We hope that violence, poverty and other social evils will diminish; we hope to have humane government policies; we hope that people will be accorded protection in this nation; we hope that justice will reach the poor and the voiceless. We dare to hope. This, of course, is a creative battle, a creative battle of sharing hope with those whose lives seem devoid of it! For triumph in the life of one individual can impact the lives of many. Hope fosters hope.

We need this hope in all our ministries today, and our hope does not arise because of the problems around, but because of our trust in the Divine Master. And we hope that *contra spem spero* vibrates in every human heart.

July 5, 2023

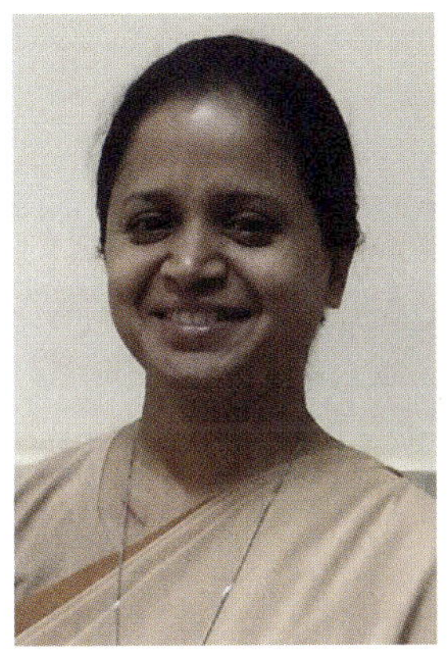

Lavina D'Souza is a Canossian sister working in Belgaum, India. She is presently the secretary of St Joseph's Society in Belgaum, which administers educational institutions. She also takes up research assignments in social work. Her postgraduate degree in social work comes as an additional help to the various rights-based approaches and community development programs that she embraces through her socio-pastoral ministries with the urban and rural poor.

Reflection

When have you experienced any kind of hopelessness? Have you felt a sense of "against all hope, I hope"? Did some sense of possibility come from that?

People who work for peace or justice or in areas that address issues that seem insurmountable are rooted in hope. They have faith the truth will be revealed; they dare to hope. For them, faith and hope are inseparable. Where do you see that kind of witness locally or globally? Do you have an area in your own life where you offer that kind of impact?

Have you changed the world today?

By Dorothy Fernandes

Have you changed the world today?

What does this mean? I wonder: How can you change the world when you are working in a very difficult situation, with many hurdles and barriers? But as I deeply reflect on what is happening around us, I feel there are a number of good things happening, so many positive initiatives to bring about change.

I like to sit down and reflect on my own life and what I do each day. Then I look around and see what is happening to the people around me. I was doing this meditation in March, and so my focus went to women—how they are doing and how they are organizing their lives.

Not just March 8 is International Women's Day, and not just March is our month!

I can think of thousands of women who have changed my perceptions, my thinking, my understanding of spirituality, and I especially appreciate those who have silently challenged me to blossom out into the woman I have become today.

When I think of the women who live in the slums, I realize they too have come a long way on this journey called change. From being engaged only in their homes, they have dared to move out in search of livelihood.

The women of the resettlement colony Bhikha Chak had just lived in their one-room houses, spending their time on household chores or sitting around gossiping. We asked them to become part of our organization, Aashray Abhiyan (which campaigns for shelter rights) and we invited them to visit the office downtown.

Earlier, they had known only their immediate neighborhood and the vegetable market; those were their boundaries. The usual practice is for the man to earn the money and do the shopping for the family.

They exclaimed, "By calling us to the office, for the first time, we have come to Gandhi Maidan!" (Gandhi Maidan is the heart of the city of Patna.) "By making us part of this organization, you have exposed us to a new world."

Today, they have gone beyond those boundaries and have reached what must have seemed the impossible.

From being confined to her house, this is the new Indian woman emerging to find her space.

"Being part of Aashray Abhiyan is awakening us to our rights; by inviting us to become part of collective struggles for housing and space in the city you are exposing us to another new world."

A world that goes beyond caste and creed! We now have one focus—that we have rights and that we will not get them unless we come together. The common factor is that we are all economically poor; we don't have enough money to own a house or to buy land.

When we, as weaker individuals come together, there is a power within the group. We have learned from each other as we live in the same situations and have become empowered by listening to each other's stories of struggle.

These women—Geeta, Pratima, Asha, Sunita, Sangeeta, Anita—have with our assistance formed their own self-help groups. We showed them how to link up with the Punjab National Bank. They have learned to do their bank transactions independently and take out loans for their economic growth.

This exposure has helped them advance as they have also joined the work force of the Labor Department of the government of Bihar. This has brought a tremendous change in their families. All their children are pursuing their studies and have aspirations to become someone in life.

Then, there are women in the rural area of Islamganj, near Patna. They are the ones who have risked moving out of the confines of their homes. They believe that since they moved out and have become "exposed," they have discovered their hidden strength.

Bedami Devi is a widow. She lost her husband some 25 years ago. By sewing clothes and then later working with women, she was forced to move to places she had not been.

I supported her by saying, "You can do it," when she was called to the speaker's dais for the first time and asked to share her experiences. She was diffident at first, but once she spoke out and there was a huge applause, she realized that I was right.

I had never realized that what I said had impacted the lives of these women, until I sat and reflected on these experiences, on these women's stories. I personally believe that there is a power within you, and it is only when you are put to the test, that the best comes out in you.

Yes, I have changed the world, I have tried to enable them to discover their inner strength, have helped them move one pace beyond.

It's true that once a woman dares to move out of the confines of her home, there is no turning back; she changes and becomes an agent of change in turn.

Very often, we are not recognized; the patriarchal mindset can never accept the contribution of women. Indian women have undertaken a long journey and there is no turning back.

April 30, 2018

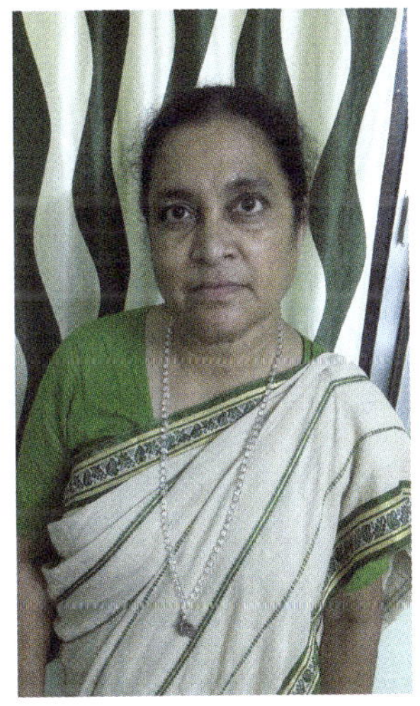

Dorothy Fernandes is a Sister of the Presentation of the Blessed Virgin Mary and a social activist who has been working in Patna since 1997 with communities on the periphery, with the goal of making their cities inclusive, so that no one is left behind. She is also the National Convener of the Forum of Religious for Justice and Peace, a solidarity group of religious activists in India, and a member of the National Alliance of People's Movements.

Reflection

In your own life, what women have changed your own perception, thinking or understanding—or perhaps even been a witness to you for change in the world? How have any of those persons shown you a way to make an impact, perhaps even in your own specific area?

Change can happen when we realize that boundaries can be crossed or new paths can be forged. Change can also happen when we listen to a story different from our own. How can you stretch yourself to recognize change, perhaps even welcome it, even if it is disconcerting or uncomfortable at first?

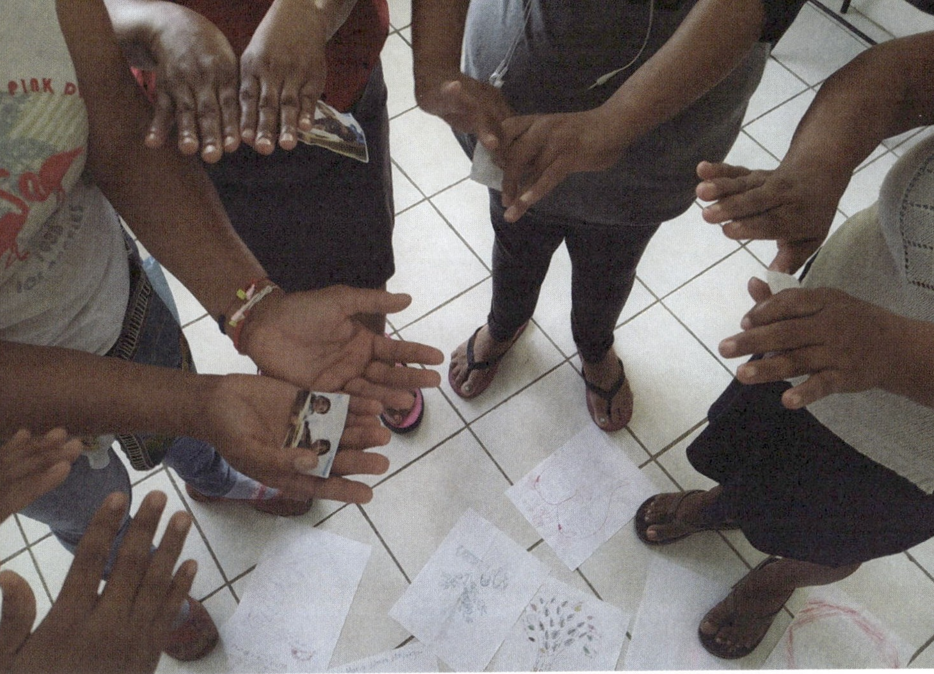

A group of women take part in a prayer to bless absent loved ones, as part of the Comboni Missionary Sisters' "Effatá" program to assist migrants in Tapachula, in the state of Chiapas, Mexico.

(Courtesy of Pompea Cornacchia)

"Effatá" program supports migrant women

By Pompea Cornacchia

Let us put our hands together: let all those who love Jesus Christ share the same desire, the same goals, the same commitment.

—St. Daniel Comboni

Every day, hundreds of migrants—young women, boys, and children arrive at the Bethlehem Shelter Center. The Tapachula Diocesan Center is not their destination, however. Coming from Honduras, El Salvador, Cuba, Nicaragua, Guatemala, and Haiti, they have something in common: they want to pursue the "American dream."

Tapachula, a city situated in the state of Chiapas, is a place of transit. It is among the most dangerous Mexican border cities. Neighboring Guatemala, this small city witnesses daily the crossing of thousands of migrants from Central America, the Caribbean, Africa, and Asia.

The Comboni Missionary Sisters established a crisis intervention program called "Effatá" at the Bethlehem Shelter to assist and serve migrants. "*Effatá*" ("be opened")—the Spanish form of the Aramaic word "*Ephphatha*"—is a powerful word that expresses a desire for and a commitment for life. A community of four Comboni Missionary Sisters from Costa Rica, Mexico, and Italy welcomes and provides support and compassionate care.

Three of the sisters are dedicated to listening and healing. Through spiritual and therapeutic accompaniment, migrants strive to integrate their trauma. Under the sisters' care, migrants renew their hope, self-esteem, and courage. Another sister teaches handicrafts. Most adults and children engage joyfully in art therapy and develop their creativity.

The intervention focuses on two stages. One is the accommodation of the population in shelters or refugee camps. The other is the repatriation to their countries to help in the reconstruction process or prepare them to continue their journey. The first stage of the intervention includes training health promoters and community leaders. Then, they learn to promote "crisis interventions" directly with affected populations.

The goal is to alleviate, empower and journey with them and share life while they wait for the documents to continue their journey of hope towards safer destinations. The program helps migrants in the following ways:

- Offers spaces to let off steam, manage stress and project themselves positively into the future;
- Facilitates the acquisition of hope, initiative, and self-esteem to cope with whatever they will experience;
- Promotes and strengthens their psychosocial support networks;
- Empowers them to search for alternative, post-disaster solutions;
- Helps them become instruments of change with their fellow migrants, even if they are repatriated back to their places of origin.

The Mexican border is filled with the tears, nightmares and dreams of those who cross it daily. According to the National Institute of Migration, about 460,000 migrants crossed into Mexico in the first half of 2019 alone. Migrants seek asylum or ask to continue their way up north. In addition, young people flee gang violence while others are forcibly displaced. Poverty, inequality, social unrest and lack of opportunities are other factors that cause people to leave their families and country.

Before the arrival of the caravans of migrants to the southern Mexican border in 2018, the Comboni Missionary Sisters participated in the campaign of humanitarian attention. From this experience, the sisters observed that the reception accommodations for migrants in Tapachula were few and limited. People encountered severe difficulties in finding shelter and food. Vulnerable migrants such as single mothers with young children, large families, pregnant women, unaccompanied children and adolescents, older people, LGBTI persons, and survivors of sexual violence face even more precarious situations. Tapachula is also home to the Siglo XXI ("21st Century") migration station, where thousands of migrants are detained.

In response to the humanitarian emergency, the opening of the Comboni Missionary Sisters community in Tapachula began in mid-May 2019. Since then, our sisters have committed themselves to promoting migrants' human rights in partnership with the shelter Hospitalidad y Solidaridad ("Hospitality and Security"), a space for refugees and asylum-seekers.

In the last two decades, migratory transit through Mexico has become a critical human mobility phenomenon, both for its magnitude and the conditions under which it occurs. The massive migration flows have attracted the attention of academics and media. Understanding the causes and effects of migration, and the risks and vulnerability of those who enter the Mexican territory irregularly is crucial.

The "ordinary" transit of Central Americans, the so-called "caravans" or "exoduses" that started in 2010 and continued in 2018, 2019, and 2020, received mixed messages from the Mexican government. The government promised support and temporary residency to immigrants, but it did not provide security; instead, it detained and deported them.

In 2020, the pandemic lockdown put migrants and refugee claimants at risk at the border and in detention centers. Stuck in the middle of the pandemic, they became even more vulnerable to violence, robbery, human trafficking and organized crime in the local Mexican cities they passed through.

When borders were closed, migrants were left unattended as centers failed to provide them with safety. Migrants also faced this situation in Tapachula. Feelings of incomprehension and despair, and loss of direction turn into open defiance. For the moment, stranded people, asylum-seekers, and refugees say that they are exchanging the "American dream" for the "Mexican dream."

Through the women's healing program, we see that when women lighten their emotional "backpack" load, their energy flows and healing happens. Some women arriving at the center carry an accumulated amount of pain, and at times, they cannot even breathe. As they process their pain, loss and grief, they regain a sense of worth, strength and courage.

Some help other women who are at the first stages of the healing process. We have seen women assisting fellow travelers. Some of the women who have been in the center become healers themselves. Migrant women know the importance of healing at this stage as their journey is still long. Once healed, they hold on to their dreams, even though they lack the resources to carry them out.

Much work remains to be done in the Effatá Crisis Intervention Program at the Bethlehem Shelter in Tapachula. Yet, we Comboni Missionary Sisters know that we are not alone. The spirit of Jesus and the solidarity of the world community strengthen us for service. To you, migrant *woman*, we say with tenderness, open yourself with renewed hope for a more humane world—*effatá*.

September 30, 2021

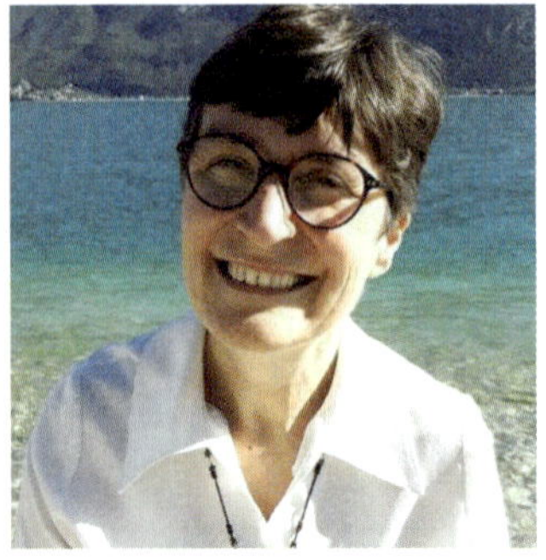

Pompea Cornacchia is an Italian Comboni Missionary Sister who has worked for more than 20 years in Latin America: Ecuador, Colombia and currently in Tapachula, Mexico. Working as a psychospiritual therapist, she has dedicated herself to the ministry of listening and accompaniment. Along with pastoral work with vulnerable people, she spent 13 years in vocation and formation ministry for her congregation. She worked briefly in Isiro, Democratic Republic of Congo, and presently is sharing life with migrant women as she serves on the border between Mexico and Guatemala.

Mago Contreras of the Comboni Missionary Sisters provided translation assistance for this column.

Reflection

Read the Scripture story in Mark 7:31-37. Jesus says to a man who is both deaf and mute, "Ephphatha" *or be opened. How are we called to either open deaf ears to hear or find the voice to speak for those who are in need as the Comboni Missionary Sisters have in their ministry center? Where might you be called to listen to or speak for others in your own neighborhood?*

The author describes the situation in a specific area of the world. But migrants, refugees, victims of violence or trafficking, or those affected by trauma exist in every part of the world. All are in need of healing and recovery. From your own life experience, where have you found healing and help to recover from a painful or traumatic experience? If you could write a prayer for all those, especially women and children, who are in need of hope, what would you say?

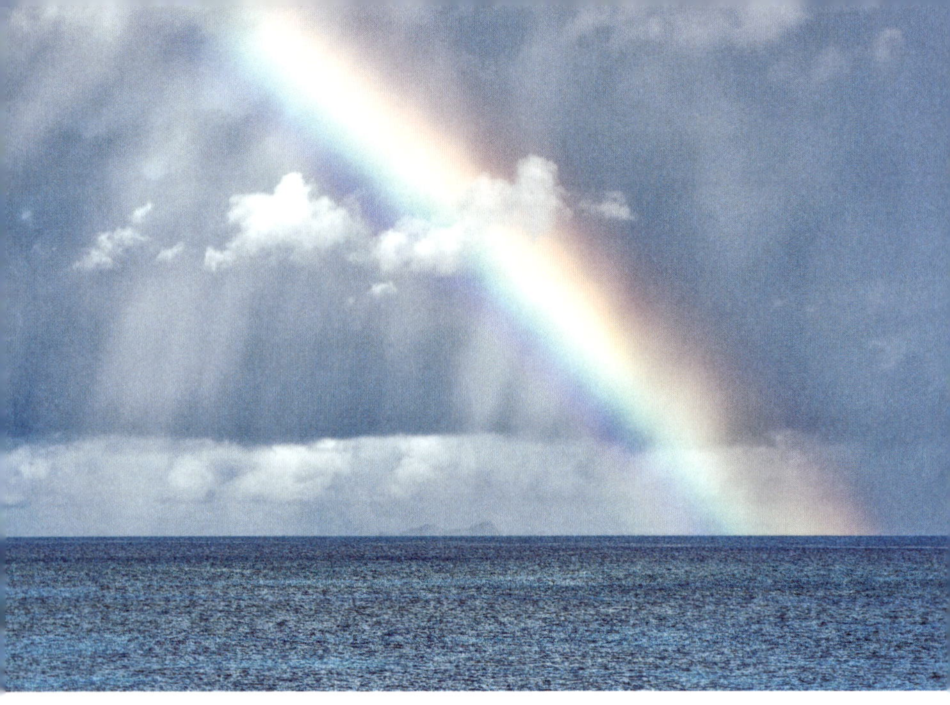

(Pixabay/Kanenori)

Care is the greatest treasure we can give to one another

By Molly Fernandes

"OK, bye. Take care. See you soon!" All short and simple phrases, yet, those two words—"take care"—have become part and parcel of our common vocabulary. The words "take care" play an important role for every person, village, state, nation and country.

Care is important. Without it, one can expect a disaster, failure—even death. Yes, these two words have implications for all creatures and creation. All that is created under the sun, be it human beings, trees, environment, animals, water, air or any other things, need care. But today, I wish to reflect on human beings.

Even so, the life of human beings is incomplete without trees, environment, water, air; all these factors contribute to human well-being, and we cannot survive without them.

The phrase "Take care" is spontaneous and casually said to someone expressing emotions of love to us, but it isn't easy for us to say it to those we don't like! It is also used as a semi-formal salutation at the end of any event.

The phrase has become well-used in today's society and in families, and it has been destroyed due to vested interests. The word "care" has been replaced with "me, me and me."

In this crumbling economy and today's world, fraught with denials and lies, greed seems to have become eternal. Human beings are frantically looking for ways to become No. 1 on the Forbes list of the richest people while the world is sick and ailing with man-made disasters. The latest earthquakes in Turkey and Syria are yet another reminder for the world—especially for those who have turned it into concrete jungles—to care for what is in our care. For the Word of God tells us that God put humans in the Garden of Eden to till it and take care of it (Genesis 1).

In Genesis 9:8-17 God promised Noah that he would never again destroy the earth with the flood. This was a commitment God made with Noah to maintain his relationship with the Creator and the creation. It was signed with the sign of a rainbow – His signature!

But then, why do we still have natural disasters or see destruction of the earth in other ways? That, to me, is the million-dollar question.

The answer is as simple as ever, spelled out with an addition of one word to the phrase where God says, "take care of it": It is not taken care of!

In any situation, all of us are called to do our part in taking care of our common home in simple ways. For example, we should be accountable for the waste we throw out and make all that we do sustainable. But we see the impact of people like the farmer in the golden goose story. The farmer killed his golden goose, which had been giving him one golden egg a day, in hopes that he would find many golden eggs inside the goose and become richer than his village banker.

As I reflected on the phrase "take care," I remembered a story I read some time ago that gave a heart-rending message about our primary responsibility toward our beloved parents or family members. It really moved my heart.

In the story, a son took his father out to eat. His father, old and weak, dropped food on himself. Diners looked on with disgust. After the meal, the son took his dad to the restroom and helped him clean up. As they left the restaurant, an old man noted that the son had modeled a message about caring for others, saying: "You left a lesson for every son and hope for every father."

Sure enough, we leave footprints behind, for every act noticed or unnoticed, wherever we go, in whatever we do and whatever we say. Even a word or two can make or break, one act can build or destroy. It all depends on me. As St. Paul wrote in 2 Tim 1:13-14, carefully guard our rich trust—His very own self—through the Holy Spirit, which in return will enable us to take care of creatures and creation.

Let us take care of our heart, mind, body and soul. It's only when I love myself wholeheartedly, when I take care of myself, that I can reach out in love and take care of others—whether things, people or creation.

Because care is the greatest treasure we can give to one another.

June 21, 2023

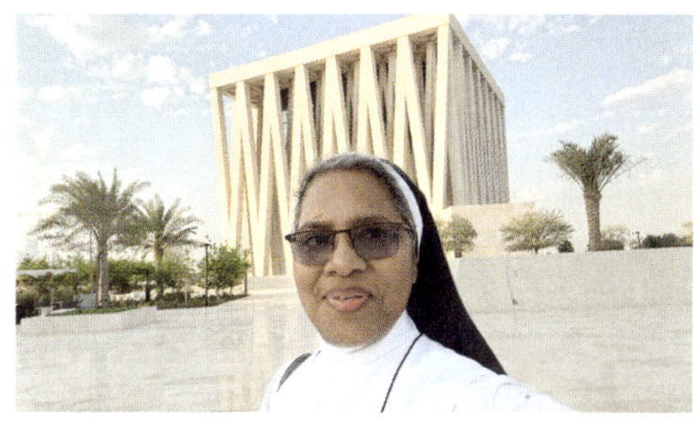

Molly Fernandes is a member of the Congregation of the Sisters of Holy Family of Nazareth, Sancoale-Goa, India. Besides teaching preschool and primary, she has done youth ministry, pastoral work and catechesis, and secretarial work in many dioceses and organizations. She is the director of the Sisters of Holy Family of Nazareth communications center and editor of their magazine, is a speaker and writer, and evangelizes through mass media.

Reflection

The author reflects on many areas where all of God's creation is not taken care of. But she emphasizes that each of us has a responsibility and a part to play in the care of the earth and all of life including humanity. Where might you make a change—even the smallest one—that would ensure that all of God's creation is protected and treasured?

What lesson or what footprint are you leaving by your witness even if it might appear that no one notices?

Acknowledgments

Global Sisters Report would like to thank all the sisters who have written for us as columnists over the years, particularly those whose work appears in this book and are listed below. We'd also like to thank all the Catholic sisters around the world who live out the Gospel message to care for "the least of these." You are truly an inspiration to us all!

Teresita Abraham
Teresa Anyabuike
Magda Bennásar
Jane Marie Bradish
Kathleen Bryant
Joan Chittister
Pompea Cornacchia
Lavina D'Souza
Ilia Delio
Judy Dohner
Dorothy Fernandes
Molly Fernandes
Susan Rose Francois
Margaret Gonsalves
Marjorie Guingona
Laura Hammel
Corbin Hannah
Kathryn James Hermes

Tracey Horan
Quincy Howard
Scholastica Oleksandra Hulivata
Begoña Iñarra
Caterina Ingelido
Tessy Jacob
Sujata Jena
Mūmbi Kīgūtha
Marilyn Lacey
María de Lourdes López Munguía
Eucharia Madueke
Jane Maisey
Mary John Mananzan
Lissy Maruthanakuzhy
Teodozija Myroslava Mostepaniuk
Scholasticah Nganda
Mary Nguyen Thi Phuong Lan
Celine Paramundayil
Kathryn Press
Cecilia A. Ranger
Mary Catherine Redmond
Linda Romey
Cheryl Rose
Jennibeth Sabay
Blanca Alicia Sánchez Olvera
Joan Sauro
Christine Schenk
Mercy Shumbamhini
Nancy Sylvester
Christin Tomy
Nicole Trahan

Julia Walsh
Rosemary Wanyoike
Jennifer Wilson